4/20

Faithful Christians must not be discouraged, nor can they conform to the spirit of the world. Instead, they are called upon to acknowledge the supremacy of God and his law, to raise their voices and join their efforts on behalf of moral values, to offer society the example of their own upright conduct, and to help those in need.

— Pope John Paul II

Catholicism and Society

Rev. Edward J. Hayes
Rev. Msgr. Paul J. Hayes
and James J. Drummey

"The Ad Hoc Committee to Oversee the Use of the Catechism, National Conference of Catholic Bishops, has found this catechetical series to be in conformity with the Catechism of the Catholic Church.*"*

C.R. PUBLICATIONS INC.
345 PROSPECT STREET
NORWOOD, MASSACHUSETTS 02062

C.R. Publications
345 Prospect Street
Norwood, MA 02062

Excerpts from the New American Bible, Copyright © 1970 by the Confraternity of Christian Doctrine, Washington, D.C., are used with permission. All rights reserved.

Excerpts from the English translation of the *Catechism of the Catholic Church* for the United States of America copyright © 1994, United States Catholic Conference, Inc. — Libreria Editrice Vaticana. Used with permission.

NIHIL OBSTAT
Msgr. William E. Maguire
Censor Librorum

IMPRIMATUR
+Most Reverend John C. Reiss
Bishop of Trenton
December 20, 1996

The Nihil Obstat and Imprimatur are official declarations that a book or pamphlet is free of doctrinal or moral error. No implication is contained therein that those who have granted the Nihil Obstat or Imprimatur agree with the contents, opinions, or statements expressed.

Third Printing September 1999

Cover design by Jeff Giniewicz
Printed in the United States of America

ISBN 0-9649087-5-1

Contents

Preface vii

1. The Christian Call to Holiness 1
2. Every Life Is a Vocation 13
3. The Future of Christian Marriage 27
4. Between Husband and Wife 39
5. Between Parent and Child 57
6. The Teenage Years 71
7. Between Family and Society 87
8. Between Family and God 107
9. The Modern Woman 121
10. The Senior Citizen 137
11. The Eighth Person 149
12. Christian Stewardship 163
13. Morality in Public Life 175
14. Cults and the New Age Movement 183
15. Advocates of Atheism 195
16. A Movement that Changed the World 205
17. Marxism and Religion 217

18. The Christian Response 225

19. The Perfect Prayer 233

20. You Can Make a Difference 245

Epilogue — Pope John Paul II 250

Bibliography 251

Index 255

Preface

"One loving soul sets another on fire," declared St. Augustine. And in more recent times Arnold Lunn, in his book *Now I See*, made this incisive and thought-provoking observation: "Christianity can sometimes be caught no less than taught." This book aims to present Christian teachings in a way that can be caught and lived.

Perhaps the underlying spirit might be expressed in the teaching of Vatican Council II in its *Dogmatic Constitution on the Church* as reiterated in the *Catechism of the Catholic Church*:

> "By reason of their special vocation it belongs to the laity to seek the kingdom of God by engaging in temporal affairs and directing them according to God's will .... It pertains to them in a special way so to illuminate and order all temporal things with which they are closely associated that these may always be effected and grow according to Christ and may be to the glory of the Creator and Redeemer" (n. 898).

This same spirit was echoed by Pope John Paul II during a visit to San Francisco in September 1987:

> It is within the everyday world that you, the laity, must bear witness to God's kingdom; through you the Church's mission is fulfilled by the power of the Holy Spirit. ... You are called to live in the world, to engage in secular professions and occupations, to live in those ordinary circumstances of family life and life in society from which is woven the very web of your existence. You are called by God himself to exercise your proper functions according to the spirit of the Gospel, and to work for the sanctification of the world from within, in the manner of leaven. In this way, you can make Christ known to others, especially by the witness of your lives.

This book is arranged in twenty chapters so that teachers of religion may effectively utilize it as a one-year course, either for Catholic high school students, those in parish religious education programs, or for adult discussion. There is regular reference to the Second Vatican Council, to recent papal pronouncements, and to the *Catechism of the Catholic Church*. Scripture quotations are from the New American Bible.

In three other books in this series (*Catholicism and Reason*, *Catholicism and Life*, and *Catholicism and Ethics*), the authors give a popular explanation of the Creed, Commandments, Sacraments, and medical issues. *Catholicism and Society* applies basic Catholic moral and ethical principles to some fundamental aspects of society in our day, such as vocations, marriage and the family, womanhood, the aging, racial justice, stewardship, morality in public life, cults and the New Age Movement, and the atheistic assault on religion as typified by Marxism and socialism.

Some might wonder why the book includes chapters on communism when that movement is supposedly dead. But even if it is dead — although as these lines are written the practitioners of communism, whether they call themselves communists or not, still hold significant power in various nations of the world — there are important lessons to be learned from the way in which this movement became the scourge of the twentieth century. As a wise man once said, those who ignore history are condemned to repeat it.

Frs. Edward and Paul Hayes have been writing throughout their priestly lives. James Drummey, a family man with nine children, has taught high school and adult catechetics, is the editor of "Catholic Replies," a question-and-answer newspaper column on religion, and is the author of a book by the same title.

In preparing sections of this volume, the authors owe a debt of gratitude to the Little Sisters of the Poor for some practical thoughts based on their years of experience in caring for thousands of elderly.

One complaint we hear today is that Christianity does not speak to the everyday problems of the modern world. *Catholicism and Society* seeks to do just that by singling out some areas where the teachings of Christ and his Church must be put into practice. G. K. Chesterton once said that "Christianity has not been tried and found wanting. It has not been tried." This book will suggest ways of making Christianity a vital force in many areas of modern living.

BOOKS IN THIS SERIES

Catholicism and Reason
and
Leader's / Catechist's Manual

Catholicism and Life
and
Leader's / Catechist's Manual

Catholicism and Society
and
Leader's / Catechist's Manual

Catholicism and Ethics
and
Leader's / Catechist's Manual

Additional books in this series may be ordered by writing to the address below, by calling (781) 762-8811, or by sending a fax to (781) 762-7890. There is a 20 percent discount for schools, parishes, and church groups, and a 40 percent discount for bookstores. Major credit cards are accepted. Otherwise, send check or money order (U.S. funds only) to:

C.R. Publications Inc.
345 Prospect Street
Norwood, MA 02062

Chapter 1

The Christian Call to Holiness

> God calls everyone to holiness. He has very precise plans for each person, a personal vocation which each must recognize, accept, and develop. — Pontifical Council for the Family, *The Truth and Meaning of Human Sexuality*, n. 100

Many Christians judge their lives on the basis of how many evils and wrongdoings they have avoided. All too few ever confront themselves with the question of how much good they have left undone. Cardinal Reginald Pole, at the time of the opening of the Council of Trent in 1545, challenged his fellow cardinals and the people of the world with these words: "We are responsible for the words we ought to have said and did not; for the things we ought to have done and did not do; for the things we ought to have uprooted and left grow; for the things we ought to have planted and did not plant."

The Penitential Rite at the beginning of Mass incorporates this same thought when we confess that we have sinned not only in thought, word, and deed but also "in what I have failed to do." But how many of us, at this point in the Mass, really stop to think of the kind word that we failed to speak or the good deed that we neglected to perform? Is there any one of us who has not walked by a new neighbor or a new employee on the job or a new student in school without saying a word? Who among us has not gone to a wake or a funeral and said to a bereaved friend or relative, "Be sure and let me know if there is anything I can do to help"? But this is little more

1

than a gesture. The sorrowing party is seldom able to think on the spot of something we can do and is hesitant to impose on us anyway. Instead of just asking, we could act. We could send a meal to the family or arrange to take care of the children or do any number of things that would be greatly appreciated.

Anyone who has ever been in the hospital has heard the familiar refrain afterwards, "I was sorry to hear that you were sick. I really wanted to get to visit you, but the time just got away from me." Talk like this is cheap; it is action that counts. Interestingly, excuses of this kind usually come from people who are not very busy, who have very little to occupy their time. Busy people somehow make the time to do things for other people.

Catholic lay persons in the world today have a solemn responsibility to God, to the Church, and to others to help "restore all things in Christ." They must begin with their own lives and then let their Christian spirit overflow and permeate everything around them. The Second Vatican Council put it this way:

> The laity are called in a special way to make the Church present and operative in those places and circumstances where only through them can she become the salt of the earth. Thus every layman, by virtue of the very gifts bestowed upon him, is at the same time a witness and a living instrument of the mission of the Church herself (*Dogmatic Constitution on the Church,* n. 33).

The Council, in another of its sixteen documents, made a rather startling statement about the serious responsibility the laity have to spread the message of Christ everywhere. After noting that every member of the Mystical Body of Christ, "which is the Church," has a share in the functions as well as in the life of the body, the Council Fathers said that "so intimately are the parts linked and interrelated in this body (cf. Eph. 4:16) that the member who fails to make his proper contribution to the development of the Church must be said to be useful neither to the Church nor to himself" (*Decree on the Apostolate of the Laity,* n. 2).

The obligation of Christian lay persons is clear. They are to bring the teaching and holiness of Christ to all and to influence society and its institutions in such a way as to lead everyone to salvation. The blueprint for this apostolate was given to us by Christ himself in the Sermon on the Mount, particularly in the Beatitudes:

When he saw the crowds he went up on the mountainside. After he had sat down his disciples gathered around him, and he began to teach them:

How blest are the poor in spirit: the reign of God is theirs.

Blest too are the sorrowing; they shall be consoled.

Blest are the lowly; they shall inherit the land.

Blest are they who hunger and thirst for holiness; they shall have their fill.

Blest are they who show mercy; mercy shall be theirs.

Blest are the single-hearted for they shall see God.

Blest too the peacemakers; they shall be called sons of God.

Blest are those persecuted for holiness' sake; the reign of God is theirs.

Blest are you when they insult you and persecute you and utter every kind of slander against you because of me. Be glad and rejoice, for your reward is great in heaven; they persecuted the prophets before you in the very same way (Matthew 5:1-12).

Christ then indicated the impact on the world of those who live these principles:

You are the salt of the earth. . . . You are the light of the world. . . . Your light must shine before men so that they may see goodness in your acts and give praise to your heavenly Father (Matthew 5:13-16).

St. Matthew tells us that when Jesus finished the Sermon on the Mount, he "left the crowds spellbound at his teaching. The reason was that he taught with authority and not like their scribes" (Matthew 7:28-29). The scribes always quoted former rabbis, but Jesus spoke in his own name, as one who had supreme authority: "You have heard the commandment, 'You shall not commit adultery.' *What I say to you is:* anyone who looks lustfully at a woman has already committed adultery with her in his thoughts" (Matthew 5:27-28). And again: "You have heard the commandment, 'You shall love your countryman but hate your enemy.' *My command to you is:* love your enemies, pray for your persecutors" (Matthew 5:43-44) [emphases added].

The crowds must have also been astounded at Christ's praise

for the poor and the lowly, the merciful and the single-hearted, the peacemakers and those who would turn the other cheek when they were insulted, persecuted, and slandered. For they lived in a land under the control of the powerful, swaggering, and vengeful Roman Empire. The Romans were, in the words of St. Paul, "men without conscience, without loyalty, without affection, without pity" (Romans 1:31).

Those listening to Jesus knew the nature of the Romans only too well. As on other occasions, they must have found Jesus' words hard to accept. But this did not deter our Lord from speaking the hard truth. He softened the effect, however, by telling the people that "anyone who hears my words and puts them into practice is like the wise man who built his house on rock. When the rainy season set in, the torrents came and the winds blew and buffeted his house. It did not collapse; it had been solidly set on rock" (Matthew 7:24-25). The people must have been impressed with the previously unheard of principles enunciated by Jesus, for "when he came down from the mountain, great crowds followed him" (Matthew 8:1).

If the reaction of the people hearing the Beatitudes for the first time seems strange to us two thousand years later, it is only because we are familiar with them and, one hopes, have put them into practice in our own lives. However, it would not be unreasonable to say that for many people living in this century, the words of Christ are still hard to accept. People are too caught up in the pursuit of material and sensual pleasures to think about serving God instead of self, to reflect on the good that they are leaving undone.

It is the duty of the Catholic lay person to jar these people loose from their attachment to the world and its pleasures; to remind them that a house built on sand will crumble and be destroyed; in other words, to let the light of Christ shine before all and lead them through the "narrow gate" to eternal happiness with God. Each beatitude is a beacon of light in a world darkened by sin and its effects: war, hatred, racism, immorality, greed, exploitation, indifference, persecution, and contempt for human life.

The Beatitudes form the basis for true Christian holiness; they must be promulgated by word and example because they are "at the heart of Jesus' preaching" (*Catechism of the Catholic Church*, n. 1716).

Blest Are the Poor in Spirit

The word "blest" is an Aramaic expression of Christ that implies a sense of well-being, a true interior happiness. Those who follow these principles, Christ is saying, will be genuinely happy and their reward will be great in heaven. The word "poor" has an economic connotation in modern English. In the Bible, however, and as used by Christ, this word refers to those who are not enmeshed in the things of this world, who realize the fruitlessness of material goods, who even have become disillusioned with the world and have placed themselves completely in the hands of God. The poor in spirit are not those in abject poverty, although some may be. They are the humble of the earth; they realize their nothingness before God and their total dependence upon him. They are like little children, trusting in God and grateful for what he is and what he does in their daily lives.

"In fidelity to the spirit of the Beatitudes," Pope John Paul has said, "the Church is called to be on the side of those who are poor and oppressed in any way. I therefore exhort the disciples of Christ and all Christian communities—from families to dioceses, from parishes to religious institutes—to carry out a sincere review of their lives regarding their solidarity with the poor" (*Redemptoris Missio,* n. 60).

The emphasis on acquiring material goods today is nothing short of overwhelming. On radio and television, in newspapers and magazines, there is a deluge of propaganda urging us to buy the latest car or appliance or clothes, or vacation in some exotic and faraway land. We are invited to live the "good life," to deny ourselves nothing, to eat, drink, and be merry. And yet, despite our affluence, many people are not happy. They are desperately searching for some meaning to life in the pursuit of material wealth, but the search frequently ends in disappointment, despair, and even death.

How many rich and prominent people who appeared to be sitting on the top of the world have committed suicide? The millionaire owner of a camera company was found at his desk, a suicide, with the gun still in his hand. A suicide note left on the desk said, "I have had all that life has to give. Life has no more to offer me, so I want no more life." The words of Jesus are appropriate: "Not on bread alone is man to live but on every utterance that comes from the mouth of God" (Matthew 4:4).

Blest Too Are the Sorrowing

A man who converted to the Catholic Faith was asked by a friend from his wild youthful days if he was happier now that he was a Catholic. The convert replied, "If you mean, am I spiritually more happy, yes; but if you mean physically, no. Sometimes this loyalty to Christ is like walking through hell. But I would rather be walking through hell than toward it."

This story offers us some insight into the second Beatitude. The sorrowing are those who remain loyal to Christ and steadfast in their faith no matter what difficulty, sadness, or tragedy may confront them. They are the ones who, in Shakespeare's words, suffer "the slings and arrows of outrageous fortune" without complaint; who grit their teeth as they struggle through school to obtain an education, or on their job to earn a living, or in their family to keep peace and harmony; who resist the temptations to neglect the worship of God, to succumb to the lure of the flesh, to cheat and steal and lie; who accept willingly the crosses that have been placed on their shoulders because they now can share in some small way in the suffering of their Savior.

They are the ones to whom Christ said, "I tell you truly: you will weep and mourn while the world rejoices; you will grieve for a time, but your grief will be turned into joy" (John 16:20).

Suffering and sorrow have no value in themselves; it is the reaction of the subject which can turn them to good. The spirit of resignation and union with Christ can turn adversity into virtue. Our Lord promised that the sorrowing would be consoled. How? They would have peace of mind, for one thing. A clear conscience, one that allows a person to sleep at night, is fervently desired by many people in our society. But they will not find this peace of mind until they are willing to walk through hell instead of toward it, until they can say to God, "Not my will but yours be done." The sorrowing, of course, will receive their greatest consolation in heaven, where all pain and sadness will be wiped away and they will enjoy an eternity of happiness.

Blest Are the Lowly

The word "lowly" in the Aramaic language which Christ spoke has the same meaning as "poor" in the first Beatitude. The lowly or the meek are those who are submissive to God, docile to his will. They are also able to control their temper when provoked. Their refusal to do battle with everyone who crosses their path results in a generally peaceful atmosphere wherever they go.

The reward promised the lowly is the same in all the Beatitudes, but in each it is presented a little differently. To inherit the land meant in the Old Testament to take possession of the Promised Land, which was the goal of Moses and the chosen people as they wandered through the desert. For Christ and his listeners it meant to obtain those things of which the Promised Land was a symbol—supernatural life and the Kingdom of God.

Blest Are They Who Hunger and Thirst for Holiness

The words "hunger" and "thirst" in the Bible signify a deep internal yearning for spiritual things. In the Old Testament, holiness was tied in with ritualistic external righteousness. Christ, on the other hand, emphasized the striving for internal goodness: "Be on guard against performing religious acts for people to see. Otherwise expect no recompense from your heavenly Father. . . . Keep your deeds of mercy secret, and your Father who sees in secret will repay you" (Matthew 6:1-4).

This Beatitude also implies that it is impossible to attain interior holiness in God's sight by our own efforts alone. One does not eagerly desire that which he can have for the doing. The implication is that our daily life must be lived hand in hand with God. Then, as Christ said, we shall have our fill. The greater our hunger and thirst for holiness, the more grace God will bestow upon us.

Pope John Paul reminded the People of God that the "prime and fundamental vocation" of every lay person is "the vocation to holiness, that is, the perfection of charity. Holiness is the greatest testimony of the dignity conferred on a disciple of Christ. . . . Everyone in the Church, precisely because they are members, receives and thereby shares in the common vocation to holiness" (*Christifideles Laici*, n. 16).

Blest Are They Who Show Mercy

This Beatitude is linked with the previous one since there can be no real holiness without mercy. To be merciful means more than just showing compassion for the less fortunate and the sinful. It is the sum total of many virtues. "Because you are God's chosen ones, holy and beloved," said St. Paul, "clothe yourselves with heartfelt mercy, with kindness, humility, meekness, and patience. Bear with one another; forgive whatever grievances you have against one another. Forgive as the Lord has forgiven you. Over all these virtues put on love, which binds the rest together and makes them perfect" (Colossians 3:12-14).

Every time we say the Our Father we should be reminded that we must be merciful to one another: "Forgive us our trespasses as we forgive those who trespass against us." If we are merciful, Christ declared, then the mercy of God shall be ours. This promise is expressed throughout the Old and New Testament. For example, the prophet Jeremiah tells us: "With age-old love I have loved you; so I have kept my mercy toward you" (31:3). So too, in her canticle of praise, Mary, the Mother of God, exclaims: "God who is mighty has done great things for me, holy is his name; his mercy is from age to age on those who fear him. . . . He has upheld Israel his servant, ever mindful of his mercy" (Luke 1:49ff).

Blest Are the Single-hearted

There is only one purpose in life: to know, love, and serve God. Whatever we do—pray, play, work—must be directed to the same ultimate end. The single-hearted are those who serve God loyally for his own sake and not primarily out of self-interest. They are true and faithful to God and to neighbor. In them there is no guile or duplicity; they are honest and sincere. Single-hearted means:

- conquering of ambition and pride—attachment to position
- conquering of unchastity—attachment to sex
- conquering of avarice—attachment to money
- conquering of sensuality—attachment to sensual pleasures.

The single-hearted shall see God, Christ promised. In this life, this means receiving gifts and favors from God and enjoying an intimate friendship with him. Possessing God through grace now will enable us to see him face to face in eternity.

Blest Too the Peacemakers

More than two hundred years have gone by since Patrick Henry strode to the pulpit of St. John's Episcopal Church in Richmond, Virginia, and declared, "Gentlemen may cry peace, peace—but there is no peace." He was referring, of course, to the imminent war with England, but his statement is equally true today. In our own time men and women cry peace, peace—but there is no peace: not in the world, not in our own land, not in our communities, frequently not in our families, sometimes not even in our own hearts. The latter domain is the most important of all, for unless we have peace in our own hearts, there will not be peace anywhere else. There are no conflicts outside us that are not first waged inside us.

Peace is an essential Christian ideal and can be achieved only by living the divine principles enunciated by Christ—the Prince of Peace at whose birth the angels sang "Glory to God in high heaven, peace on earth to those on whom his favor rests" (Luke 2:14); the Prince of Peace who told his Apostles at the Last Supper, " 'Peace' is my farewell to you, my peace is my gift to you; I do not give it to you as the world gives peace. Do not be distressed or fearful" (John 14:27).

The peacemaker is not only at peace with himself; he also prevents strife and promotes harmony in the human community. He is patient, conciliatory, and tolerant. The role of the peacemaker has been well set forth by St. Paul: "Remain at peace with one another. We exhort you to admonish the unruly; cheer the fainthearted; support the weak; be patient toward all. See that no one returns evil to any other; always seek one another's good and, for that matter, the good of all" (1 Thessalonians 5:13-15).

The reward promised the peacemakers is that "they shall be called sons of God," with all the privileges that this implies. The peacemakers belong to God in a special way, they are his adopted children and heirs. "You did not receive a spirit of slavery leading you back into fear, but a spirit of adoption through which we cry out, 'Abba!' (that is, 'Father')" (Romans 8:15).

Blest Are Those Persecuted for Holiness' Sake

This was a revolutionary idea introduced by Christ, that those who are persecuted while striving to carry out the will of God are to be considered blest. Contrast this Beatitude with the previous one, which reminds the world that peace is a keynote of Christianity and that individual Christians must work for peace within themselves, among neighbors and nations. The paradox is that those who labor for the peace of Christ may expect persecution from the world. This should not surprise any follower of Christ, for he warned that "they will harry you as they harried me" (John 15:20).

St. Peter recognized the blessings of persecution. "Do not be surprised, beloved, that a trial by fire is occurring in your midst," he said. "It is a test for you, but it should not catch you off guard. Rejoice instead, in the measure that you share Christ's sufferings. When his glory is revealed, you will rejoice exultantly. Happy are you when you are insulted for the sake of Christ, for then God's Spirit in its glory has come to rest on you" (1 Peter 4:12-14).

Over the past twenty centuries, countless people have cheerfully given their lives rather than renounce Jesus or his Church. From the early Christian martyrs whose bodies were coated with pitch and set on fire to light the gardens of the cruel Emperor Nero, to the suffering souls undergoing persecution and death at the hands of tyrants today, we have thrilling examples of people whose reward will be great in heaven. "Whoever loses his life for my sake," Jesus promised, "will find it" (Matthew 16:25).

A Blueprint for Reform

The sublime wisdom and great potential of the Beatitudes are admitted by many but practiced by few. "Sensible" people say that such a lifestyle is not practical; it demands too much and offers so little reward here and now. They tell us that other things are more important—power, prestige, position, pleasure. But Christ knows better. "What man thinks important," he warned, "God holds in contempt" (Luke 16:15).

Our Lord not only taught the Beatitudes, he lived them. He was poor in spirit, lowly, merciful, and suffered persecution. Yet he will not force us to keep the Beatitudes. That is a choice we will have to make ourselves. Knowing our human hearts as he does, however, Christ knows that there will never be peace in those hearts, that we will never be truly happy until we follow his ideals, his way of life. Vatican II, urging "the laity to express the true spirit of the Beatitudes in their lives," reaffirmed this truth:

> Following Jesus who was poor, they are neither depressed by the lack of temporal goods nor puffed up by their abundance. Imitating Christ who was humble, they have no obsession for empty honors (cf. Gal. 5:26) but seek to please God rather than men, ever ready to leave all things for Christ's sake (cf. Lk. 14:26) and to suffer persecution for justice' sake (cf. Mt. 5:10). For they remember the words of the Lord, "If anyone wishes to come after me, let him deny himself, and take up

his cross, and follow me" (Mt. 16:24) (*Decree on the Apostolate of the Laity,* n. 4).

A blueprint for the ethical and social reform of our modern society was given by Christ on the side of a mountain two thousand years ago. Application of this blueprint today is essential if we are to form correct attitudes toward marriage and the family, the religious life, the modern woman, the elderly, those of different races, public officials, those caught up in cults, and the promoters of philosophies that are diametrically opposed to the one expressed in the Sermon on the Mount.

Speaking in San Francisco on September 18, 1987, Pope John Paul gave us our challenge:

All the Catholic laity are called to live the Beatitudes, to become leaven, salt, and light for the world, and sometimes a "sign of contradiction" that challenges and transforms that world according to the mind of Christ. No one is called to impose religious beliefs on others, but to give the strong example of a life of justice and service, resplendent with the virtues of faith, hope, and charity.

Chapter 2

Every Life Is a Vocation

> In the design of God, every man is called upon to develop and fulfill himself, for every life is a vocation. —Pope Paul VI, *On the Development of Peoples,* n. 15

Human society with all its various stages of life is like the human body, each member of which has its own function to perform. Every member of the human body is working, each in its own way, toward a common goal—the good of the human being. Every member of human society—physician, lawyer, secretary, seamstress, truck driver, teacher, laborer, salesperson, married, unmarried—is working each in his or her own way toward a common goal: happiness here and hereafter.

No one, of course, no matter how seemingly lofty their vocation, should look down on the calling of another. In the words of the Vatican's *General Catechetical Directory:* "Every vocation is worthy of honor and is a call to the fullness of love, that is, to holiness; every person is endowed with his own supernatural excellence, and must be given respect" (n. 66). Or to put it in less sublime terms, consider the remark made some years ago by Oliver Nelson of Yale University Divinity School: "If all the garbage men and all the preachers quit at the same time, which would you miss first?"

God calls each of us to a particular state in life and gives each all the grace and help necessary for that state. That state is a person's vocation. In other words, your vocation is that state in life in which you can best find a measure of happiness here and secure your eternal happiness hereafter. Note the phrase, "a measure of happiness." This is important to remember because no

13

loyal follower of Christ should expect an earthly life of uninterrupted joy and bliss. Suffering and sorrow are an integral part of life, unavoidable consequences of original sin, but they can be turned to our eternal advantage if we understand and accept them in the spirit of the Beatitudes.

Since the conscientious fulfillment of a vocation is very intimately connected with our eternal salvation and happiness, the question of choosing the proper state in life and of sincerely preparing for and carrying out one's vocation should be a matter of concern to young men and women and to conscientious parents.

Saul of Tarsus was a zealous young man, of keen mind and willing to throw all his energies into the attainment of his ideals. Before his well-known conversion to Christianity, he gave himself wholeheartedly to the persecution of Christians. One day, while on his way to the city of Damascus, Saul was stunned by a great light from heaven and the voice of Christ. Fearful and astonished, he asked, "What is it I must do?" (Acts 22:10). Saul was told to go into Damascus where he would learn his true place in God's plan. The day of the Apostle's vocation was at hand.

God ordinarily does not work in such an unusual and miraculous fashion in calling a person to a vocation. But God, nonetheless, is calling each person to a definite state in life. "What is it I must do?" is a question that must be asked by each person who wishes to live his or her life according to the divine plan. The answer will not come as a bolt of light, but God does provide certain signs by which a vocation in life might be chosen.

Young people especially need the help of prudent parents to find the right answer to this question. "Children should be so educated," said Vatican II, "that as adults they can, with a mature sense of responsibility, follow their vocation, including a religious one, and choose their state of life" (*Pastoral Constitution on the Church in the Modern World,* n. 52).

The Four States in Life

There are only four states in life, or vocations, in which to serve God: the single state, the religious life, the priesthood, and married life. Of course, there are many other things to be considered under each of these. A single person or one who is married may also hold a professional position or a blue-collar job. A sister or brother may devote his or her life to teaching, nursing the sick, social work, or missionary work. A priest may work in a parish, or teach, or work in the missions, or enter a monastery. But everyone is meant to serve God in one of the four vocations.

It is unfortunate but true today that many people seeking a vocation ask only two questions: "What do I like to do?" and "Where will I make the most money?" These are considerations, of course, but one's reasons for selecting a particular state in life must go much deeper if real happiness and fulfillment are to be found.

Everyone has a job to do in life. Cardinal John Henry Newman, the famous English Catholic convert of the eighteenth century, once said,

> God has created me to do him some definite service; he has committed some work to me which he has not committed to another. I have my mission. I may never know it in this life, but I shall be told it in the next.
> Therefore, I will trust him. Whatever, wherever I am, I cannot be thrown away. If I am in sickness, my sickness may serve him; in perplexity, my perplexity may serve him; if I am in sorrow, my sorrow may serve him. He does nothing in vain. He knows what he is about.

Your vocation, then, is the state in life in which God wants you to serve him in a particular way. God wants us to work with him in carrying out his divine plan so that we may be able to work toward heaven. Whatever our vocation—single, married, priest, brother, or sister—we have a mission to carry out, one that God could have accomplished himself, but for which he has chosen us as his instruments. How we perform as his chosen instruments will determine our destiny in this life and in the life to come. A brief discussion of the four states in life may help us to prepare properly for a vocation and live it in the spirit God intended.

The Single Life

It never seems to occur to the average person that some men and women are unmarried because they want to be. There is no reason for us to become confused about people who stay single. Marriage is by its nature a right, not an obligation. If anyone wants to remain unmarried, all things being equal, he or she is free to do so.

We hear a great deal about vocations to the religious life, the priesthood, and married life, but let us not forget that God calls many people to the single state. St. Paul praised those who had chosen the single life. "I should like you to be free of all worries," he said to them. "The unmarried man is busy with the Lord's affairs, concerned with pleasing the Lord; but the married man is busy with this world's demands and occupied with pleasing his wife. This means he is divided. The virgin—indeed any unmarried woman—is concerned with things of the Lord, in pursuit of holiness in body and spirit.

"The married woman, on the other hand, has the cares of this world to absorb her and is concerned with pleasing her husband. I am going into this with you for your own good. I have no desire to place restrictions on you, but I do want to promote what is good, what will help you to devote yourselves entirely to the Lord" (1 Corinthians 7:32-35).

The majority of unmarried people who consecrate their virginity or celibacy to God are priests or brothers or sisters with public vows. But there are a number of lay people, not members of religious orders, who have made private vows of virginity or chastity. Vatican II spoke highly of them in these words:

> This total continence embraced on behalf of the kingdom of heaven has always been held in particular honor by the Church as being a sign of charity and stimulus towards it, as well as a unique fountain of spiritual fertility in the world (*Dogmatic Constitution on the Church*, n. 42).

Heaven must have a special reward for the man or woman who has for some high motive chosen to remain unmarried. Many a priest in God's service owes his success to such a person. Many a gifted individual, many an outstanding pupil was formed by a patient unmarried teacher. So the next time you hear someone talk about a man or woman who "missed the boat" on marriage, point out that perhaps they are God's chosen souls, perfectly happy in their life of consecration.

No one would deny that our age demands spiritual heroism. The Church always needs consecrated single men and women, working under the guidance of priests as spiritual directors, to help in the fight against the evils of the day. If you are single, is God calling you to serve him in this special vocation?

The Religious Life

There is not a day that goes by that Christ does not invite many young men and women to go into partnership with him, to carry on his work as brothers and sisters in Catholic schools, hospitals, charitable and social agencies, and in the missions. There is so much good to be done and not enough dedicated religious to do it. Suppose a person has thought of doing this apostolic work, how can he or she recognize whether a religious vocation is present? There are four factors that must be considered:

1. *Right intention and desire.* The potential candidate must want to dedicate his or her life wholeheartedly to Christ and share in the work that brothers and sisters are doing.

2. *Physical ability.* The demands of religious life require ordinary good health. A person need not always have been free from sickness to qualify for the religious life; normal health is sufficient.

3. *Mental ability.* The potential candidate must possess average intelligence and a willingness to study. He or she need not be the class scholar, but neither should they be below normal in class work.

4. *Moral fitness.* The interested person does not have to be a saint, or to have the spiritual qualities of a veteran brother or sister. Moral fitness means freedom from the moral ugliness of evil habits and from nasty character traits, plus a spirit of self-sacrifice, a willingness to obey, and an eagerness to please God.

If a positive response can be given to each of these points, then perhaps God is calling this young man or woman to the religious life. The next step is to discuss the matter with a priest, brother, or sister, and then to talk it over with one's parents. Parents should give guidance and encouragement all along the way, but should not interfere with the choice of a son's or daughter's vocation.

"The Church needs to make known the great Gospel values of which she is the bearer," said Pope John Paul. "No one witnesses more effectively to these values than those who profess the consecrated life in chastity, poverty, and obedience, in a total gift of self to God and in complete readiness to serve man and society after the example of Christ" (*Redemptoris Missio,* n. 69).

The Priesthood

The priest is another Christ. He alone has the merciful power to forgive sins. He alone has the miraculous power to change bread and wine into the Body and Blood of Jesus Christ. He alone, said Jean Lacordaire, the French Dominican who lived over a century ago, has a vocation "to live in the midst of the world without seeking its pleasures; to be a member of every family but belonging to none; to penetrate all secrets, share all sorrows, heal all wounds; to go from man to God and to offer him their prayers, and to return from God to man bringing pardon and hope; to have a heart of fire for charity and a heart of bronze for chastity."

It is said that the young are searching for heroes today, for people they can look up to and admire and imitate. They need look no further than the vast majority of our priests, holy and zealous men who are in the world, but not of the world; saints in the making who are doing far more good than they realize; other Christs who are always asking themselves, "What would Christ do, *now*?"

What a challenge for any young man—to be another Christ! The qualifications are the same as those for the religious life: right intention and desire, ordinary physical health, average intelligence, and moral fitness. An individual meeting these conditions should then talk over his intentions with a priest and his parents, seeking their advice and encouragement before formally making application to a seminary. An intense spiritual life, one that develops an ever-closer relationship with Christ, the Supreme and Eternal High Priest, will provide the solid foundation on which a fruitful priesthood can be built.

"In expressing the conviction that Christ needs his priests and wills to associate them with himself in his mission of salvation," Pope John Paul told a group of priests in Miami on September 10, 1987, "we must also emphasize the consequences of this: the need for new vocations to the priesthood. It is truly necessary for the whole Church to work and pray for this intention. We priests must personally invite generous young men to give their lives in the service of the Lord; they must truly be attracted by the joy that we project in our own lives and ministry."

Three years later, on October 28, 1990, the Holy Father concluded a Synod of Bishops in Rome with these words: "We can assure you, from our experience, that it is worthwhile to give one's life and strength as a priest in the service of the people of God. In spite of every difficulty, such a life can always bring joy and happiness. Jesus Christ himself has promised us that 'he who loses his life for my sake will find it.' The Church and the world need good shepherds, priests ready to serve God and the people of God with free hearts and free hands. We know that it is not easy to answer God's call to priesthood. But we must trust, dear brothers, that with God's help many young men will answer such a call."

The Vatican Council, wishing to assist priests in their service to the people of God, approved the restoration of the permanent diaconate as a rank in the hierarchy. After a lapse of many centuries, the deacon is now resuming his service to the Church in the ministries of the liturgy, word, and charity. He may administer baptism, distribute Holy Communion, witness marriages, bring Viaticum to the dying, read the Gospel and preach at Mass, officiate at funerals, administer sacramentals, preside at prayer services, and help in such specialized areas as catechetics, counseling, Church administration, and public relations.

One day early in his public life, Jesus was walking along the Sea of Galilee when he saw two brothers, "Simon now known as Peter, and his brother Andrew, casting a net into the sea. They were fishermen. He said to them, 'Come after me and I will make you fishers of men.' They immediately abandoned their nets and became his followers" (Matthew 4:18-20). Jesus is still asking men to come after him two thousand years later. Let us pray that the men of today will respond to our Lord's call as quickly as Peter and Andrew did.

The Married Life

People have no difficulty in recognizing the priesthood or the religious life as a vocation. But how many consider marriage a vocation? How many realize that the married state, like the other three states in life, is part of the divine plan and is a means of finding some happiness here and securing eternal happiness hereafter? Suffice it to say that far fewer marriages would end up in the courthouse and divorce if more serious thought were given to the choice of a marriage partner.

Since marriage is in the fullest sense a vocation, and is the vocation chosen by the vast majority of people, wisdom, care, and thoughtfulness must come into play when the time comes to pick a partner for life. Even a superficial knowledge of the modern marriage situation clearly indicates that many present-day husbands and wives have not been too successful in choosing a partner. There are several reasons for this unhappy state of affairs.

First, many young people are confused by the warped theories of love promulgated through books and magazines, movies and television—theories that condone immorality and sinfulness as long as the participants allegedly love each other. This confusion prevents young people from seeking the true and solid qualities in a prospective husband or wife. Some females are looking for the perfect physical specimen, the "man of their dreams" with whom they can rush headlong into marriage and a lifelong honeymoon. Some males are looking for a glamorous woman who will satisfy their sexual desires. Love becomes strictly a physical attraction and fades quickly as the physical bond deteriorates and there is no spiritual, intellectual, cultural, or emotional bond to fill the void.

Second, many modern youth seldom consult parents, priest, or a prudent adviser on such an important matter. And many parents are reluctant to give any advice at all. Not that parents should interfere or force their will on their children, but a youth contemplating marriage may well benefit from the experience and maturity of a parent or adviser. Would a youth select a certain college or apply for a job without asking some knowledgeable person for an evaluation of the college or job?

Third, not a few young men and women enter marriage rashly, hastily, and lacking the necessary knowledge of their future spouses. The usual scenario is boy meets girl; courtship is spent almost exclusively in places of entertainment where liquor flows freely; and marriage follows after a short association built largely around "fun and games." The young man or woman is not marrying an individual or a personality, but rather a set of circumstances. When the circumstances change, when the "good life" is interrupted by some unforeseen crisis, a spouse may discover that the individual he or she married is not able to function very well under adverse conditions.

Fourth, many young men and women have lost sight of the very purpose of the American "dating" system and engagement period. Couples out on a date generally do not think about anything more than having a good time that evening. There is little or no thought given to the qualities one would like to see in a life-time marriage partner. Similarly, during the engagement period, couples concentrate too much on enjoying themselves and not enough on some of the vital matters that should be discussed and agreed upon before marriage. At the very least, couples contemplating marriage ought to have reached agreement in the following areas: the purpose and sanctity of marriage, religious practice, standard of living and finances, in-laws, rights and duties of parents, outside activities, and the number of children, how they should be raised, and their religious training. Failure to settle differences on these issues before marriage will lead to problems later on.

Fifth, many couples do not have a strong determination to make marriage work. They do not understand that marriage is an indissoluble arrangement. They hear a lot today about "trial marriages," about marriage contracts that are renewable every few years, about living together before marriage to see if a couple is compatible. The absurdity of this latter arrangement should be obvious: people who know that they can get out of a situation if the going gets tough will never try very hard to smooth over the rough spots that show up whenever two individuals try to live together as one. No marriage can be successful without a firm resolve on the part of each spouse to overlook the idiosyncrasies of the other and to overcome any difficulties with large doses of love, understanding, and patience.

"The Person I Marry"

Coming to the positive side, what are some of the qualities which a young man or woman should look for in a future spouse? What are some of the attributes which parents must know and emphasize—and exemplify? What are some of the underlying factors that can contribute to a happy marriage? We can find the answers to these questions by considering four different categories: physical health, mental health, intellectual qualities, and emotional qualities.

1. *Physical health.* It is clear that a prospective husband or wife should possess moderately sound physical health. Only under extraordinary circumstances should a person consider marriage with one who cannot undertake the ordinary tasks of mar-

ried life. Neither should a person lightly link his or her life with another who is suffering from a disease which is likely to prove fatal within a few years' time. The prospective husband and wife should be free from contagious diseases, especially those of a venereal nature.

Just as the husband in a traditional family must be able to earn a living to support his family, so the wife must be able to discharge the duties of homemaking. She must also be able to bear and rear children without abnormal difficulty. On the other hand, minor health difficulties should not prevent a woman from having children. Modern medicine has solved virtually all the problems of pregnancy and childbirth.

2. *Mental health.* It is equally clear that no man or woman should marry a person who is emotionally disturbed or who is likely to become so in the near future. If marked abnormalities in emotional make-up show themselves during the courtship or engagement period, a young man or woman would do well to seek expert advice on the subject. However, a person should not regard himself or herself as unfit for marriage because of insanity in some other members of the family.

3. *Intellectual qualities.* It is generally desirable that husband and wife be more or less on a par in their intellectual ability. This does not mean that college graduates should marry only college graduates. Equality of native intelligence is more important than equality of education. But if a very brilliant man or woman is matched with a dull and slow-witted partner, they will not have much true companionship and will be unable to share information and ideas about their respective careers and activities.

4. *Emotional qualities.* The number of marital problems that arise under the first three categories are miniscule compared to the marriages that have been destroyed by emotionally immature individuals. There are too many men and women who are adults in body and mental ability, but always remain children in their emotional development.

They are changeable, addicted to moods and tantrums, oversensitive, given to excessive jealousy, irresponsible, and sometimes hysterical. They make unsatisfactory husbands or wives, and are extremely unsatisfactory as parents. As fathers and mothers, they often place children in an emotional environment which leads to delinquency, alcoholism, and mental or emotional unbalance.

Some Good Qualities

It is obvious then that maturity and balance are emotional qualities to be sought in a mate. Evenness of temper, without excessive alteration of moods, is also desirable. Emotional balance should not be confused with coldness or absence of emotional response. A capacity for affection is very necessary; real coldness (as opposed to shyness) is a bad thing in a husband or wife. Warmth and heartiness, cheerfulness and enthusiasm, and a sense of humor are all pluses. But marked changes in emotions, sudden rages for reasons that would not move the ordinary person, as well as extreme jealousy and suspicion, should be warning signals that an individual is emotionally unstable.

It is clear, too, that the future partner must be a good man or woman. Unselfishness is a prime quality and the major ingredient of true love—always wanting to give rather than to get, always thinking of the other person first, always wanting to make that person happy even if you do not feel like it. Honesty ranks near the top of the list, as does sincerity, understanding, patience, respect, and gentleness. Perseverance in a task and faithfulness to a promise are important. So is generosity coupled with a reasonable thrift that is free from miserliness. Modesty, in its special sense of the proper respect for sex, is an ornament both before and after the wedding day.

No person wants to marry a drunkard or a drug addict; no one should. People are sometimes trapped by pity into marriage with substance abusers; they secretly flatter themselves into believing that they will be able to change the potential alcoholic or drug addict. They are like the man who built a new home on a swamp and expected that the swamp would dry up just because he built his home there. Before entering into marriage with a heavy drinker or drug user, make sure that he or she shows positive proof of reform over a long period of time.

No man or woman should marry a person of loose sexual habits under the fond belief that he or she will change after the marriage vows have been taken. It is true that God forgives and that with his grace we can reform. But before accepting a spouse with a notorious record of sexual escapades, the other person must demand positive proof of a change of ways over a lengthy period.

The man who is to succeed as husband and father should be truly masculine. In the dislocated society of today, we are producing a crop of masculine women and feminine men. Being masculine is not the same thing as being rough, brutal, or unfeeling. Tenderness and compassion do not conflict in any way with a really masculine temperament. The man should be vigorous, decisive, and capable of exerting leadership. He must accept the responsibility of being protector and provider to his wife and children. He should be interested in his job, proud of his workmanship, and have a reasonable desire for advancement in his chosen field. He should also accept his responsibility as a citizen in the community.

A good wife and mother should be feminine. True femininity is something quite different from fine clothes or expensive perfumes and the image of the modern woman commonly set forth in the media. Real femininity involves the qualities which go with a woman's maternal role: generosity, tenderness, sympathy, sacrifice, and total gift of self.

Far from shunning the role of motherhood, the true woman welcomes it eagerly. She should be professionally competent, not only in her homemaking tasks, but also in those outside activities which complement her role in the home. She must exercise her responsibility as a citizen, following the example of those housewives and mothers who have had a significant impact on public issues over the years, including efforts to halt abortion and restore respect for human life.

If these fundamental qualities and attributes are carefully considered and put into practice, the foundation of a successful marriage will have been established. Men and women should not enter into marriage on a mere whim or superficial attraction. Their vocation should be based on common sense, prudent judgment, sound advice, and persevering prayer. Regarding the latter, a strong religious faith is absolutely essential in candidates for the married life. Every Christian marriage is a triple union—a union of two bodies, a union of two hearts, and a union of two souls. Take away any one of these and the marriage will be in trouble. Keep them intact and the married state in life will be a true vocation, bringing a measure of happiness here and leading the Christian couple to eternal happiness in heaven.

Every Life Is a Vocation

Life can be beautiful for any man or woman who strives to serve God and to follow the teachings of Christ in one of the four vocations. Pope Paul VI gave the world an inspiring summary of the dignity of everyone's vocation:

In the design of God, every man is called upon to develop and fulfill himself, for every life is a vocation. At birth, everyone is granted, in germ, a set of aptitudes and qualities for him to bring to fruition. Their coming to maturity, which will be the result of education received from the environment and personal efforts, will allow each man to direct himself toward the destiny intended for him by his Creator.

Endowed with intelligence and freedom, he is responsible for his fulfillment as he is for his salvation. He is aided, or sometimes impeded, by those who educate him and those with whom he lives, but each one remains, whatever be these influences affecting him, the principal agent of his own success or failure. By the unaided effort of his own intelligence and his will, each man can grow in humanity, can enhance his personal worth, can become more a person (*On the Development of Peoples,* n.15).

Paul VI was echoed by John Paul II two decades later:

In Church communion, the states of life, by being ordered one to the other, are thus bound together among themselves. They all share in a deeply basic meaning: that of being the manner of living out the commonly shared Christian dignity and the universal call to holiness in the perfection of love. They are different yet complementary in the sense that each of them has a basic and unmistakable character which sets each apart, while at the same time each of them is seen in relation to the other and placed at each other's service (*Christifideles Laici,* n. 55).

Chapter 3

The
Future of
Christian Marriage

> The well-being of the individual person and of both human
> and Christian society is closely bound up with the healthy
> state of conjugal and family life. — *Catechism of the
> Catholic Church*, n. 1603

Why should we bring up the subject of Christian marriage and
family life in the context of Christianity and society today? Are
not the average parents trying to live a decent life with their family, trying to earn a living, manage a home, raise children properly, enjoy a happy life, and not interfere in anybody else's problems? Besides, if there are problems in the world, in our country,
in our city or town—what can we do about them? After all, every
generation has said, "We hardly know what this world is coming
to." Why begin raising that old cry today?

Is everything going along today just about as it always has? Or
are there certain fundamental problems eating away at the very
structure of family life in America, problems that must be solved?
What is happening today? And what is the future of Christian
marriage and the Christian family at the turn of the century?

The Picture Today

Suppose in our age of space travel a visitor from another planet
were to arrive in the United States to study our family life. What
would he find? He would find the whole Christian tradition concerning the family and married life under relentless attack. He

would find contempt for human life through widespread contraception, abortion, and euthanasia; venereal disease at epidemic levels; rampant alcoholism and drug addiction; widespread juvenile criminality; an appalling record of child abuse; and a high suicide rate among young people.

He would also find loud demands for acceptance of homosexuality and lesbianism as "alternate lifestyles" and even for same-sex "marriage"; a large number of couples living together outside of wedlock; permissive parents who have failed to instill in their children a respect for authority; a veritable flood of pornographic films and literature; and sex education programs that ignore moral teachings and promote promiscuity by distributing condoms in public schools.

Our space traveler would discover that the annual number of divorces has more than doubled since the 1970s. Divorce has become socially acceptable. Cards offering "congratulations on your divorce" can be purchased in stationery stores. Gone are the long and involved legal proceedings. Many states have passed "no fault" divorce laws which allow couples to split up without first proving that one is to blame for the breakup. There are even "do-it-yourself" divorce kits that contain all the forms needed for the handling of a divorce without a lawyer, along with instructions on filling them out.

Even Catholics cannot escape this indictment, for the divorce rate among Catholics has been just as high as the national average. The reason for this is clear: too many Catholics base their actions on the false images presented by the media, rather than on the Gospel and its teachings.

"Human beings are not the same thing as the images proposed in advertising and shown by the modern mass media," said Pope John Paul in his *Letter to Families*. "They are much more, in their physical and psychic unity, as composites of soul and body, as persons. They are much more because of their vocation to love, which introduces them as male and female into the realm of the 'great mystery' " (n. 20).

Some people, when confronted with these facts, will point out the other side of the coin—that most marriages do not end in divorce. But how many of these marriages are happy? How many couples are fulfilling the plan for marriage handed down by God himself? How many parents are raising their children to become responsible citizens and parents themselves? How many mothers and fathers, by word and example, are demonstrating to their children that marriage and the family offer the only real security for young people and the only real hope for the future of society?

Today there is an obvious breakdown in the influence of the Church over Catholics in general and youth in particular. Young people hear one thing from the Church and another from society. They are taught the virtues of purity, honesty, and truthfulness by the Church, but are then exposed to immoral videos, books, magazines, and music. They read about corrupt politicians or watch as public figures in all walks of life are brought down by lies, lust, and greed. And of course, the sexy and the sensational always get more media coverage than the modest and the mundane.

The picture we have been painting, in all its discouraging details, shows that the institution of marriage and the family is in trouble. This does not mean, however, that the institution is obsolete or expendable. It is under stress but it can be defended and strengthened if those already married and those who will marry recognize the problem areas and work at making marriage and the family what God intended them to be. The current situation indeed offers a challenge to all thinking people—to those who still have left even a spark of love for Christian family ideals.

"Every effort should be made so that the family will be recognized as the primordial and, in a certain sense, 'sovereign' society!," said Pope John Paul. "The 'sovereignty' of the family is essential for the good of society. A truly sovereign and spiritually vigorous nation is always made up of strong families who are aware of their vocation and mission in history. The family is at the heart of all these problems and tasks. To relegate it to a subordinate or secondary role, excluding it from its rightful position in society, would be to inflict grave harm on the authentic growth of society as a whole" (*Letter to Families*, n. 17).

What Is Christian Marriage?

Anyone desirous of strengthening Christian marriage must have a clear understanding of the divine origin and sacramental nature of marriage. We can easily arrive at this understanding by consulting such landmark Church documents as Pope Pius XI's encyclical on Christian marriage *Casti Connubii* (1930), the Second Vatican Council's *Pastoral Constitution on the Church in the Modern World* (1965), Pope Paul VI's prophetic encyclical on the regulation of birth *Humanae Vitae* (1968), Pope John Paul II's apostolic exhortation *The Role of the Christian Family in the Modern World* (1981) and his *Letter to Families* (1994), and the *Catechism of the Catholic Church* (1992).

The same theme runs through all of these documents: marriage owes its existence to God, and its origin dates from the very beginning of the human race; Christ later elevated the state of marriage to a sacrament through which Christian spouses receive the grace to fulfill their marital and family obligations and lead each other to God; and the Christian family is the foundation of society and manifests to all the presence of Christ in the world.

In the earliest pages of the Bible, we find God instituting marriage by bringing the first man and woman into existence and telling them to "be fertile and multiply; fill the earth and subdue it" (Genesis 1:28) Many centuries later, the Son of God came on earth and confirmed his Father's plan: "At the beginning of creation God made them male and female; for this reason a man shall leave his father and mother and the two shall become as one. They are no longer two but one flesh. Therefore let no man separate what God has joined" (Mark 10:6-9).

Jesus also showed us his respect for the institution of marriage when, at the beginning of his public life, he attended the wedding feast at Cana. Our Lord, whose three years of public life were so crowded, still took time to be present at the village of Cana not only for the sake of recreation and sociability, but even more to give his stamp of approval, to consecrate and elevate matrimony by his presence.

Still further evidence of Jesus' high regard for marriage is his reply to the question about why his disciples did not fast. "How can wedding guests go in mourning so long as the groom is with them?" he asked. "When the day comes that the groom is taken away, then they will fast" (Matthew 9:15). Christ found it altogether appropriate to compare himself to the bridegroom and his disciples to the guests at a marriage feast.

What God the Father ordained, and Jesus upheld, St. Paul taught. The Apostle saw the intimate love between a husband and wife as symbolic of the love between Christ and his Church. He said that a wife should submit to her husband as the Church submits to Christ, and that a husband should love and care for his wife as Christ loves and cares for his Church. Calling attention to the passage from Genesis about a man leaving his parents and clinging to his wife, St. Paul said that "this is a great foreshadowing; I mean that it refers to Christ and the church" (Ephesians 5:32).

What St. Paul taught two thousand years ago, Pope John Paul II taught in our day. During a visit to San Antonio in September 1987, the Holy Father said:

> This sacrament [of marriage] forms the stable basis of the whole Christian community. Without it, Christ's design for human love is not fulfilled; his plan for the family is not followed. It is precisely because Christ established marriage as a sacrament and willed it to be a sign of his own permanent and faithful love for the Church that the parish must explain to the faithful why all trial marriages, merely civil marriages, free unions, and divorces do not correspond to Christ's plan.

Marriage, then, even as a human contract, has a divine dignity by reason of its very nature, by reason of its origin from God, and by reason of Christ's elevation of it to one of the seven sacraments. That is the difference between marriage and matrimony. Matrimony confers grace—a sharing in the life and love of God—upon baptized persons who enter this state.

The sacrament of matrimony was instituted by Christ as an outward sign both of God's grace and our faith. When the bride and groom administer this sacrament to each other, they begin sharing together in Christ's grace. They will have this supernatural assistance for all the years of their married life, to help them overcome difficulties or disappointments and to cope with every situation. The bishops of Vatican II summed up the significance of matrimony this way:

> Christian spouses have a special sacrament by which they are fortified and receive a kind of consecration in the duties and dignity of their state. By virtue of this sacrament, as spouses fulfill their conjugal and family obligations, they are penetrated with the spirit of Christ. This spirit suffuses their whole lives with faith, hope, and charity. Thus they increasingly advance their own perfection, as well as their mutual sanctification, and hence contribute jointly to the glory of God (*Pastoral Constitution on the Church in the Modern World*, n. 48).

The Twofold Purpose of Marriage

Happiness in marriage depends on your philosophy of marriage, on what you think marriage is all about, on what you see as the purpose of marriage. The secular society in which we live says that the purpose of marriage is pleasure—what can I get out of it? In their selfish pursuit of pleasure for its own sake, the secularists condone and encourage a wide variety of immoral actions—contraception, sterilization, abortion, adultery, and finally, if none of these aberrations can guarantee maximum carnal pleasure, there is always divorce. The results of this false outlook on marriage are painfully apparent today.

The Catholic Church, on the other hand, faithful to the teachings of its Founder, presents a philosophy of marriage that views the married state as a symbol of the union between Christ and his Church and an opportunity for the couple to attain happiness and holiness in this life and in eternity. Marriage, the Church teaches, has a twofold purpose: (1) the procreation and education of children, and (2) the development of mutual love and sanctity between husband and wife. If either purpose is compromised, the marriage and the family will suffer. The two aspects of marriage are inseparable.

The same can be said of the marital act itself. Marital intercourse has a twofold meaning—life-giving and love-giving—and it is a mutilation of the act to deprive it of either meaning. A person who forces sexual acts on a spouse against his or her reasonable wishes deprives the act of its love-giving aspect. So, too, spouses who practice contraception deprive the act of its life-giving meaning. The two purposes of the sexual act were designed by God the Creator. To disregard either one is to contradict not only the nature of both man and woman and their most intimate relationship, but also the plan of God and his divine will.

"Because of the inseparable connection willed by God of the unitive and procreative meaning of the conjugal act," said Pope John Paul during a visit to Canada in 1984, "the Church proclaims that there can be total self-giving in marriage only if these two elements are not artificially separated. In the plan of God, respect for the meaning of the body and openness to life is a necessary condition for ensuring the full dignity of the human person, the full dignity of human life."

The correct philosophy of marriage can be illustrated by drawing a large triangle. Put the word "husband" in the left corner and the word "wife" in the right corner. Put the word "God" at the top and the word "children" in the center of the triangle. There is the true Christian philosophy of marriage—a partnership in sanctity, a union with God.

Never forget that triangle. No matter what you hear the "media people" say, that triangle is the only true philosophy of marriage, and consequently the only one upon which a man and woman can build their happiness. Any Christian marriage that falls short of this ideal will flounder helplessly. When these fundamental components of marriage are rejected, then family life, the individual, and the nation suffer. There cannot be a violation of God's moral norms, of his divine plan, without repercussions. And when God's laws are rejected on a wide scale, the nation suffers.

The Plague of Divorce

In an age of widespread licentiousness and rejection of traditional moral values and traditional marriage, the Catholic Church's prohibition of divorce must seem old-fashioned and foolish. To couples with seemingly insurmountable marital problems, this prohibition must seem particularly harsh and lacking in compassion. Does the Church have to be so strict? Is it not time for the Church to reevaluate its position on divorce and remarriage?

The simple answer to all of these questions is the same: the Catholic Church cannot allow divorce because Jesus Christ rules it out. The Catholic Church prohibits divorce because Christ himself prohibited it. Jesus knew well the devastating effect that divorce would have on family life and society, and so he spoke repeatedly and clearly on the nature of marriage and the question of divorce.

Two places where our Lord's teaching on divorce can be found are the Sermon on the Mount and when a group of Pharisees asked him a question to test his credibility. In the first instance, Jesus, comparing the teaching of the old law and the prophets with his own teaching, said, "It was also said, 'Whenever a man divorces his wife, he must give her a decree of divorce.' What I say to you is: everyone who divorces his wife—lewd conduct is a separate case— forces her to commit adultery. The man who marries a divorced woman likewise commits adultery" (Matthew 5:31-32).

The apparent exception for lewd conduct has puzzled people for centuries. Biblical scholars are not agreed on the meaning of the phrase. That Jesus was not sanctioning divorce for this reason, however, is clear from his other statements, and from the teaching of St. Paul, the teaching of the early Church, and the consistent reaffirmation of his prohibition by his Church down to our own day.

The incident involving the Pharisees gave Jesus another opportunity to state his position on divorce. The Pharisees, trying to trip Jesus up, asked him whether it was permissible for a husband to divorce his wife. Our Lord replied that when a man and woman marry, "they are no longer two but one flesh. Therefore let no man separate what God has joined" (Mark 10:8-9). Later, when his disciples began to question him about this, Jesus told them, "Whoever divorces his wife and marries another commits adultery against her; and the woman who divorces her husband and marries another commits adultery" (Mark 10:11-12).

St. Paul, in his preaching, reiterated Christ's prohibition of divorce and emphasized that it was our Lord's prohibition and not his own: "To those now married, however, I give this command (though it is not mine; it is the Lord's): a wife must not separate from her husband. If she does separate, she must either remain single or become reconciled to him again. Similarly, a husband must not divorce his wife" (1 Corinthians 7:10-11).

Twenty centuries later, the Second Vatican Council labeled divorce a "plague" and a profanation of the sacrament of matrimony (*Pastoral Constitution on the Church in the Modern World*, nos. 47, 49). Pope John Paul, in his letter on *The Role of the Christian Family in the Modern World*, declared that "it is a fundamental duty of the Church to reaffirm strongly . . . the doctrine of the indissolubility of marriage." He said that Christian spouses must "remain faithful to each other forever, beyond every trial and difficulty, in generous obedience to the holy will of the Lord" (n. 20).

And the *Catechism of the Catholic Church* reaffirmed this teaching:

> Divorce is a grave offense against the natural law. It claims to break the contract, to which the spouses freely consented, to live with each other till death. Divorce does injury to the convenant of salvation, of which sacramental marriage is the sign. Contracting a new union, even if it is recognized by civil law, adds to the gravity of the rupture: the remarried spouse is then in a situation of public and permanent adultery" (n. 2384).

The *Catechism* went on to say that "divorce is immoral also because it introduces disorder into the family and into society. This disorder brings grave harm to the deserted spouse, to children traumatized by the separation of their parents and often torn between them, and because of its contagious effect which makes it truly a plague on society" (n. 2385).

Necessity of an Indissoluble Bond

Jesus's strict teaching on divorce, like all of his teachings, makes good sense in the practical order. The very nature of marriage and the family demands an indissoluble bond. The good of both husband and wife and of the children must stand or fall with the marriage tie. What would become of children if parents could separate at their own pleasure? A look today at the homes of divorced parents, and the consequences for the children involved, proves the need of marriage for life.

Divorce has brought with it far more hardships and much more unhappiness in the world than marriage fidelity with its trials and sacrifices. Experience and observation show that by and large the most unhappy and discontented people in the world are not those who are married to one partner for life, but those who have been divorced one or more times.

There are many reasons why married couples seek a divorce: lack of true love, sexual immaturity, marital infidelity, false ideas and practices of responsible parenthood, lack of money, drinking or drugs, and so forth. Most of these excuses could be listed under the first one, lack of true love or, in a word, selfishness. None of these problems is insurmountable. Their solution can be found by studying any successful marriage with its qualities of large-heartedness and forgiveness and true spiritual love—a benevolent love that consists of giving and sacrificing, of always being solicitous for the happiness and salvation of the spouse.

Every law made for the general welfare may mean some hardship in a particular case. Quarantine laws, for instance, frequently impose inconvenience on individuals, but we do not for that reason abolish the laws. Similarly, the Church cannot change its divorce laws just because certain hardship cases exist—and they do exist. The only thing that the Catholic Church can do in such extreme situations is to allow the husband and wife to separate but not of course to remarry.

At the same time, the Church, through its priests and religious, its laity and its agencies, shows compassion and concern for the victims of broken marriages. There is a great need for understanding and assistance for men and women who suddenly find themselves alone in a new lifestyle with no companionship, few friends, little money, new responsibilities, and a sense of loneliness and despair.

What divorcees or separated people want most at a time like this is acceptance by others, to be treated with respect and dignity and not scorned as a pariah. They also need competent and sympathetic help, financial aid, moral support, and spiritual guidance to remain faithful to their Catholic religion. (Bear in mind that it is not divorce but remarriage that bars a Catholic from the Eucharist.) Positive efforts are being made today to cushion the traumatic effects of a broken marriage; they deserve support and participation by all Catholics.

Irregular Marriages

In a 1994 letter to the world's bishops regarding reception of Communion by divorced-and-remarried Catholics, the Sacred Congregation for the Doctrine of the Faith said that "the difficulties and sufferings of those faithful in irregular marriage situations merit special attention. Pastors are called to help them experience the charity of Christ and the maternal closeness of the Church, receiving them with love, exhorting them to trust in God's mercy, and suggesting, with prudence and respect, concrete ways of conversion and participation in the life of the community of the Church" (n. 2).

The letter cautioned, however, that since "authentic understanding and genuine mercy are never separated from the truth, pastors have the duty to remind these faithful of the Church's doctrine concerning the celebration of the sacraments, in particular the reception of the Holy Eucharist" (n. 3). It then spelled out that doctrine:

> The faithful who persist in such a situation may receive Holy Communion only after obtaining sacramental absolution, which may be given only to those who, repenting of having broken the sign of the covenant and of fidelity to Christ, are

sincerely ready to undertake a way of life that is no longer in contradiction to the indissolubility of marriage.

This means, in practice, that when for serious reasons, for example, for the children's upbringing, a man and a woman cannot satisfy the obligation to separate, they take on themselves the duty to live in complete continence, that is, by abstinence from the acts proper to married couples. In such a case they may receive Holy Communion as long as they respect the obligation to avoid giving scandal (n. 4).

What of the Future?

There are serious problems facing Christian marriage today. One could try to ignore these problems, or to wish them away, or to despair of ever solving them. But this is not the Christian way. As in so many other areas of our society, the Christian is called to holiness — first to put his own spiritual and moral house in order, and then to permeate society with Christian principles and example.

Christian marriage will surive this and future crises if married couples understand, promulgate, and live the true philosophy of Christian marriage; if they meet the problems head on and work within their own families and with other families to solve them; if they demonstrate that Christian marriage is vitally important for the spiritual and social well-being of the couples themselves, their families, and society in general.

"The history of mankind, the history of salvation, passes by way of the family," said Pope John Paul in his *Letter to Families*. "In these pages I have tried to show how the family is placed at the center of the great struggle between good and evil, between life and death, between love and all that is opposed to love. To the family is entrusted the task of striving, first and foremost, to unleash the forces of good, the source of which is found in Christ the Redeemer of Man."

He said that "every family unit needs to make these forces their own so that, to use a phrase spoken on the occasion of the Millenium of Christianity in Poland, the family will be 'strong with the strength of God' " (n. 23).

Chapter 4

Between Husband and Wife

> Marriage to be sure is not instituted solely for procreation. Rather, its very nature as an unbreakable compact between persons, and the welfare of the children, both demand that the mutual love of the spouses, too, be embodied in a rightly ordered manner, that it grow and ripen. — Vatican II, *Pastoral Constitution on the Church in the Modern World*, n. 50

At times the discussion of the subject of marriage and the family is so concerned with the modern evils of divorce, artificial birth control, and neglect of parental duties that we are apt to get an unbalanced picture. There is a danger today, even among good people, that a negative instead of a positive attitude may be created. Certainly we must avoid the moral diseases and errors prevalent today. But we must do more. We must look at the positive side and build up a strong, healthy, revitalized family. The first step in this process involves a discussion of the proper relationship between husband and wife.

Marriage is a sacred vocation. It is the state in life to which husbands and wives have been called by God from all eternity. Their meeting, attraction to each other, and decision to set up a Christian home are not the result of blind chance, but are part of the Creator's divine plan. As instruments of God, husbands and wives are involved in a holy and noble undertaking. They have a responsibility not only for their own salvation, but also that of their spouses and their children. How important it is then that husbands and wives understand the earthly and heavenly ramifications of their state in life, and work to mold their marriages into the supernatural unions that God wants them to be.

Three Pillars of Marriage

Where do we begin? How does a couple go about building a happy and holy marriage? Are there certain basic foundations upon which a successful marriage can be constructed? People who have studied marriage and marriage problems are generally agreed on the importance of three foundation stones or pillars that should undergird all marriages: information, communication, and application.

Information. If there is one subject about which there is voluminous information, it is the subject of marriage. From every corner of the printed and electronic media we are deluged with suggestions on how to improve marriages. Much of this material is worthless. No normal husband or wife would ever have the time to go through all of this information, and to sort out the good from the bad. So where do conscientious spouses look for sound information on marriage?

One obvious source, to which we have already referred a number of times, is the Bible, particularly the New Testament. Much valuable and reliable information on marriage, and all phases of life, can be found in the Gospels and the letters of St. Paul. A related source of solid information is the teaching authority of the Church, that is, the writings of the popes and the bishops.

Such documents as the *Catechism of the Catholic Church*, Vatican II's *Pastoral Constitution on the Church in the Modern World*, nos. 47-52, Pope Paul VI's encyclical letter *Humanae Vitae*, Pope John Paul's apostolic exhortation *The Role of the Christian Family in the Modern World*, and his *Letter to Families* are of great value to couples seeking the Church's attitude towards married life and the family.

John Paul has also published a book, *Love and Responsibility*, that contains a series of lectures he delivered over a period of twenty years on sexuality and love.

Finally, married couples can learn by observing other married couples, especially those who appear to have attained a happy and holy marriage. Such lucky couples are more numerous than you think. They might be in your own family, or next door.

You have already noticed them, the way they talk to each other, the joy they experience in doing things together, the way their children reflect credit on them. There is an unmistakable aura of love and happiness about them. They are not perfect; once in a while you catch them acting very humanly. But for the most part, they are in complete control of their situation and offer a shining example of a true matrimonial partnership with God.

Communication. Marriage counselors are agreed that the vast majority of problems between spouses can be traced to poor communication between them. One survey concluded that 87 percent of all marital problems originate in the failure of husbands and wives to communicate adequately with each other. The following complaints are typical: "My wife doesn't understand me." "My husband won't talk to me." "We can't carry on a civil discussion, we always wind up fighting."

By communication we do not mean conversation. Many couples have no difficulty talking to each other, but they do not communicate. They discuss all kinds of trivial matters in order to avoid the major problems that are really troubling them. Other couples do communicate—verbally, with facial expressions or gestures—but they never reach a mutual understanding of each other or their problems. They argue or shout or give each other the silent treatment. Instead of listening to what their partner is trying to say, they are busy thinking of a retort that will put their spouse in his or her place.

What then do we mean by communication? *We mean a constructive and open attempt to reach a mutual understanding and knowledge of each other.* The main consideration in this process, as in all aspects of married life, must be the thoughts, feelings, and reactions of the other person. True communication exists when both spouses are sincerely interested in what the other partner thinks. And when there is disagreement, they discuss their differences calmly and lovingly. There are no harsh or unkind words; there is no ridicule; one partner does not say to the other, "How can you be so stupid as to think such a thing?" Putting it at its simplest: Spouses should treat each other as they would like to be treated.

The only way that a man and woman can really get to know each other and to grow in love is to talk openly and constructively about the things that are most important to them—love and sex,

God and children, money and work, relatives and friends, politics and play. On most things couples will agree. When they do not, each will have to give a little, or perhaps a lot. This giving should not be done grudgingly or resentfully, but generously. It will not be easy; it could be very painful. Spouses who truly love each other, however, will make the sacrifice, and will unselfishly put their partner's feelings ahead of their own. The result will be a peaceful and happy marriage.

Here are a few basic principles to keep in mind:

1. *Always bring grievances into the open.* If a husband is annoyed because his wife's family comes to dinner every Sunday, or a wife is angry because her husband never calls when he has to work late, they should discuss the difficulty openly with each other. Ignoring the problem will not make it go away. It will only fester and may break out later in a violent manner. Bring the grievance out in the open where it can be discussed and resolved.

2. *Do not magnify minor irritations.* All of us are confronted with petty annoyances every day. They are not worth getting excited about and should be overlooked, or handled in a low-key manner.

3. *Always make the meaning of your words clear.* Just as debaters should define their terms, so couples interested in improving their communication should make sure that they are not being misinterpreted or misunderstood. Never assume that your partner knows what you are talking about. An amazing number of marital problems could be avoided if spouses were clear and precise in their communication. In the same vein, spouses should never attempt to read more into a remark than was intended. "I heard what you said," says one mate, "but I know what you really meant." Try not to be like the two psychiatrists who said, "Good morning," as they passed on the street and then walked away thinking, "I wonder what he meant by that."

4. *Avoid angry words and bitter statements.* Guard against harsh and cutting words that you will regret later. No matter how many words may be spoken in the months and years after a shouting match, somehow we never forget the nasty remarks. Spouses who find themselves on the verge of losing their temper should say a prayer for patience or, as a last resort, take a walk. There is a story about an eighty-year-old man who went to the doctor for a check-up and was found to be in excellent health.

Asked for an explanation, the old man replied: "When my wife and I were married, we made a promise that whenever she got angry, she would leave the room and do her housework elsewhere. Whenever I got angry, I would leave the house and take a long walk. And, Doc, for sixty years I've had the greatest outdoor life you ever did see."

5. *Never let bitterness carry over until the next day.* Even if you cannot agree on a problem, grant your partner's sincerity, exchange a good-night kiss, and resolve to resume the discussion on a friendly basis the next day.

6. *Keep disagreements between yourselves.* Nothing will destroy communication between husband and wife faster than involving relatives, friends, or neighbors in disagreements. What mate would speak freely again after having confidential statements carried to outsiders? There is one exception to this rule: if serious problems continue unresolved over a long period of time, endangering the stability of the marriage, then a qualified priest or a trained marriage counselor should be consulted.

Application. Once married couples have acquainted themselves with sound information, and have established constructive lines of communication, the other requirement necessary for a successful marriage is application, not just when troubles arise, but every single day. It is usually small and seemingly unimportant things, such as daily displays of moodiness, lack of consideration, disinterest in a partner's activities, that lead to the deterioration of a marriage, not major crises or disasters.

Hence, a happy relationship demands day-by-day evidence of cheerfulness, concern for a spouse's feelings, and genuine interest in jobs outside the home or in the household routine. One of the worst things a couple can do is to take each other for granted. Little things do mean a lot. Frequent compliments and indications that you care will go farther than huge displays of generosity and attention only on a birthday or an anniversary.

We all can whip up enthusiasm for a major event now and then. The hard part is concentrating on the small details without which the major event would be a failure. The same is true of marriage. Getting excited about a birthday party or an anniversary celebration is comparatively easy; devoting attention to the minor matters that influence the success or failure of a marriage the other 363 days of the year is difficult.

There was a popular song many years ago, one verse of which went like this:

Will someone kindly tell me,
Will someone let me know,
Why I picked a lemon in the garden of love,
Where they say only peaches grow!

That song, in a humorous way, reflects what is happening all too often today when we consider the skyrocketing divorce rate. Of course, the question of matrimonial peaches or lemons is at times relative. A person who is a peach to one may be a lemon to another. But here are certain qualities which, when present, will make a "peach" of a husband or wife, mother or father. In a Christian sense, we might consider five such basic qualities—chastity, unselfishness, affection, sexual love, and humility.

Chastity

If the Christian ideal of chastity before marriage strikes many in our sex-saturated society as old-fashioned and repressive, they must be incredulous at the thought of chastity within marriage. "Are you kidding?" one can hear them say. "Anything goes in marriage. There are no restrictions." The plain fact is, however, that chastity is an essential requirement for a happy and holy marriage.

Couples who enter the married state with visions of unlimited sexual pleasure are in for a big surprise. Like any other bodily appetite, sex can be abused and must be curbed at times for the physical, social, and spiritual well-being of the spouses. For instance, during times of illness, or unavoidable separations, or before and after the birth of a child, couples must practice continence, that is, they must abstain from sexual relations. For unselfish spouses, these temporary situations will pose no serious problems.

There will also be cases where the wife may be unable to bear children without grievous risk to her health or even to her life, or where couples may be financially unable to support another child, or where there may be other serious reasons for spacing out births. Under these conditions, there are only two possible solutions: the moral practice of continence or the immoral practice of contraception. The choice Catholic couples make will depend on several factors: their spiritual life, their responsiveness to the teachings of their Church, and their strength of character.

If couples have never practiced any Christian self-denial, if God has no place in their married life, if they consider the teaching of the Holy Father as just one of many options, if they accept the view of the "media people" that sexual gratification is the ultimate goal of a man-woman relationship, then continence will seem like an impossible, unreasonable, and even detrimental practice. Again, however, the facts are at variance with the prevailing attitude in our modern society, as thousands of happily married couples can testify.

Continence is not only possible, it is desirable in married life. With the mutual consent and affirmative support of both partners, it can enhance the enjoyment of the marital act and raise it from a purely mechanical function to a deeply spiritual union. Furthermore, continence is an absolute requirement for Christian living, offering an alternative to such illicit practices as contraception and adultery.

It must be conceded, however, that continence, in and of itself, is a negative concept. Viewed strictly in this light, it is not difficult to understand why it would seem repressive and out of reach by those who live in spiritual mediocrity, who are obsessed with a hedonistic philosophy of life, who are governed by selfishness rather than by love. But this is not the case when continence is linked with the positive virtue of chastity. In marriage chastity means the integration of sexual love with the procreative end of marriage, as God intended, instead of selfishly seeking sexual pleasure as an end in itself.

It is much easier to make such a statement than it is to live up to it. No one in his right mind would ever suggest that the practice of continence and chastity in marriage is not a terrific struggle. But to couples with strong convictions about life and love, who seek the help of God through constant prayer and frequent reception of the sacraments of Penance and the Holy Eucharist, the ideal of chastity will become, if not easy, at least attainable.

The discipline of chastity, "far from harming conjugal love, rather confers on it a higher human value," Pope Paul said. "It demands continual effort, yet thanks to its beneficent influence, husband and wife fully develop their personalities, being enriched with spiritual values. Such discipline bestows upon family life fruits of serenity and peace, and facilitates the solution of other problems; it favors attention for one's partner, helps both parties to drive out selfishness, the enemy of true love, and deepens their sense of responsibility" (*Humanae Vitae*, n. 21).

Unselfishness

Of all the traits necessary in family life, wholehearted unselfishness has to rank near the top of the list. There can be no successful family life without it. The good of one's partner and the common good of the family must come first, and that means generosity and at times self-sacrifice. Anyone who is really earnest about marriage and family will put his or her own wishes and desires in second place rather than first. An excellent illustration of this quality can be found in the short story, *The Gift of the Magi*, written by the famous author O. Henry.

A young husband and wife living in one of the poorer sections of New York were struggling to get along financially. Della had one thing she prized very much, her beautiful hair; Jim was very attached to one of his few earthly possessions, a pocket watch. These things were very dear to them—little things, perhaps, but they meant a lot to them. It was Christmas Eve and Della had only a few dollars to get a present for Jim. Jim had a meager income and had little left to get a present for Della. While he was at work, Della went to a beauty parlor and sold her hair. With the money she bought a beautiful watch chain that Jim had wanted for some time. Jim came home on Christmas Eve and was dumbfounded when he saw Della's hair. He handed her a package. It contained an expensive set of combs which he had bought with the money he obtained by selling his watch. Della then gave Jim the watch chain.

The point of the story is that both were willing to give up their most precious possession for the sake of the other. This principle is also summed up well in the instruction that for many years was given to couples before marriage:

It is most fitting that you rest the security of your wedded life upon the great principle of self-sacrifice. . . . Henceforth you belong entirely to each other; you will be one in mind, one in heart, and one in affections. And whatever sacrifices you may hereafter be required to make to preserve this common life, always make them generously. Sacrifice is usually difficult and irksome. Only love can make it easy; and perfect love can make it a joy. We are willing to give in proportion as we love. And when love is perfect, the sacrifice is complete.

Affection

According to the dictionary, affection means love, a word very much misunderstood today. Ask ten people to define love and you will probably get ten different answers. Someone has put it this way: "Love is a certain force within a person leading him to lay all he is and all he has at the feet of the one he loves." And that is a good test of love. It is not so much measured by sentiment, physical attraction, or mere words, but by how much you are willing to give, how much you are willing to sacrifice for the one you love.

The true Christian family must be based on this solid love expressed by deeds. Never once in the Gospels is Mary reported as saying to her Son, "I love you." Her love was obvious from the way she acted. Thus the important thing is not so much what is said, but what is done, what is sacrificed willingly.

St. Paul, himself unmarried, gave a summary of love that married couples would do well to take to heart: "Love is patient, love is kind. Love is not jealous, it does not put on airs, it is not snobbish. Love is never rude, it is not self-seeking, it is not prone to anger; neither does it brood over injuries. Love does not rejoice in what is wrong but rejoices with the truth. There is no limit to love's forbearance, to its trust, its hope, its power to endure" (1 Corinthians 13:4-7).

Affection in marriage can be expressed in countless ways. There are physical expressions, such as spontaneous kisses and thoughtful actions; intellectual expressions, such as constructive discussions of all matters which affect husband, wife, and family; and spiritual expressions, such as praying together and living together in the way that God intended.

Sexual Love

One of the great ironies in our sex-saturated society is that so many people are so woefully ignorant about the facts of life and love. Hence the popularity of sex manuals and videos and of men and women who claim to be "experts" in this field. The availability of this information, however, has not diminished the number of people who are confused about their sexuality, primarily because the material is concerned almost exclusively with the physical aspects of sex and hardly at all with its spiritual dimensions.

Sexual intercourse in marriage is a sacred act that was designed by God to provide mutual pleasure to a husband and wife and at times a new life. There is no other proper way to bring children into the world. In the words of Vatican II, "The actions within marriage by which a couple are united intimately and chastely are noble and worthy ones" *(Pastoral Constitution on the Church in the Modern World,* n. 49).

Husbands and wives must treat each other as persons, not things. They must be gentle, patient, considerate, and sensitive to each other's feelings. Love-making without mutual affection and tenderness is nothing more than having sex. Love must be more than just the marital act itself; it must be a morning, noon, and night endeavor by both spouses that includes frequent signs of affection and concern.

If there is true love, understanding, tenderness, patience, and spiritual and emotional rapport between a husband and wife, their relationship will nearly always result in pleasure and joy. Married couples should occasionally reexamine their own attitudes toward love. They should honestly discuss their needs and difficulties with each other and work to improve their relationship if it needs improving. If they are unable to resolve problems, they should consult a qualified marriage counselor.

Humility

The late Cardinal James Gibbons once said: "If we examine the sources of our troubles and agitation, we find that they almost invariably spring from a desire of appreciation or a fear of contempt." Witness the reaction of the wife whose husband has forgotten to bring home flowers for her birthday. "You don't love me any more!" she says. Or the husband whose toast is burned says, "I guess the honeymoon is over!" Many a family difficulty could be averted, many a heartache done away with if humility were put into practice.

Humility does not mean becoming a "shrinking violet" or walking around the house with your head down, telling all who will listen how terrible you are. Humility is truth; it is realizing that we have good qualities and bad qualities, and that the good is from God and the bad from us. If humility of this kind is practiced in the home, then God becomes a part of family life. And what better model of humility could we look up to than our Blessed Lord, "who humbled himself to share in our humanity"? The Son of God became man, was born in a stable when he could have been born in a palace, and died as a criminal on a cross. What more evidence do we need that humility must be a part of our life?

It takes a humble person to admit error, to give in when wrong, to put up with life's constant annoyances. How many marriages would improve tomorrow if both spouses swallowed their pride and resolved to introduce some humility into their lives? It was to those who can overlook the minor faults of others because they are so very aware of their own faults that Christ said, "Blest are the lowly; they shall inherit the land" (Matthew 5:5).

The success or failure of the lifelong partnership of marriage depends on many factors. Holding an important place among those factors, as we have seen, is mutual understanding. It is precisely here that so many couples fail. They do not understand the important differences between men and women. As a result, husbands try to fit wives into a masculine pattern, and wives look at husbands from the feminine viewpoint. This is a mistake because men and women differ in many ways—in their respective vocations, their intellectual processes, and their emotional natures. A mutual understanding of these differences will go a long way towards guaranteeing a happy marriage.

Respective Vocations

Nearly two thousand years ago, St. Paul summed up the roles of Christian wives and husbands:

Wives should be submissive to their husbands as if to the Lord because the husband is head of his wife just as Christ is head of his body the church, as well as its savior. As the church submits to Christ, so wives should submit to their husbands in everything.

Husbands, love your wives, as Christ loved the church. He gave himself up for her. . . . Husbands should love their wives as they do their own bodies. He who loves his wife loves himself. Observe that no one ever hates his own flesh; no, he nourishes it and takes care of it as Christ cares for the church (Ephesians 5:22-29).

These words of St. Paul have been the subject of much controversy down through the centuries and especially in recent years. The reaction of "liberated" people is familiar to all of us. "Wives submit to their husbands! Don't be absurd. That stuff went out with slavery. This is the twentieth century. Why should anyone listen to some male chauvinist who lived at a time when women were treated like dirt?"

St. Paul needs a good public relations firm, for the implication of his words is not what his modern critics would have you believe. He never said or implied that wives were inferior to their husbands. What he did say was that wives should serve their husbands as the Church serves Christ, and that husbands should love their wives as Christ loved the Church. How did Christ show his love for his Church? He suffered and died for it in the greatest demonstration of love the world has ever known.

The true meaning of St. Paul's words is that Christian marriage symbolizes the intimate relationship between Christ and the Church, that wives should serve their husbands in the same spirit that the Church serves Christ, and that husbands should care for their wives with the same devotion that our Lord has for his Church. What other analogy could St. Paul have used that would have conferred higher praise on husbands and wives?

A true wife, then, submits to her husband by her own free decision, not as a result of any demand from him. She trusts her husband completely and is quite happy to follow him. She is an inspiring companion, praising her spouse when he wins a battle, consoling him when he suffers defeat or disappointment, but always encouraging him and demonstrating her faith in him. A good wife is always careful, however, to inspire her husband so that he grows spiritually and emotionally, rather than pushing him only to gain material benefits for her and the family.

The wife's vocation is motherhood. By nature she is ordained for physical and spiritual motherhood. God has entrusted to her the sublime task of bringing children into the world, of fostering the child during its formative years, of guiding it and becoming a loving friend and confidant of her offspring. That is why the Creator gave women an abundance of tenderness and compassion.

A wife is also a manager, a teacher, a nurse, and a creative and versatile playmate for her children. Add to this her role as a gracious and thoughtful helpmate for her husband and you will know why wives are very special people. And husbands are very lucky to have them, as an inspired author of the Old Testament noted centuries ago:

> Happy the husband of a good wife, twice-lengthened are his days; a worthy wife brings joy to her husband, peaceful and full is his life. A good wife is a generous gift bestowed upon him who fears the Lord; be he rich or poor, his heart is content, and a smile is ever on his face (Sirach 26:1-4).

The husband's vocation is leadership. Man, in the ordinary providence of God, was meant to be head of the home. A husband, as the leader of his family, must be strong, but not domineering; he must be a good provider, a teacher to his children, and a source of inspiration to his wife. He must recognize the spiritual and emotional needs of his wife and children and strive always to fulfill those needs. Words of praise and encouragement should never be far from his lips.

God has entrusted to husbands the serious responsibility of caring for and protecting mother and child. They must be able to look to him to solve the problems and overcome the trials in their lives. He will consult with his wife in making important decisions and then carry them out. He must be the head of the family, just as his wife is the heart of the family.

Intellectual Processes

It is important for couples to realize that husbands and wives think in a different way and arrive at conclusions by different thought processes. Men ordinarily follow cold, solid reasoning, somewhat devoid of sentiment, when seeking the solution to a problem. Women usually follow spontaneous, sympathetic intuition. They are more sensitive to another's sentiments and feelings; they are attentive to details.

We do not mean to imply that a woman never reasons logically. Rather, we are saying that she reaches conclusions without thinking a matter out systematically. A judgment on her part is mingled with feelings and imagination. But she is very often correct in spite of rushing through reasoning to reach conclusions quickly. Those who scoff at a woman's intuition would do well to look at the record and to consider her almost uncanny ability to arrive at the right answer in many situations. When a problem arises, a man will slowly, by logical steps, seek a solution. A woman, on the other hand, will be prompted by her intuition to follow the most advantageous course spontaneously. A man, once having logically reached a solution, is slow to change his mind. A woman is more adaptable.

A man leans toward the abstract in his thinking, a woman towards the concrete. A father is more apt to insist on invariable rules or norms in dealing with his children, while a mother adapts herself according to circumstances. Thus father says that Mary can never go out on a school night; mother realizes that there might be a particular set of circumstances when it will be all right for Mary to go out.

These distinctive intellectual qualities in a husband and wife, strange as it may seem, actually complement each other. If there is mutual understanding of these differences between man and woman, friction will not result and couples will use them in a harmonious way to promote the good of the family.

Emotional Natures

The differences between men and women extend also to their emotions. A woman is blessed with a sensitive nature. She is moved to pleasure, sadness, fear, or anxiety by what, to a husband, are trifles. Ask her to explain her reaction and she cannot. She has a lively imagination, whereas a man leans more towards solid facts, with little reliance on his feelings. A woman will more readily laugh at anything that is amusing and cry at the drop of a handkerchief. A man, by nature, is attracted by this emotional responsiveness; a woman is attracted by the firmness and steadfastness of the man.

In the realm of love and affection, as we noted earlier, a woman seeks to be loved, to have constant affection and attention showered on her. This is especially true when she is pregnant and frequently just after the birth of a child. At these times, husbands must outdo themselves in tenderness and consideration. Women also desire to give themselves completely in love, in wholehearted sacrifice, in total devotion. A husband's love may be just as deep, but it is less external or expressive. A man seeks someone to love; a woman seeks someone who will love her. To summarize what we have said:

Man is Characterized

from the physical aspect	by	strength
from the intellectual aspect	by	logic and reason
from the emotional aspect	by	protective love
		stability

Woman is Characterized

from the physical aspect	by	gentleness
from the intellectual aspect	by	intuition
from the emotional aspect	by	desire to love
		responsiveness
		sensitivity

For Better or for Worse?

The Polish have an old proverb: "Before going to war, pray; before going to sea, pray twice; before getting married, pray three times." This proverb simply recognizes the fact that marriage is one of the most serious steps in one's life and that God must have a part in it from beginning to end. "Unless the Lord build the house," the psalmist said, "they labor in vain who build it" (Psalm 127:1). Young couples about to establish a home and a family must not ignore this sound advice.

When couples approach the altar on their wedding day, they have stars in their eyes. They can see nothing but good times and happy experiences ahead of them. It is doubtful that this rosy outlook ever paled even when the priest once instructed newlyweds that the future, "with its hopes and disappointments, its successes and its failures, its pleasures and its pains, its joys and its sorrows, is hidden from your eyes. You know that these elements are mingled in every life, and are to be expected in your own. And so, not knowing what is before you, you take each other for better or for worse, for richer or for poorer, in sickness and in health, until death."

More recent marriage rites are less foreboding. Either the bride and groom state their promise to be true to each other "in good times and in bad, in sickness and in health," all the days of their life, or the priest elicits an "I do" from each of them to the same promise presented in the form of a question.

But newlyweds seldom think about problems that might arise in the future. Or if they do think about them, they assume that they will be able to cope with such problems when the time comes. And if they try to live up to the Christian ideals of marriage, if God is an important factor in their lives, and if they have tried to develop a deep love for and mutual understanding of each other, there is a good chance that their marriage will turn out for better and not for worse.

Bearing Crosses in Marriage

But what if in the course of time one party finds himself or herself joined to a partner in marriage for worse instead of for better? Perhaps the husband has become an alcoholic, or is running around with another woman, or is gambling away his week's pay. Or maybe the wife is having an affair, or has become a drug addict, or has decided to "liberate" herself from her domestic responsibilities. What then?

Or suppose one spouse is horribly crippled in an automobile accident, or suffers a severe mental breakdown, or is afflicted with a chronic disease, or they have a badly deformed or retarded child who requires constant care. What happens to that glorious picture of marriage they shared on their wedding day?

The immediate answer of the "media people" is divorce. They say that no person should have to remain in a marriage that has gone sour; that no one should do anything unless he can get something out of it; that God does not expect any person to live in such an unhappy situation.

The "media people" conveniently ignore the words of Christ: "If a man wishes to come after me, he must deny his very self, take up his cross, and begin to follow in my footsteps" (Matthew 16:24). They are so self-centered and selfish that they look with disbelief at those people who, in the words of St. Francis, do not "so much seek to be consoled as to console; to be understood as to understand; to be loved as to love."

Many a cross in marriage can be borne and survived if deep spiritual and Christian love is present. The cross may be a blessing in disguise. The patient and courageous bearing of that cross may bring a shower of graces on the one willing to bear it, and perhaps even the reform of the other party. There have been many cases of sincere and loving spouses following the advice of St. Paul: "Help carry one another's burdens; in that way you will fulfill the law of Christ" (Galatians 6:2).

The humble acceptance of crosses, trials, and sufferings can be of tremendous spiritual value, not only in large difficulties but also in the small annoyances of each day. Little by little, husbands and wives can learn to see the hand of God in every part of their lives. A harsh remark, a child's sickness, a spoiled dinner, difficulties at work—all are permitted by God and can be offered up in a spirit of sacrifice and love. Every situation, large or small, can be a means of bringing the family closer to the model of the Holy Family.

If crosses should come in married life, the answer is not to sever the bond, for God has made that permanent. The answer is to unite these crosses with Christ to sanctify yourself, to make yourself a spiritually better and stronger person, to help your children, to convert and redeem your spouse. Great love can do it as it has done it in the past. "The unbelieving husband is consecrated by his believing wife; the unbelieving wife is consecrated by her believing husband," St. Paul has said (1 Corinthians 7:14).

The Apostle also had good reason for comparing the love of husband and wife to the love of Christ for his Church. Christ delivered himself up, gave himself completely for the Church and for us. So some wives and husbands are asked to make great sacrifices. They cannot make them unless they call on God for help. "Apart from me you can do nothing," our Lord has told us (John 15:5). The answer to great trials or petty difficulties in marriage is not to give up or to become embittered; it is to recognize the faults and failings in each spouse, to make the most of the good things and to accept the bad, and to work and pray for a marital relationship that will provide some true happiness here and eternal happiness hereafter.

One young couple of our acquaintance has a very beautiful custom based on real love and Christ-like understanding. Before each meal, the husband says grace and then kisses his wife. Only after this ritual do they sit down at the table for a meal. This custom is practiced whether there are visitors for dinner or not. No petty difficulty can last for long when such calling on God and the expressing of mutual love are an intimate part of every day. The same can be said of couples who pray and frequent the sacraments together. The closer a couple is to Christ, the closer they are to a happy and holy marriage.

A One Hundred Percent Proposition

The task of making a success of marriage rests on both husband and wife. It is not a fifty-fifty proposition, as some people contend, but a full-time task that demands one hundred percent from both spouses. "Success in marriage," says a time-honored proverb, "means not only finding the right mate but also being the right mate." A good test of a marriage is to ask each partner who gives the most to the marriage. If both partners give credit to the other, they have a happy and successful marriage.

A happy marriage does not eliminate all of life's problems, but it can make them more bearable. Certainly a house full of harmony and happiness is smiled upon by God. In the words of the Old Testament: "With three things I am delighted, for they are pleasing to the Lord and to men: harmony among brethren, friendship among neighbors, and the mutual love of husband and wife" (Sirach 25:1).

Chapter 5

Between Parent and Child

> By its very nature the institution of marriage and married life is ordered to the procreation and education of the offspring and it is in them that it finds its crowning glory. Children are the supreme gift of marriage and contribute greatly to the good of the parents themselves. —*Catechism of the Catholic Church*, n. 1652

It is indeed true that the family is the basic unit of society, and its influence on the well-being of the individual, the Church, and the nation is widely recognized. The importance of the family extends into many fields, but when we look at the proper mission of the family as established by God, namely, the procreation and training of children, then we must acknowledge that the relation of the family to youth is of the highest importance. The training and attitudes which are conveyed to young people within the family circle will affect significantly the future of our Church and our country.

Unfortunately, we must concede at the outset that everything is not as it should be with the family today. There are serious problems to face and Christian parents and children should take the lead in confronting and solving them. Alcoholism, crime, drugs, juvenile criminality, mental illness, suicide, lack of respect for authority, and the weakened influence of religion are troubles only too familiar to the present generation of children and adults. These problems have always existed, of course, but never have they been so widespread, never have they seemed so overwhelming, never has the response to them seemed so timid and uncertain.

Even good parents do not seem anxious to make the necessary effort to protect their children from these problems or to bring the level of family life up to the Christian ideal. Instead, some parents, perhaps without even realizing it, seem resigned to lowering the level of family life to pagan depths. They have lost their will to fight. They are like the man walking along the street who saw a drunkard lying in the gutter. The man looked at the drunkard for a minute and then said, "I can't lift you up, but I tell you what I'll do. I'll lie down beside you!"

So often, sincere parents look at some youthful activities today—their viewing of degrading and dirty movies, their use of foul language, their reading of immoral books and magazines, their attachment to alcohol and drugs, their involvement in early and prolonged sexual experiences, their contempt for the property and possessions of others—and then, with a shrug of the shoulders, say, "Oh, well, young people are different these days. I guess I can't be too strict with my children."

We are not implying that all young people fall into these categories. There are many boys and girls who are a credit to their families, their Church, and their God. But even these children find it increasingly more difficult to buck the tide of immorality and licentiousness. They are often subjected to ridicule and scorn and even physical abuse for not doing what "everybody else" is doing. These children need the support and encouragement and example of a true Christian family to do the right thing in a society that is intent on doing the wrong thing. With the proper education and training at home, Catholic boys and girls can become witnesses to Christ in the world. They can let the light of his teachings shine before their friends and acquaintances in an increasingly paganized society. This is their mission and the mission of every follower of Christ.

In order to deal with the problems confronted by parents and children, it is necessary to discuss the purpose of the family and the roles and duties entrusted to mothers, fathers, and children by God himself. Only by starting from the foundations and working up can we draw a blueprint for the ideal Christian family.

The Purpose of the Family

It is and always has been the teaching of the Catholic Church that a prime purpose of the institution of marriage is the begetting and upbringing of children. In the words of Vatican II: "The true practice of conjugal love, and the whole meaning of the family life which results from it, have this aim: that the couple be ready with stout hearts to cooperate with the love of the Creator and the Savior, who through them will enlarge and enrich his own family day by day" (*Pastoral Constitution on the Church in the Modern World*, n. 50).

What an exalted vocation marriage and family life is! God could have decided to bring new lives into the world by direct creation as he did with Adam and Eve. But instead, he chose to have human beings work in partnership with him. A husband and wife have a unique position in God's scheme of things. They cooperate with God in creation. The parents work with God in producing the body; he produces the soul. Marriage cannot accomplish this fundamental purpose without the contribution of Almighty God.

Pope John Paul on many occasions called young people "the hope of the Church." This very simple but significant statement points up another purpose of the family: the upbringing and training of children. Husbands and wives not only share in the creation of children with God, but they must then work with God to educate and prepare their children for their proper role in life.

People make headlines today if they discover a new medicine to cure a deadly disease, if they write a best-selling book, if they pitch a no-hitter in the World Series, or if they win a tennis championship. Prominent people from all walks of life are held in esteem. But their accomplishments pale into insignificance when compared with the task of training a soul for God, of joining with God in bringing new souls into the world and molding them according to the plan of God for their eventual return to him. Children are the truly important people of our day and our hope for the future.

The Christian family should be a team, with each member having certain responsibilities to fulfill. When one or more members of a baseball team neglect their duties and fail to execute their proper role, the team runs into trouble. The same is true of the family. In the game of life, however, the consequences of poor teamwork are far more devastating than those experienced in an athletic event.

Hence the need for spelling out the duties and responsibilities of each member of the family. Only when these roles are fully understood and faithfully lived will the family be strong enough to

bring about the Christianization of our society (cf. Pope John
Paul's *Letter to Families*).

The Role of Parents

The goal of Christian parents must be to help their children
become Christian men and women in the fullest sense. To have
any hope of accomplishing this goal, parents must first of all be
completely Christian themselves. They must be models worthy of
imitation by their children. The importance of good example, of
practicing what you preach, can never be overemphasized. It is
not enough for parents to point out the way to their children; they
must lead the way.

If they want their children to pray, they must pray; if they
want their children to go to church, they must go to church; if they
want their boys and girls to be truthful and honest, parents must
be truthful and honest; if they want them to respect the name of
God and refrain from cursing, they must do likewise; if they want
their children to read decent literature and watch wholesome
movies and television programs, parents must not violate these
conditions themselves.

The most obvious role of parents is that of providing children
with the necessities of life—food, shelter, clothing, medical care,
education, and so forth. All of these things are important in giving
a child a sense of security and well-being. Children must be
taught, however, the value and proper use of the material goods
of this world.

They must never get the idea that life is just one long pursuit
of material wealth. They must be encouraged early and often to
thank God for the material blessings that have come their way.
They must be told of their obligation as followers of Christ to
share their earthly goods with those who are less fortunate. "I
assure you," our Lord said, "as often as you did it for one of my
least brothers, you did it for me" (Matthew 25:40).

Parents must give their children love and affection. There is a
story of a little girl named Laura who lived in an orphanage. Her
playmates often made fun of her because of an unsightly birthmark on her face, and so Laura preferred to play by herself. One
day, one of the teachers at the orphanage saw the little girl climb
the fence that enclosed the property, reach over the top, and place
an envelope on the branch of a tree just beyond the fence. After

Laura had returned to the building where she lived, the teacher retrieved the envelope. In it was a note with these words: "To anybody who reads this, I love you! Laura."

Children crave love and affection. If they do not find these feelings at home, they will seek them outside the home. The love of parents for their offspring can have a great influence on them. This love and affection can be shown in many ways. It may consist of understanding and support for children; it may involve giving them a sense of worth and self-esteem; it may mean openness and sympathy, advice and direction, encouragement in their school work or in their hobbies, and respect for their privacy, their good reputation, their personal religious life, and their choice of vocation.

Whether by word or deed, parents must communicate their love to their children. They must, in fact, just plain communicate. They must be approachable, they must show an interest in what their children are saying, they must answer their questions honestly and fully, they must listen, listen, listen. There should be family conversation times, as well as opportunities for private talks. Parents should never refuse a child's request for private conversation. It is through open and honest dialogue that children will gain confidence in their parents, and parents will gain confidence in their children.

Not every conversation between parents and children will result in complete agreement on both sides. All opinions should be voiced in a spirit of charity, and once a decision is reached, the discussion should be terminated. Children will find some decisions hard to accept, but if they feel that their parents have been open and fair and attentive to their views, they will usually abide by whatever decisions are reached. It is when parents refuse even to discuss the matter in a candid and reasonable way that unhealthy conflicts arise in the family and children feel less and less inclined to seek parental advice about some problem or situation that has arisen.

The Role of Children

Just as parents have certain duties and responsibilities to their children, so children have duties and responsibilities to their parents. There is no one, with the exception of God, to whom children owe more loyalty and devotion than their parents. The parents who, from the day they were born, have fed, clothed, sheltered, and educated them, have taken care of them when they were sick, and have given them just about everything they could ever reasonably want or need. It is doubtful that most children could ever do as much for their parents as has been done for them.

Children should honor their mother and father, said Pope John Paul in his *Letter to Families*, "because for you they are in a certain sense representatives of the Lord; they are the ones who gave you life, who introduced you to human existence in a particular family line, nation, and culture. After God, they are your first benefactors. While God alone is good, indeed the Good itself, parents participate in this supreme goodness in a unique way. And so, honor your parents!" (n. 15).

The best way that children can repay their parents is by always showing them love, respect, and obedience, especially when they disagree on something, and by taking time now and then to say thank you. They can repay their parents by discussing things with them, asking their advice, keeping them informed of their activities, and generally being open and honest with them. Genuine communication is a two-way street. Children who expect their parents to listen to them must listen to their parents. They must be polite and courteous, understanding and patient. When discussion has ended and a decision has been made, children must accede to their parents' wishes because parents stand in the place of God. In the words of St. Paul: "Children, obey your parents in the Lord, for that is what is expected of you. 'Honor your father and mother' is the first commandment to carry a promise with it—'that it may go well with you, and that you may have long life on the earth'" (Ephesians 6:1-3).

Children who keep open the lines of communication with their parents and with their brothers and sisters will avoid many of the problems and heartaches which plague so many young people today.

Children also should help mom and dad with the household chores—making the beds, cleaning the house, doing the dishes, preparing the meals, mowing the lawn, running errands, taking care of the younger children, and so forth. These chores should be done automatically and voluntarily and not only after mom or dad has to yell or threaten to a take away some privilege. These tasks are not always pleasant, but neither is getting up for work every morning or washing clothes or putting meals on the table.

Doing the chores willingly and with a smile might not make them any more pleasant, but it will go a long way toward making your house a happy home.

To sum up the roles of the members of a family, we can turn to the advice of the kindly Pope John XXIII:

> Let the father of the family take the place of God among his children, and not only by his authority but by the upright example of his life also stand clearly in the first place.
>
> Let the mother, however, rule firmly and agreeably over her offspring by gentleness and virtue in the domestic setting. Let her behave with indulgence and love towards her husband and, along with him, let her carefully instruct and train her family, the most precious gift given by God.
>
> The children are always to obey the parents who bore them, as is fitting, and love them, and be to them not only a comfort but, in time of need, a real support.
>
> Within the walls of the home let there be that warmth of love which existed in the family at Nazareth (*Ad Petri Cathedram*).

The Education and Training of Children

There is no educational institution more important for a child than the family. No school can compensate for what is lacking there. The home is the natural education element and the parent is the teacher appointed by God. In the words of Vatican II: "Parents must be acknowledged as the first and foremost educators of their children. Their role as educators is so decisive that scarcely anything can compensate for their failure in it" (*Declaration on Christian Education*, n. 3).

The task of training children and transmitting values to them in today's society is an awesome one. It begins at birth and continues until children become of age to make a life for themselves. The task belongs to both parents and is one more reason against divorce. The upbringing of children cannot be safeguarded except through a stable marriage bond.

We do not exaggerate when we say that a child's training must begin at birth. A famous prison warden once observed that "it is in the high chair not the electric chair that crime must be fought." And psychologists assure us that a child is pretty well formed by the age of six. These pre-school years are vitally important and should be a matter of serious thought and concern for parents.

The family is the first and best school of faith and morals because it is there that children first learn of God, learn to love him and pray to him, learn of the Church, learn the wholesomeness of human companionship, and learn to love their neighbor. Or at least children will learn these things if their parents are oriented toward God in their daily lives. In a truly Catholic family, the word "God" should be as familiar to children as "mom" and "dad."

As soon as children begin to understand, prayers should be taught and stories told of God and Jesus, Mary and the saints. Small children find Bible stories fascinating and religious and moral principles can be taught by reading to them of God the Creator, Adam and Eve, Moses, Daniel, and the events in the life of Jesus.

Children will have many questions about these stories and about God. Parents can use these opportunities to impart a world of valuable knowledge about God and our relationship with him to their youngsters at a time when their minds are like sponges, just waiting to soak up information. Parents who neglect these important years may regret it later when they are confronted by teenagers who have little or no interest in God or his Church.

When the time comes for children to enter school, Catholic parents have the duty "to entrust their children to Catholic schools, when and where this is possible, to support such schools to the extent of their ability, and to work along with them for the welfare of their children" (*Declaration on Christian Education*, n. 8). Where Catholic schools are not available, parents should enroll their children in parish programs of religious education, and should become involved in these programs themselves.

Parents cannot completely delegate the religious education of their children to any school or program. The role of the parent as a religious educator does not cease when a child enters school. The parent must continue the training and moral formation of the child at home and make sure that the child's classroom instruction does not contradict or undermine correct doctrine or sound morality. Parents should also take advantage of good Catholic literature and adult education courses to keep themselves informed and prepared to teach their children.

Among the spiritual duties of parents is the obligation to pray for and with their children. The power of prayer can be astounding. Many problems could be solved if some of the time spent in undue concern and anger was devoted to prayer. St. Monica had a problem child, the future St. Augustine. She prayed for him for many long years and through those prayers saw him return to the God from whom he had drifted far away.

Family life should be one constant prayer, from the Morning Offering, to grace before and after meals, to the family rosary, to evening prayers and spiritual readings. The family that prays together stays together. Important, too, is frequent recourse to the sacraments—Mass and Communion regularly, Confession frequently. This daily striving for holiness cannot help but make the duties and responsibilities of family life easier to shoulder.

Since we have mentioned the sacraments, parents should be reminded of their important spiritual duty of having a child baptized promptly. Following upon this is the obligation to arrange for a child's First Penance, First Communion, and Confirmation, and to take an active part in the child's preparation for these sacraments. With proper instruction and encouragement from parents, these sacramental encounters with Christ can be joyous and fruitful occasions for children that will stay with them for the rest of their lives.

Finally, parents and guardians are bound to observe and correct youths entrusted to their care. To put this in a practical light, it means, for instance, to supervise the children's school work, to know who their friends are, to find out where they are going when they leave the house. Any mother or father who takes the attitude that as long as there is peace and quiet in the house, little effort need be made to find out where their boys or girls are, or with whom they are spending their time, or what they are doing, will be answerable to God for neglecting important parental responsibilities.

Parents must check what their children are reading, what television shows they are watching, what movies they are viewing. Parents who are indifferent to having their children read morally objectionable books and magazines, or view filthy and degrading programs and films, share in the guilt. Massive quantities of morally objectionable materials pour out in a polluted stream each year. Adults are bound before God not only to avoid such materials themselves but to steer their children away from them, too.

This obligation of correcting and training is by no means easy, and that is all the more reason why parents should rely on prayer and the sacraments to seek God's special help in this all-important job. With God's help parents can be just, merciful, patient, and considerate in dealing with their children.

Effective Discipline

Failure to discipline a child and to show that he or she cannot always have their own way is no favor to the child. When an undisciplined child runs into serious difficulties, and finds that these difficulties cannot be resolved immediately, he often becomes angry and even violent. He is so used to having his own way that he cannot tolerate resistance to his demands.

Children need and want limits. It is vital for their security and well-being that they know what is expected of them, what the boundaries are which govern their activities. Limits, boundaries, and expectations must be pointed out very early in a child's life and then the reins can be loosened as the child grows older and more mature.

Discipline to be effective must be fair, firm, consistent, and constructive. *Fair* means that the punishment should fit the crime. *Firm* means that the punishment should be decisively and promptly administered. *Consistent* means that the same infraction should always be treated in the same way, not punished one time and overlooked another; not resulting in an easy punishment for one child and harsh sentence for another. It also means that both parents agree on the disciplinary system, and support each other in its enforcement. *Constructive* means that discipline should not be strictly negative. An explanation of why the conduct was bad should accompany the punishment so that the child can learn from the experience.

Finally, discipline must be balanced with love. Just as a husband and wife should not let disagreements and conflicts carry over until the next day, so parents should not allow children to go to sleep at night without discussing the incident or without expressing their continued love and affection for the offender. Parental firmness does no psychological harm to children. On the contrary, it shows youngsters that parents really care about them.

A word of advice to parents and future parents: Children respond to praise much quicker than they do to criticism. Establish a system of rules and responsibilities for the family, and enforce it. But do not constantly nag the children about little things. And when they are good, reward them with praise, affection, treats, and extra privileges. Children generally aim to please their parents and win their approval, so frequent expressions of that approval will accomplish more than constant criticism and ridicule. Firm leadership coupled with love, understanding, and patience will result in happier and well-behaved offspring and a peaceful family environment.

Sex Education—When, What, and How Much?

There are few matters more controversial today than education in human sexuality. People are generally agreed on the need for sex education for children, but they are far apart when it comes to the best way of meeting this very important need. Some feel that it should be the exclusive prerogative of parents; others that the schools ought to help out. Some feel that the moral dimensions of sexuality must be included; others say that morality should have little or nothing to do with it, that only clinical details and contraceptive techniques should be presented.

What does the Church expect of Catholic parents in this sensitive area? It expects, in the words of Vatican II, that as children advance in years, they will be given "positive and prudent sexual education" (*Declaration on Christian Education*, n. 1). Pope John Paul expanded on this instruction in 1981, calling on parents "to give their children a clear and delicate sex education." He said that "sex education, which is a basic right and duty of parents, must always be carried out under their attentive guidance, whether at home or in educational centers chosen and controlled by them" (cf. *Catechism of the Catholic Church*, n. 1632).

The Holy Father also said that "the Church is firmly opposed to an often widespread form of imparting sex information dissociated from moral principles. That would merely be an introduction to the experience of pleasure and a stimulus leading to the loss of serenity—while still in the years of innocence—by opening the way to vice" (*The Role of the Christian Family in the Modern World*, n. 37).

It is not within the scope of this book to offer detailed instructions on how to educate children in human sexuality; sound literature along these lines is readily available. However, we would like to offer a few basic thoughts and suggestions. They are taken from the Pontifical Council for the Family's 1995 document *The Truth and Meaning of Human Sexuality*.

"Each child is a unique and unrepeatable person and must receive individualized formation" (n. 65).

"Each child's process of maturation as a person is different. Therefore, the most intimate aspects, whether biological or emotional, should be communicated in a personal dialogue" (n. 66).

"Experience shows that this dialogue works out better when the parent who communicates the biological, emotional, moral, and spiritual formation is of the same sex as the child or young person" (n. 67).

"The moral dimension must always be part of their explanations. Parents should stress that Christians are called to live the gift of sexuality according to the plan of God, who is love, i.e., in the context of marriage or of consecrated virginity and also celibacy. They must insist on the positive value of chastity and its capacity to generate true love for other persons .... Only a person who knows how to be chaste will know how to love in marriage or in virginity" (n. 68).

"In talks with children suitable advice should always be given regarding how to grow in the love of God and one's neighbor, and to overcome any difficulties: These means are discipline of the senses and the mind, watchfulness and prudence in avoiding occasions of sin, the observance of modesty, moderation in recreation, wholesome pursuits, assiduous prayer, and frequent reception of the sacraments of Penance and the Eucharist. Young people especially should foster devotion to the immaculate Mother of God" (n. 71).

"Parents should provide this information with great delicacy, but clearly and at the appropriate time .... Giving too many details to children is counterproductive. But delaying the first information for too long is imprudent because every human person has natural curiosity in this regard, and sooner or later everyone begins to ask themselves questions, especially in cultures where too much can be seen, even in public" (n. 75).

The document also discusses the principal stages in the development of children (innocence, puberty, and adolescence), urges parents not to allow educators or anyone else to interfere with their children's "right to chastity" (n. 118), declares that "no material of an erotic nature should be presented to children or young people of any age, individually or in a group" (n. 126), and warns against methods and ideologies, such as "values clarification" (n. 140), that would threaten the rights of parents and the moral life of their children.

This document is must reading for those who wish to understand the Church's teaching on the truth and meaning of human sexuality.

Parenthood Means Sacrifice

There was a story in the newspapers not long ago of an eight-year-old boy who fought his way three miles through deep snow to a neighbor's house to seek help for his mother, who lay dying at home. Help was obtained, the mother was rushed to a hospital, and her life was saved. "It was one of the most remarkable things I've ever seen a boy do," the neighbor said.

The point of the story is that parents never know how their children will react in certain situations. Mothers and fathers can only give their offspring good example and good training, teach them to love God and their neighbor, to treat others as they would like to be treated—and pray. Having done all of these things, parents can then stand before God and say that they did all they could to return to God this soul entrusted to their care.

The task of parenthood requires all-out service and sacrifice. In a world where men and women are brought up surrounded by an attitude of selfishness and individualism, parents need gallant hearts that dare to be different. But any goal worth obtaining means sacrifice and daring to do what is right instead of what "everyone else" is doing. And the goal of a successful family life surpasses the earthly success of any other human endeavor. A good home, where rights and duties of both parents and children are honored, comes as close to earthly paradise as anything we might hope for in this life.

A false picture, a caricature, of marriage and the family is being presented to us today by the pleasure-seekers in our society. We must be on guard not to be influenced by this phony portrait. The sooner the world gets back to the true Christian ideals of marriage and the family, to the recognition and realization of the primary purpose of the family — cooperation with God in the pro-creation and education of youth — the better it will be for the world.

St. Francis de Sales gave this important bit of advice to mothers and fathers:

Parents ought often to speak of God to their children, but yet more often to speak to God of their children.

Family life is important. Christ himself spent thirty out of his thirty-three years on earth in the midst of a family. The ideal of Christian family life was set by Jesus, Mary, and Joseph of Nazareth. But Nazareth is set on a hill, and you have to climb to get there.

Chapter 6

The Teenage Years

> Young persons exert very substantial influence on modern society. . . .They themselves ought to become the prime and direct apostles of youth, exercising the apostolate among themselves and through themselves and reckoning with the social environment in which they live. —Vatican II, *Decree on the Apostolate of the Laity,* n. 12

From the time of Adam the raising of children has been a difficult task, particularly during the teenage years. The reason for this is simple: parents and children come from different generations and tend to view their situations from different perspectives. This so-called "gap" will cause no more than the usual disagreements and annoyances if parents and children maintain a mutual respect, understanding, consideration, and love for each other.

The rearing of teenagers is more complicated for parents today, however, because of increasing pressures and influences from outside the family. These may come from teachers, from the children's peers, or from the mass media, especially from television, which some observers have termed "the third parent" in the average family. It is a fact that by the time a child reaches the age of sixteen, he or she will have spent about fifteen thousand to twenty thousand hours in front of the television set. Imagine if the Church could have this much influence over the development of a child!

When you consider, too, the kinds of information and propaganda that are conveyed to the child by television, is it any wonder that parents find it hard to develop Christian attitudes in their offspring?

Parents who are sincere about educating and training their children must realize that outside influences, not all of them good, have a major impact on the development of their teenagers. Parents must do all they can, therefore, to screen out the bad influences as much as possible and increase their own good influence, and that of the Church, on their sons and daughters. This is one of their first and foremost duties. Taking such steps will frequently pit responsible Catholic parents against friends, neighbors, and society, but parents must have confidence in their own judgment and the courage of their convictions. For only they, not friends, neighbors, or society, will have to answer to God for the way in which their children were brought up.

The Crisis of Authority

The revolt against authority has reached frightening levels today. Christians have to be concerned at the widespread contempt for authority, a contempt that has infected many teenagers and even children in their pre-teen years. The situation that exists in many of our schools today, where the ABCs have come to mean assaults, burglaries, and crimes, is just one illustration of the problem that exists. Nor has the Christian family been immune from this disease, and it is in the family that the revolt must be stopped first if we hope to correct the situation in society at large.

What do we mean by authority? *Authority is the right to command and enforce obedience.* In the family, authority is the foundation of discipline. Without it, family life would be chaotic. It is vitally important, however, that we not neglect to mention the place of love in this picture. Authority with love is a firm but gentle molding of a child's character after the pattern of Jesus Christ.

Parents, by training and experience, know more than their children and are their offspring's most important advisors. What a tragedy it is when there is little or no communication between parents and children, and the opportunity is lost for mutual understanding and sharing of each other's burdens. Those who have survived the trials of adolescence should sympathize with the new generation of teenagers and do all they can to help their sons and daughters to come through this experience as painlessly as possible.

Another point worthy of note is that most teenagers like their parents, even though they would have trouble telling them so. Teenagers should show their love for their parents. Why hide it? Just as the love of a husband and wife can wither if it is not expressed, so too with the love between parents and children. And that love should be expressed now — not when it's too late and you find yourself at the funeral of a parent, wishing that you had another chance to tell them how much they meant to you.

Authority does not have to be the bugaboo that many people make it out to be. Many teenagers want parental supervision. They need limits and boundaries. They can handle only so much freedom and they crave the security of knowing what is expected of them. They will rebel at times, and concerned and loving parents, exercising the authority given to them by God, will stand firm, while at the same time trying to see and understand the teenager's point of view. Teenagers will then respect, obey, and love their parents for being firm but fair in enforcing discipline.

The general guideline in these situations is that parents should be strict enough to keep children in line, and lenient enough to allow them to make some decisions for themselves—and to allow them to take the consequences when their decisions do not turn out as expected. Parents make a mistake when they try to remove or cushion all the bumps on the road of their teenager's life, for they give their child a false picture of life and ill prepare him for adulthood.

We all learn from the rough spots on the road of life, and no child should be raised with the idea that life is just one long, wide, and smooth superhighway. Parents must be honest and truthful with their children, particularly their teenagers, if they expect to gain their trust and confidence.

There is a story about a twenty-year-old man who was discussing his parents with a friend. "You know," he said, "when I was sixteen, my father didn't know anything. And today he knows quite a bit. It's amazing how much he learned in just four years." After the son had made a few mistakes of his own, he began to realize that none of us is perfect and that perhaps his father was a pretty smart individual after all.

It is too bad that so many parents and children have to go through these difficult stages before they come to appreciate and understand each other. Let us turn to four problem areas in the life of teenagers and offer some guidelines to parents and adolescents that might be helpful in facing and solving these problems in a Christian manner. The troublesome areas might be classified as the "Four Ds"—Dating, Drinking, Drugs, and Driving.

The Teenager and Dating

We know very little about the life of St. Valentine, except that he was martyred for his faith in the third century. How he became the patron saint of lovers, why we exchange tender notes on the fourteenth of February every year, are questions whose answers have been lost in the misty corridors of time. What we do know, however, is that young people will be attracted to each other, will exchange love notes, and will be a delight to see when they are together. It was so in the days of St. Valentine, it is so today, and it will be so until the end of the world.

The romantic attraction between young people of the opposite sex is perfectly natural and good because it is part of the Creator's divine plan. It is only the abuse of the divine plan that should be feared. Parents and teenagers should not be afraid of youthful relationships with the opposite sex. There are many pitfalls to be avoided, to be sure, but on the other hand, wholesome companionship between boys and girls is the beginning of good marriages. To insure such wholesome companionship during the adolescent years, here are some words of advice that might be helpful to parents, guardians, and teenagers during those years.

1. *Parents should start with the presumption that their children are morally good and then provide them with all the information they need in the matter of sexuality.* To set a child adrift in the sex-saturated modern world without any moral guidance from the home is an outrage. Positive and prudent sex education should begin in the home, by word and example, long before a child enters school. It should be expanded and adapted to the child's age and maturity (cf. *The Truth and Meaning of Human Sexuality*).

2. *The youth of today are as confused and unsure of their sexuality as their counterparts of generations gone by.* They have been exposed to a lot more of the facts and terminology and techniques than their predecessors, but few understand and appreciate the place of sex in the divine plan of God. They have been inundated with the physical side of sex but hardly touched at all by the spiritual dimension. They are easy prey for the purveyors of pornography, permissiveness, promiscuity, and perversion.

3. *Parents have an obligation to help their teenagers form their consciences.* This can be done by discussion of moral prob-

lems from a common sense and logical point of view, and through discussion of morality as revealed in the Scriptures and in the teaching of the Catholic Church. It is not enough merely to impart information on sex to young people. The goal should always be *formation*—the cultivation of respect and reverence for the sexual powers given to us by God, and for our bodies as temples of the Holy Spirit.

Instead of providing their children with the latest contraceptive drugs or devices, parents should encourage chastity and self-control. The world says that the sexual appetite cannot be controlled; Christianity says that it can, and offers the shining example of millions of its adherents over the centuries as clear evidence of that fact. Young people are very idealistic today and they ought to be given some exposure to Christian ideals, instead of being dragged down to the lowest moral and social common denominator.

4. *Young people need to know that there are objective standards of morality, that the rightness or wrongness of an act does not depend solely on the situation.* The specifics of Christian morality can be found within the overall framework of the Ten Commandments of God and the Sermon on the Mount, especially the Beatitudes.

"In the area of sexuality," the Catholic Bishops of the United States have told us, "the Christian is to be modest in behavior and dress. In a sex-saturated society, the follower of Christ must be different. For the Christian there can be no premarital sex, fornication, adultery, or other acts of impurity or scandal to others. He must remain chaste, repelling lustful desires and temptations, self-abuse, pornography, and indecent entertainment of every description" (*Basic Teachings for Catholic Religious Education*, n. 19).

5. *The ground rules for dating ought to be thoroughly discussed and carefully worked out by parents and their teenagers.* Parents ought to know who their children are going out with, where they are going, what they intend to do, and when they will be home. Parents seek this information not to pry or snoop but because they love their children and accept the responsibility of watching out for their spiritual and moral well-being.

Parents, who were once teenagers themselves, know that there are certain persons (boys and girls of loose morals) and places (parked cars, homes where the parents are out) that can be occasions of sin for their offspring. They know that sex is a powerful urge, not unlike a runaway locomotive, and that even the strongest-willed teenager will not always be able to resist opportunities and temptations if he or she is confronted with them often enough. Parental supervision means keeping children out of situations where adult decisions will have to be made.

6. *Young people who begin dating in the sixth, seventh or eighth grades are on the road to serious moral trouble.* This would be true even if teenagers today were not exposed to such massive propaganda about the joys and pleasures of sex. The basic reason for saying this is the problems that arise from too early exposure, on a one-to-one basis, to members of the opposite sex. Individual dating should not begin until at least the junior or senior year of high school, and even then double dating is to be preferred.

Prior to that time, boys and girls should involve themselves in group activities—parties, dances, athletic events—all properly chaperoned, of course. This may sound old-fashioned and out of tune with the times, but sensible and honest teenagers will recognize the wisdom of the advice.

7. *"Going steady" is dangerous to the moral, emotional, and intellectual health of teenagers.* By going steady, we mean keeping company exclusively with one person. It is actually the same as the courtship or engagement period in which a man and woman evaluate each other as potential marriage partners for life. So unless a couple is contemplating marriage in the near future, going steady should be forbidden.

There are advantages to going steady, such as never having to worry about getting a date or being lucky enough to have a "steady" who is kind and attentive and fun to be with. But these are outweighed by the disadvantages, including the normal difficulty of avoiding sexual intimacy. The frequent contact often leads to increased sexual excitement and sexual experimentation. Parents who encourage this kind of exclusive arrangement share responsibility for any sins committed.

Other disadvantages of going steady include the risk of complete dependence on one another, the failure to make new friends, the lack of participation in exciting interests and hobbies because they do not appeal to the other person, the retardation of mental and emotional growth, and the devastated feeling when the relationship that was going to last forever breaks up, as most of them do. Who needs that kind of traumatic experience at the age of sixteen or seventeen? Those who mix with a number of people of both sexes undergo a more normal development and are much happier in the long run.

8. *Premarital sex is not the fulfilling experience that the promoters of promiscuity would have you believe.* The advocates of early and frequent sex never mention the practical problems that have wreaked havoc in the lives of so many young people—the unwanted pregnancies, the staggering number of abortions, the physical and emotional complications of abortion, the alarming incidence of venereal disease, the heavy burden of a guilty conscience, and the harm to a future marriage.

How many boys and girls, urged into premarital sex by the lie that "everybody is doing it," have come away from the experience bitterly disappointed and wishing that they had waited? How many young people have fallen for the oldest line of all—the one that says that sexual intercourse is required to prove the depth of their love? What kind of "love" is it that asks a girl to give up cheaply the precious gift of her virtue, that exposes her to a possible illegitimate pregnancy, that causes her to abandon her moral convictions, that asks her to jeopardize her eternal salvation? It is not love, of course, it is lust, and the lustful one, having succeeded in his conquest, usually moves on to try the same line on another unsuspecting girl.

9. *Purity is security.* The struggle to attain purity has never been an easy one to win. It is doubly difficult for the youth of today because they see impurity praised and glorified everywhere. We are living in an age where, as someone has said, they stone the virgins instead of the harlots. To resist the pressure of their peers and of the sex pushers in the media, teenagers must build up their moral strength. They must work just as hard to keep their immortal souls in shape as they do to keep their mortal bodies in trim.

They can do this, first, by finding out exactly how and when God expects them to use the sexual powers he gave them; second, by forming a right conscience to guide them through the situations they will encounter; third, by giving good example to others and never, by word, action, or provocative dress, leading another person into sin; fourth, by avoiding persons, places, and things that could be occasions of sin; fifth, by concentrating on the development of their personalities, talents, brains, and holiness, rather than their physical and sexual attributes; and sixth, by constantly seeking God's help both to restrain their own passions and to act as his apostles in the modern world.

This divine assistance, without which we can do nothing, can be obtained in many ways: through the Mass, the sacraments of Penance and the Holy Eucharist, prayer, good works, and spiritual reading, especially the Bible. How ironic it is that so many teenagers neglect these vital sources of help at a time when they need such help the most. With God's grace, purity is within the grasp of young people. And purity is security insofar as it guarantees what sin can never guarantee—true happiness in this life and in the next life.

The Teenager and Drinking

If you were to ask a number of people to name the most dangerous drug they know of, you might get such answers as marijuana, heroin, "crack" cocaine, and so forth. And these certainly are dangerous drugs, but speaking broadly the most dangerous drug of all today is alcohol because it is socially and legally acceptable even though it is potentially habit-forming and deadly. Alcohol is dangerous because it is involved in more than half of all the crimes committed in the United States, many of the highway accidents and deaths, and many home accidents.

There are more than ten million known alcoholics in this country who have brought untold heartache and disaster to themselves, their families and friends, and society. By some estimates, the cost of alcoholism in the United States in terms of health care exceeds $400 million a day.

Furthermore, the problem is not getting better; it is getting worse, especially as heavy drinking moves down the age ladder even into the pre-teen years. It is estimated that at least half a million teenagers are problem drinkers.

Some parents can be heard expressing a sigh of relief at reports that many teenagers are switching from drugs to alcohol. That's like taking consolation from the fact that the person about to mug you is carrying a knife instead of a gun. And how many parents know that some adolescents are mixing alcohol with barbiturates, thus becoming addicted to both drugs?

The teenage alcohol scene is bleak, but it is not hopeless by any means. Conscientious, informed, and prayerful parents and their children can handle the problems of alcohol by facing the facts, discussing the situation calmly and intelligently with each other, and giving good example. Parents and teenagers might consider the following points:

1. *Parents should tell children the truth about alcohol.* Like so many other things, it is not the use of alcohol that is bad, but rather the abuse of it. If the use of alcohol is evil and sinful, would Jesus have changed water into wine at the wedding feast in Cana? Parents who drink should do so moderately. They should indicate to their children that alcohol is one of life's pleasures, not a crutch or the central point of life. Creating the proper attitude at home is very important.

2. *Parents should impress upon their children that teenage drinking is inadvisable and dangerous and should be avoided until the children are of legal age.* In addition to the hazards of alcohol already related, parents ought to stress that alcohol can be a moral danger in that it breaks down religious convictions, dulls the conscience, and often leads to serious sin. Drinking should be taboo for high school students.

3. *The reasons for teenage drinking should be clearly understood and acted upon if necessary.* The most common reasons why young people drink include: a desire for acceptance among their peers; to show how grown up and sophisticated they are; to overcome a feeling of failure or to ease the pain of growing up; and to get high. The first two reasons are neither new nor very profound. They can usually be handled by deglamorizing drinking and the alleged maturity and sophistication it supposedly brings, and by pointing out that peer acceptance is not worth endangering one's physical, emotional, and spiritual health. Unfortunately, these lessons are usually learned the hard way. The third and fourth reasons suggest problems much deeper than the drinking itself and ought to be treated immediately and, if necessary, with professional help.

4. *Teenagers must dare to be different.* They must resist the pressure to drink. They should stay away from those who drink or who have access to alcohol. Those who are of drinking age should never make alcohol available to younger persons, thereby creating problems for other children and their families. People who truly love their neighbor would never do anything to corrupt or destroy another person's life. Teenagers who find themselves with a drinking problem of their own, or in their family, should

seek advice and assistance from their priest or reliable relatives, friends, or organizations which specialize in helping those afflicted with alcoholism. Help is always available, of course, from God, if we but ask him.

The Teenager and Drugs

In recent years, many parents have been horrified to find that their children, from college age down to the elementary grades, have become confirmed users of drugs. And even though the dangers of hard drugs have been broadcast far and wide, still the number of young people surrendering their bodies and souls to drugs continues to increase.

The teenage drug scene, like the youthful alcohol scene, is frightening, but it can be substantially improved through the mutual efforts of parents and teenagers. Some suggestions:

1. *Parents should be knowledgeable about drugs and drug abuse.* They should communicate this knowledge to their children in an honest and forthright manner, should not abuse alcohol or pills themselves, should confront their children if they recognize signs of drug usage (loss of weight, aches and pains, runny nose, vomiting, unnatural amount of sleep, lack of interest in the things that ordinarily interest boys and girls, and long and deep periods of depression, followed by short periods of elation), and should seek professional help in treating the problem. Parents should also try to find out where the drugs were obtained and inform the local police so that steps may be taken to apprehend the criminals who are selling narcotics to teenagers.

2. *The reasons for teenage drug usage should be determined and acted upon accordingly.* The reasons for using drugs are basically the same as for drinking: a desire for acceptance, to escape from the problems and failures and disappointments of real life, and to get high. Again, the last two reasons conceal much deeper motivations and demand immediate analysis and treatment. But whatever the reason for drug usage, immediate action is imperative, first, because drugs can enslave and destroy a person much faster than alcohol, and second, because feeding a drug habit is very expensive and more often than not drives young people into a life of crime, with boys becoming thieves and pushers, and girls becoming prostitutes.

3. *Teenagers must dare to be different.* They must say a firm no to the use of drugs, including marijuana, whose dangers have been confirmed by scientific studies. Teenagers must not run away from the problems of life and try to find escape in drugs. They must face up to the deplorable conditions in society and work to improve them. They must be prudent in their choice of companions and places they frequent, avoiding those which would lead them away from God and into trouble and sin. They should never take a drink or a cigarette from a stranger because some young people have become addicted in this way. They should bring their friends home with them to meet their parents, and should be encouraged by parents to consider the home as a place for wholesome social and recreational activities.

4. *The best preventive medicine against drug abuse is a solid family life and religious stability.* It is a fact that in homes where there is love and understanding and honest communication between parents and children, as well as family prayers and religious training, there is far less trouble with drug abuse than in homes where such an atmosphere does not exist. Parents and children who place their trust in God and ask for his divine assistance every day will be able to cope with whatever difficulties arise.

The Teenager and Driving

Teenagers are often blamed for evil deeds they do not do and for bad intentions they do not have. When such false accusations are hurled at young people, we come quickly to their defense. But there is one accusation that the strongest supporters of teenagers cannot refute; namely, that some teenagers are a menace when they get behind the wheel of a car. This undeniable fact is reflected in the death and accident toll on the highways and in the higher insurance rates that teenagers must pay. Another indication is the dramatic increase in the number of fatal car accidents triggered by teenagers who had been drinking.

The most aggravating thing about the bad driving record of teenagers is that they ought to be the best drivers on the road. The typical teenager is the one best equipped by nature to drive a car. Teenagers learn quickly, their senses are sharp and alert, their responses are fast, and they are able to perform mechanical functions with the greatest of ease. Since there is nothing wrong with their physical ability to drive, the problem must involve either their brains or their consciences.

As teenagers, perhaps all of us, or certainly some of us, were unaware of the unbelievable number of teenage drivers who killed or injured people; unaware that there is a human limit to our ability to control a car; unaware of the ever-present possibility of a child running in front of our car, or some elderly person unable to jump out of our way, or a deaf person who cannot hear our horn, or a little child with poor vision who did not see us coming.

Drop in at your local ambulance squad some day, or the fire and police rescue squads. They will be happy to see you, and willing to describe some of the accidents they have seen. Or ask permission of your local hospital to spend a few minutes talking to the Emergency Room staff, who can tell you about arms ripped off, people blinded and decapitated, children dying in the arms of their parents, and countless sad and sickening things often caused by reckless driving. Once we realize that a car is a dangerous weapon, then it becomes a matter of conscience, a moral obligation, to drive carefully and at a safe and appropriate speed at all times.

Although more than fifty thousand persons die in automobile accidents every year, teenagers—and many adults, too—do not seem to realize that the vehicle they are operating can be a lethal weapon. They engage in speeding, reckless driving, driving under the influence of alcohol or other drugs, using the car to vent anger and frustration, driving with utter disregard for traffic laws, and operating as if they owned the road. They offer convincing proof of the statement that it takes thousands of bolts to put a car together but only one nut to take it apart.

That kind of driving, whether people know it or not, is a sin. It is a violation of the Fifth Commandment, which forbids not only murder but also actions which could cause bodily harm. Perhaps Driver Education courses should include an explanation of the Fifth Commandment.

The moral implications of the automobile are not limited to the Fifth Commandment either. What about the Sixth Commandment, which forbids adultery, fornication, and other impure and unchaste acts? How many teenagers have violated this law of God in a car? How many illegitimate pregnancies, how many abortions, how many cases of venereal disease, how many heartaches and bitter disappointments, how many souls have been lost, all as a consequence of using the automobile as a "motel on wheels"?

Instead of an occasion of sin, your car can be a powerful means of building up Christian charity. How many times each day, especially in city driving, do we see opportunities to practice kindness toward pedestrians, meekness toward other drivers, patience in delay, tolerance of our brothers and sisters in Christ, long suffering toward habitual offenders, restraint and justice when we are tempted to blame an entire race or sex or ethnic group for the poor driving of one person?

We can even grow in holiness by being a good driver in the best sense of the term. Did you ever consider the possibility of engaging in group prayer or saying the rosary while driving instead of spreading the latest gossip? Or suppose the next time someone cuts you off, instead of cursing him or making an obscene gesture or recklessly pursuing him, you say a prayer for the souls in purgatory? Imagine how many souls some of us would get to heaven in the course of a year!

The modern automobile is intended to serve people, not destroy them. The proper use of a car offers a tremendous challenge to teenagers and their parents. They have a choice of death, destruction, financial woes, family troubles, loss of reputation, loss of purity—or possible growth in holiness. Which road do you choose?

Young People Are Important

The Second Vatican Council saw a great opportunity for young people to influence modern society. Citing their "zest for life and abounding energies to assume their own responsibility," as well as their yearning "to play their part in social and cultural life," the Council said that if their youthful zeal "is imbued with the spirit of Christ and is inspired by obedience to and love for the shepherds of the Church, it can be expected to be very fruitful. . . . In their own way, they can be true living witnesses to Christ among their companions" (*Decree on the Apostolate of the Laity*, n. 12).

No one has reached out more to young people than Pope John Paul. Addressing a youthful crowd in New Orleans in September 1987, the Holy Father said:

You young people should be grateful to God for your freedom. But even though you can come and go as you like, and do what you want, you are not really free if you are living under the power of error or falsehood, or deceit or sin.

The Pope told his audience that "the world will try to deceive you about many things that matter: about your faith, about pleasure and material things, about the dangers of drugs. And at one stage or another the false voices of the world will try to exploit your human weakness by telling you that life has no meaning at all for you. The supreme theft in your lives would be if they succeeded in robbing you of hope. They will not succeed if you hold fast to Jesus and his truth."

The Holy Father delivered a similar message during World Youth Day festivities in Denver in 1993. Speaking to half a million young people, he said:

Christ needs you to enlighten the world and to show it the "path to life" (Ps. 16:11). The challenge is to make the Church's "yes" to life concrete and effective. The struggle will be long, and it needs each one of you. Place your intelligence, your talents, your enthusiasm, your compassion, and your fortitude at the service of life!

Have no fear. The outcome of the battle for life is already decided, even though the struggle goes on against great odds and with much suffering ....

At this stage of history, the liberating message of the Gospel of life has been put into your hands. And the mission of proclaiming it to the ends of the earth is now passing to your generation. Like the great Apostle Paul, you too must feel the full urgency of the task: "Woe to me if I do not evangelize" (1 Cor. 9:16). Woe to you if you do not succeed in defending life.

The Church needs your energies, your enthusiasm, your youthful ideals, in order to make the Gospel of life penetrate the fabric of society, transforming people's hearts and the structures of society in order to create a civilization of true justice and love. Now more than ever, in a world that is often without light and without the courage of noble ideals, people need the fresh, vital spirituality of the Gospel.

Do not be afraid to go out on the streets and into public places, like the first apostles who preached Christ and the good news of salvation in the squares of cities, towns, and villages. This is no time to be ashamed of the Gospel (cf. Rom. 1:16). It is the time to preach it from the rooftops (cf. Mt. 10:27).

The teenage years are difficult for parents and children. Those who have lived through the experience, however, know that teenagers eventually become adults and, as parents, have just as much trouble understanding their own teenagers. If you think this situation is something new, consider the following remark:

I see no hope for the future of our people if they are dependent on the frivolous youth of today, for certainly all youth are reckless beyond words. . . . When I was a boy, we were taught to be discreet and respectful of elders.

These words come from a Greek writer of the eighth century before Christ!

Chapter 7

Between Family and Society

> The importance of the family for the life and well-being of society entails a particular responsibility for society to support and strengthen marriage and the family. Civil authority should consider it a grave duty to acknowledge the true nature of marriage and the family, to protect and foster them, to safeguard public morality, and promote domestic prosperity. — *Catechism of the Catholic Church*, n. 2210

When an architect draws up the blueprint for a building, he must carefully avoid pitfalls or weak points in the plan lest the structure eventually come tumbling down. Furthermore, the contractor must use good quality materials in the construction of the building. Every now and then you read in the newspapers about a building that collapsed, trapping or killing people under the rubble. Usually, there is an investigation and sometimes a trial at which those responsible for the faulty planning and construction are convicted of negligence and either fined or sent to jail.

The family structure must also be based on a perfect blueprint (God's divine plan) and must be built with good quality materials (love, prayer, work) if it is to stand tall and strong in our modern world. It must rest on the foundation of God's moral law if it is to avoid the pitfalls of selfishness and inordinate seeking of pleasure. And it must strive to resist such destructive and false doctrines as contraception, sterilization, abortion, and euthanasia. If these moral termites are successful in undermining the structure of the family, it will lead to the erosion and collapse of our society just as surely as the widespread acceptance of these illicit practices brought down earlier civilizations.

There is in our land today what Pope John Paul called a "conspiracy against life" (*Evangelium Vitae*, n. 17). It has been brought about by the actions of influential people in government and the news media, by some members of the medical and scientific professions, and by the failure of Catholics and other people who look upon God as the Creator and Ruler of all life to mount a united and vigorous campaign to protect innocent life from the moment of conception until natural death.

There are many facets of this anti-life, and anti-family, conspiracy: conception of life in the laboratory; widespread voluntary use of birth control drugs and devices; the dissemination, by government, of contraceptives to dozens of nations around the world; increased use of sterilization by individuals and forced sterilization of "mentally retarded" or "incompetent" persons; the slaughter of thousands of unborn babies every day by abortion; the starvation of handicapped infants; and the extermination of the elderly and comatose via euthanasia and "assisted suicide."

These threats to the dignity of human life need to be examined further if we are to prevent a "culture of death" from becoming entrenched in our country.

In Vitro Fertilization

The birth of Louise Joy Brown as the world's first "test-tube baby" in 1978 was a major step on the road to the "Brave New World" envisioned by Aldous Huxley in his fictional account of the creation of human beings in the laboratory. Since Louise's birth in Britain, thousands of babies have been conceived by the process known as in vitro fertilization (IVF). The public reaction has been a combination of wonder at the extraordinary scientific achievement and joy for couples unable to conceive children in the natural way.

Not as well known to the public are the negative aspects of IVF, which include experimentation on and destruction of tiny human embryos, freezing of embryos for later implantation, genetic manipulation of human gametes with other human cells and with animals, tissue and organ transplants from aborted babies to infants and adults, sperm banks that enable single women and lesbians to impregnate themselves, and "surrogate mothers"—women who rent out their wombs to carry children for other women who are either unable or unwilling to experience pregnancy. The well-being of the child has taken a back seat to the desperation of childless couples, the frustration of physicians trying to cope with infertility, and the eagerness of entrepreneurs to make a profit on these new technologies.

The Vatican Congregation for the Doctrine of the Faith responded to this troubling situation in 1987 with an *Instruction on Respect for Human Life in Its Origin and on the Dignity of Procreation*. While recognizing "the suffering of spouses who cannot have children," the Church said that "the act of conjugal love is. . . the only setting worthy of human procreation." It called the IVF process "illicit and in opposition to the dignity of procreation and of the conjugal union, even when everything is done to avoid the death of the human embryo." The *Instruction* declared that the child conceived "must be the fruit of his parents' love. He cannot be desired or conceived as the product of an intervention of medical or biological techniques; that would be equivalent to reducing him to an object of scientific technology."

Contraception

There is a story told of a well-to-do and influential pagan Roman woman, Cornelia, who lived many centuries ago. On one occasion, she was entertaining a group of friends, attired in their finery and adorned with jewels. The group asked their hostess, "And now won't you show us your jewels?" Cornelia's answer was to call her children and introduce them: "These are my most precious jewels."

Those who favor the practice of birth prevention cite a number of reasons: financial difficulties, physical or emotional health, stability of the marriage, desire to give the fullest possible upbringing and education to already existing children, and the dangers of unchecked population growth.

There is no question that there are some true hardship cases where the birth of a child could pose serious problems. But for many people practicing contraception, let us be honest, the reasons given are not valid. The financial difficulties mentioned all too often mean not a denial of necessities but of luxuries; the emotional problems, which most parents experience at one time or another, are seldom insurmountable; the stability of the marriage cannot really be improved by undermining its holiness and rebelling against God; several children in a family does not mean sacrificing quality for quantity (consider how many famous people would never have been born if their parents had had only two children—St. Ignatius, St. Francis, St. Catherine of Siena, St. Therese, Fr. Jacques Marquette, John Paul Jones, Washington Irving, Sir Walter Scott, Alfred Lord Tennyson, Mozart, Wagner, Schubert, Pope John XXIII); and population projections into the future have been notoriously inaccurate.

Population growth can bring economic prosperity to developing nations, but some governments want to limit population by using coercive methods. In a message to an international population conference in 1984, Pope John Paul rejected this approach, saying that "development should not be interpreted simply in terms of population control, nor should governments or international agencies make development assistance dependent on the achievement of family planning goals." He said that contraceptive programs "have increased sexual permissiveness and promoted irresponsible conduct with grave consequences especially for the education of youth and the dignity of women."

The Holy Father said that "the Church condemns as a grave offense against human dignity and justice all those activities of governments or other public authorities which attempt to limit in any way the freedom of couples in deciding about children."

The answer to population growth and starvation is social and economic development, not birth control and abortion. There is truth in the old saying: "Give a man a fish and he will eat for one day; teach him how to fish and he will eat for a lifetime." Furthermore, responsible economists have pointed out that there is little validity to the propaganda poured forth by the advocates of population control. In her book *The War on Population,* Dr. Jacqueline Kasun of Humboldt State University in California has presented copious evidence to refute the almost hysterical claims of the population controllers:

> Resources, far from being limited, are abounding. No more than one to three percent of the earth's ice-free land area is occupied by human beings, less than one-ninth is used for agricultural purposes. Eight times, and perhaps as much as twenty-two times, the world's present population could support itself at the present standard of living, using present technology; and this leaves half the earth's land surface open to wildlife and conservation areas.

. . . Above all, the cherished notion advanced by the population programmers — of a hapless humanity, out of control, breeding itself into misery — is a far cry from the truth. Families throughout the world have balanced their childbearing to their fluctuating economic circumstances.

On July 25, 1968, the feast of St. James the Apostle, Pope Paul VI issued an encyclical, *On Human Life*, that restated the Catholic Church's centuries-old prohibition of artificial methods of birth control. Some people, led to believe that the Church was about to change a teaching that goes back to the earliest years of Christianity, expressed surprise and shock. They should not have been either surprised or shocked, for there are few teachings of the Church that have been reaffirmed more often than the teaching on the proper regulation of birth.

Just in recent decades, for example, artificial contraception has been condemned by Pope Pius XI (1930), Pope Pius XII (1951 and 1958), Pope John XXIII (1961), the Second Vatican Council (1965), Pope Paul VI (1964, 1965, and 1968), Pope John Paul II on numerous occasions, particularly during his visits to the United States and in his 1981 exhortation *The Role of the Christian Family in the Modern World*, and the *Catechism of the Catholic Church* (1992).

Humanæ Vitae has been criticized as a negative document written by a bachelor Pope who had little or no idea about the problems faced by married couples and society at large. It has been dismissed as the noninfallible opinion of one man, with whom Catholics are free to agree or disagree. It has been rejected as a not very scholarly or intellectual treatment of a matter that could be much better handled by certain "theologians." Are these criticisms valid? They are not.

The truth is that *Humanæ Vitae* is a profound treatment of life and love; a proclamation of the positive values of love, marriage, parenthood, and family; a consistent, authoritative, and morally binding statement by the Vicar of Christ; and, in the words of Pope John Paul, "a truly prophetic proclamation, which reaffirms and reproposes with clarity the Church's teaching and norm, always old yet always new, regarding marriage and regarding the transmission of human life" (*The Role of the Christian Family in the Modern World,* n. 29).

The encyclical defends human sexuality against mere sex, declares that the life-giving and love-giving aspects of marital intercourse cannot be separated, and reminds Christian married couples that the strength they need to observe this difficult teaching can be found in prayer and the sacraments.

To those who contend that Catholics do not have an obligation to follow this teaching because the Pope was not speaking *ex cathedra*, that is, from the chair of Peter, or infallibly, we call to their attention the words of Vatican II:

> In matters of faith and morals, the bishops speak in the name of Christ and the faithful are to accept their teaching and adhere to it with a religious assent of soul. This religious submission of will and of mind must be shown in a special way to the authentic teaching authority of the Roman Pontiff, even when he is not speaking *ex cathedra*. That is, it must be shown in such a way that his supreme magisterium is acknowledged with reverence, the judgments made by him are sincerely adhered to, according to his manifest mind and will. His mind and will in the matter may be known chiefly either from the character of the documents, from his frequent repetition of the same doctrine, or from his manner of speaking (*Dogmatic Constitution on the Church*, n. 25).

The Pope, either alone or in conjunction with the bishops of the world, is the only authoritative teacher and authentic interpreter of the law of God. No theologian, priest, sister, brother, or lay person—whatever their sincerity, popularity, or academic or professional credentials—can be followed if they teach a doctrine contrary to the official and authoritative teaching of the Holy Father. The teachings of those who contradict the authentic interpretations of the Vicar of Christ must be rejected

Why Is Contraception Wrong?

Contraception is any direct, positive frustration of any phase in the process of conception before, during, or after a voluntary act of intercourse. It is the clear, unmistakable, and unchanging teaching of the Catholic Church that contraception is always and everywhere evil, immoral, and sinful. The use of contraceptives of whatever type and for however long a time can never be objectively condoned or justified as a morally acceptable means of controlling births or limiting the size of a family.

Please note that we are talking strictly about the evil of contraception itself, not about the guilt of persons who practice it. This important distinction can be illustrated by recalling the three conditions for mortal sin—grave matter, sufficient reflection, and full consent of the will. We are saying only that the practice of birth control is grave matter. Whether couples fully meet the other two conditions, or whether their moral guilt is reduced by ignorance or weakness, are matters for a confessor, or God, to judge.

The evils of contraception are not confined to the violation of the divine plan and the natural law. Birth control, as Pope Paul said in *Humanae Vitae* (n. 17), is also destructive of the person and disastrous to society. It brings to a marriage selfishness, infidelity, lack of self-sacrifice, and the loss of respect for the woman, who is treated as a thing to be used and not as a person to be loved and respected.

Would any husband who truly loved his wife allow her to risk her health and even her life by taking powerful contraceptive drugs or using some potentially harmful intrauterine device? Mohandas Gandhi, the Hindu leader, was right when he said in 1946: "Contraceptives are an insult to womanhood. The difference between a prostitute and a woman using contraceptives is only that the former sells her body to several men, the latter sells it to one man."

Contraception is also disastrous to society because it brings about a general lowering of morality, places a dangerous weapon in the hands of government, and paves the way for abortion and euthanasia (*Evangelium Vitae*, n. 13). Who would deny that these grave consequences have come about since they were forecast by Pope Paul in *Humanae Vitae*? Each year that passes confirms the wisdom and foresight of the Holy Father and the absolute necessity of rejecting the contraceptive mentality and returning to the true Christian concept of married life and love.

Responsible Parenthood

At this point, the question naturally arises: How many children is a married couple expected to have? Does the Church's teaching mean that a woman has to have a baby every year? What is the Church's position on family size and responsible parenthood?

Married couples are expected to "be ready with stout hearts" to cooperate with God in bringing children into the world. This does not mean that couples must have an unlimited number of children; that they cannot have reasonable intervals between births; that they cannot take into account the harmony and peace of the family, and the welfare and education of the children they already have.

Responsible parenthood, according to the Second Vatican Council, means that couples "thoughtfully take into account both their own welfare and that of their children, those already born and those which may be foreseen. For this accounting they will reckon with both the material and the spiritual conditions of the times as well as of their state in life. Finally, they will consult the interests of the family group, of temporal society, and of the Church herself" (*Pastoral Constitution on the Church in the Modern World*, n. 50).

However, in the same paragraph, the Council went on to say that "the parents themselves should ultimately make this judgment in the sight of God. But in their manner of acting, spouses should be aware that they cannot proceed arbitrarily. They must always be governed according to a conscience dutifully conformed to the divine law itself, and should be submissive toward the Church's teaching office, which authentically interprets that law in the light of the Gospel."

Clarifying this point further, the Council said that in "harmonizing conjugal love with the responsible transmission of life . . . sons of the Church may not undertake methods of regulating procreation which are found blameworthy by the teaching authority of the Church in its unfolding of the divine law" (*Pastoral Constitution on the Church in the Modern World*, n. 51).

In other words, the practice of responsible parenthood cannot involve the use of artificial methods of birth control, or sterilization, or abortion to limit the size of a family. The firm teaching of the Church is that "each and every marriage act must remain open to the transmission of life" (*Humanae Vitae*, n. 11). For those couples who have "serious motives to space out births," Pope Paul said in his encyclical, their only recourse is natural family planning, which means abstaining from marital relations during those days when a woman is fertile and capable of conceiving a child.

The methods developed by advocates of natural family planning are safer than chemical means and more effective than mechanical means. Couples seeking information on natural methods should contact the Family Life Office in their diocese, as well as such organizations as the Couple to Couple League in Cincinnati, Ohio.

Natural family planning involves a willingness to restrain one's sexual impulses, a suggestion that is not very popular in a society that frowns on any kind of self-control. But there are definite advantages to this method, including the fact that it requires the cooperation of both parties, as opposed to other methods which place the burden of responsibility on one partner. This mutual involvement of husband and wife, which will demand real communication between them, can enhance the respect, increase the affection, and deepen the love which they feel for each other.

The Church's teaching on responsible parenthood is a hard teaching but millions of couples have tried and are trying to follow it. There are some who do not always succeed and to them Pope Paul offered this compassionate advice: "Let them implore divine assistance by persevering prayer; above all, let them draw from the source of grace and charity in the Eucharist. And if sin should still keep its hold over them, let them not be discouraged, but rather have recourse with humble perseverance to the mercy of God, which is poured forth in the sacrament of Penance" (*Humanae Vitae*, n. 25).

Vatican II also had a word of praise for those couples who choose to have large families, saying that they "merit special mention who with wise and common deliberation, and with a gallant heart, undertake to bring up suitably even a relatively large family" (*Pastoral Constitution on the Church in the Modern World*, n. 50). These couples do indeed have gallant hearts and can identify with the following humorous, but very true, observation made by entertainer Victor Borge: "People sometimes ask me if I think of myself first as a musician or a comedian. I never think of myself first—not with five children."

Abortion

Abortion is the expulsion of a nonviable fetus from the womb. We are not talking about spontaneous abortion, popularly known as miscarriage, which often results from disease or accident or some unknown cause; nor about indirect abortion, which results from a medical procedure to preserve the life or health of the mother, such as the removal of a cancerous uterus. We are referring to the deliberate killing of a developing baby for social, economic, or other reasons, most often for the convenience of the mother.

The scope of abortion very nearly defies comprehension. In the year following the infamous "Black Monday" decision of the U.S. Supreme Court on January 22, 1973, an estimated 1.5 million unborn babies were deprived of their God-given right to life in the United States. That annual death toll has continued ever since and the victims of this "silent holocaust" number in the tens of millions.

When Does Human Life Begin?

For many people, the word abortion does not have much significance because they are not aware of when human life begins or of how the child develops in the mother's womb. They have been misled by the euphemistic terminology used by the death peddlers. Instead of saying unborn child, the anti-lifers say "glob of protoplasm." Instead of a human being with potential, they say "potential human." Instead of killing an unborn baby, they say "termination of pregnancy." Instead of saying pro-abortion, they say "pro-choice." Instead of saying pro-life, they say "anti-choice." Language is used to disguise the horrific and violent nature of abortion.

In October 1967, a distinguished group of experts in the fields of medicine, law, ethics, and the social sciences met in Washington, D.C., for the First International Conference on Abortion. Asked to declare when human life begins, the almost unanimous conclusion (19 to 1) of the group was as follows:

> The majority of the group could find no point in time between the union of sperm and egg, or at least the blastocyst stage, and the birth of the infant at which point we could say that this was not a human life. [The blastocyst stage occurs shortly after fertilization.] The changes occurring between implantation, a six-weeks embryo, a six-months fetus, a one-week child, or a mature adult are merely stages of development and maturation.

Modern science has provided us with a clear description of human life from the moment of conception, when the sperm cell from the father fertilizes the egg cell from the mother. Each parent contributes twenty-three chromosomes to the fertilized ovum, which now becomes a unique being with its own genetic package that has already determined its future height, the color of its eyes, and other characteristics. The development of the unborn child takes place as follows:

1. The fertilized egg is implanted in the wall of the uterus seven to nine days after conception.

2. Blood cells are present seventeen days after fertilization.

3. The heart begins to beat at eighteen days.

4. The foundation of the brain, spinal cord, and nervous system is established by the twentieth day.

5. At thirty days, the unborn child is a quarter of an inch long, is made up of millions of cells and, under a powerful microscope, looks human. The baby is now 10,000 times larger than the original fertilized ovum.

6. Measurable brain waves can be recorded by the forty-third day, a sure sign that life is present. The child begins to move at this point, although it will be another fourteen weeks or so before the mother feels any life.

7. By the eighth week, every body system of the child is present, and all of them will be working by the eleventh week. During this period of time, the child becomes very active, kicking its legs, sucking its thumb, turning its head, squinting and frowning, drinking the amniotic fluid that surrounds it—more if the fluid is sweetened and less if it has a sour taste.

8. The child weighs about one ounce at twelve weeks after fertilization and can feel pain. Unborn children have been known to push away or grasp instruments or needles inserted into the uterus.

9. The child grows rapidly during the next few weeks, reaching a weight of one pound and a height of one foot by the twentieth week. An increasing percentage of babies born between twenty and twenty-four weeks gestation are surviving, even though they are just past the halfway point in the pregnancy.

10. If no attempt is made to kill the unborn child, he or she will grow in size and strength in the remaining months before birth.

No Good Reason for Abortion

How anyone who knows these facts of fetal development, especially the mother, who should be the natural protectress of her own child, can inflict violent death on these modern-day Holy Innocents to solve personal or social problems is difficult to perceive. The methods of abortion are cruel and barbaric whether they involve cutting, scraping, or vacuuming the child from the wall of the uterus, burning the child to death with a salt solution, or delivering all but the child's head, stabbing the back of the head with scissors, and then sucking out the child's brains with a vacuum device so as to collapse the skull and permit the extraction of a dead baby. This atrocity is called "partial-birth abortion."

The reasons given to justify the legalized slaughter of the unborn, while plausible sounding on the surface, have no validity when subjected to careful scrutiny. The reasons include the physical or mental health of the mother, pregnancy resulting from rape or incest, the child will not be wanted, the "population explosion," the possibility of a deformed child, the need to reduce the number of illegal abortions, and a woman's "right to choose" and to control her own body.

In point of fact, modern-day advances in medicine have eliminated practically every medical indication for abortion. There is no physical problem or ailment that cannot be treated while a woman is pregnant. Doctors never really have to decide whether to save the life of the mother or the baby; they do everything possible to save the lives of both their patients.

As for the mental health of the mother, there is no known psychiatric ailment that can be cured by abortion. If a woman has a mental problem, she can be treated during and after the pregnancy. And it should be noted that not a few women have developed mental problems *as a result* of abortion. The mental health excuse used to justify many abortions really means that a woman is looking for a convenient way to get rid of her baby.

Pregnancy resulting from rape or incest is rare, accounting for about one percent of the 1.5 million abortions reported each year in the United States. But even if such a pregnancy should occur, is abortion the answer? Will killing the child remove the emotional scar left by the rape, or will it add another emotional scar? And what kind of logic is it that would punish the child for the sin of the father? Furthermore, the incidence of sterility among women, particularly teenagers, having abortions is note-worthy. Would it not be better to carry the child to full term and put it up for adoption rather than risk sterility and the possibility of never being able to have another child?

Many unwanted pregnancies result in the course of time in truly wanted children. But if a woman does not want to keep her baby, she can put him up for adoption. The number of couples desiring to adopt a child far exceeds the number of children available.

Nor does abortion eliminate the problem of the battered child. A study in California some years ago of four hundred battered children showed that ninety per cent of them were wanted by their parents. Abortion is the ultimate form of child abuse.

We have already discussed the "population explosion" in the section on contraception and have seen that no population problem exists that modern society cannot solve in a moral way.

The possibility of a deformed child, while a hardship on parents, still cannot justify killing the child. Many retarded or handicapped children can lead reasonably normal lives and the love and affection shown to these children by their parents is a joy to behold. Permitting the killing of unborn children who might be defective is a dangerous step because it would lead to the killing of any defective human being, regardless of age.

A more humane approach to this problem would be to encourage continued research into birth defects, improved treatment of deformed children, and supportive measures for families raising children with such problems.

What must we say of the need to reduce the number of *illegal* abortions? By following this path of "social reform," we could do away with all crime by doing away with all laws against criminal activities. In point of fact, illegal abortions continue to be performed even when abortion is legal because some women do not want to have their abortion at a legal facility lest the fact of the abortion become known to their families or friends.

Another reason for abortion involves the "right" of a woman to control her own body. The time for a woman to control her body is before she becomes pregnant. Once she is pregnant, there is another party involved—the unborn child. This baby is not part of her body, but has its own completely separate humanity. Any discussion of rights must include the baby's rights. And speaking of the so-called "right of privacy," which the Supreme Court said allows a woman to kill her unborn child anytime in the first three months without state interference, may we suggest that even if such a "right of privacy" did exist in the Constitution of the United States, it would not supersede the right to life which is our most basic right and without which none of our other rights would have any meaning.

As for the cry for "reproductive freedom" and the "right to choose," no sane society can give its citizens the right to choose to kill those who are not wanted for one reason or another. And that is what "pro-choice" means—choosing to kill the most innocent and defenseless members of the human family. Opponents of abortion should never use the terminology of the baby-killers. Call them pro-death or pro-abortion, but never pro-choice. The Catholic Bishops of the United States have made it quite clear that "no Catholic can responsibly take a 'pro-choice' stand when the 'choice' in question involves the taking of innocent human life."

Get Rid of the Problem, not the Baby

All of this is not to deny that pregnancy does pose serious problems for some women. However, the right to life and to birth must always be protected. The answer, therefore, is to get rid of the problem, not the baby. If a woman is contemplating abortion because of seemingly desperate difficulties, she deserves positive, humane assistance to solve her problems.

Fortunately, there are organizations, both Church-affiliated and privately operated, which are providing an alternative to abortion. They offer encouragement to have the baby, help in obtaining medical and financial aid, professional counseling, a sympathetic ear during and after pregnancy, and assistance in finding housing and jobs. Getting involved with one of these groups is a wonderful opportunity to practice Christian charity. Will you accept the challenge?

Abortion is not a Catholic issue, although the Church has condemned the killing of unborn children as an "unspeakable crime" (Vatican II, *Pastoral Constitution on the Church in the Modern World,* n. 51); imposed excommunication on any Catholic who participates in an abortion with full knowledge of the Church's penalty (Canon 1398, Code of Canon Law); warned that "a Christian can never conform to a law that makes abortion legal" (Congregation for the Doctrine of the Faith, *Declaration on Procured Abortion*, n. 22), and declared with the full authority of its ordinary and universal Magisterium that "direct abortion, that is, abortion willed as an end or as a means, always constitutes a grave moral disorder since it is the deliberate killing of an innocent human being" (*Evangelium Vitae*, n. 62).

Abortion is a human issue and should be rejected by every person who values his or her humanity, regardless of religious beliefs. Failure to act on behalf of the innocent, helpless, defenseless, voiceless unborn is inexcusable, immoral, and a repudiation of the teaching of the Christ: "As often as you did it for one of my least brothers, you did it for me" (Matthew 25:40).

"Life must always be defended, welcomed with love, and accompanied with constant respect," said Pope John Paul while celebrating a "Day for Life" in Italy in February 1991. "As human beings and believers, we must never stop promoting the culture of life in the face of the culture of death. We must proclaim the inviolability of the right to life — and to a life with dignity — against abortion, an aberrant crime which has the qualities of totalitarianism in regard to the most defenseless human beings."

Euthanasia

A woman who had grown tired of caring for her old and sick mother decided to get rid of her. She called her son and told him to put his grandmother in the wagon, take her out in the woods, and leave her there in the wagon to die. The young man did as he was told, except that when he returned a few hours later, he had brought the wagon back with him. When his mother asked why, he replied: "Some day you will be old and sick and I'll need the wagon to take you out in the woods to die."

Since human life is a continuum from the moment of conception to the moment of death, it is logical, if one believes in killing the child in the womb by abortion, to argue that the life of a born person—infant, child, adolescent, adult, or senior citizen—can also be terminated. Either all life is sacred or no life is sacred.

Those who tolerated or approved contraception got abortion. Those who tolerated or approved abortion got euthanasia. And they may get it personally if some "compassionate" activist decides that they are not leading "a meaningful existence," that they have become a social or economic, or perhaps a political or religious, burden to someone. Parents may find themselves faced with three choices: be nice to their children, get on the committee that decides who shall live and who shall die, or fight the modern-day Hitlers.

Euthanasia is the direct killing of those who, while they have committed no crime deserving of death, are because of mental or physical defects considered of no further value to society. We are told that the killing is being done for the good of the patient. In fact, euthanasia is not uncommonly done for the convenience of the family, a hospital or institution, or society. Putting it simply, euthanasia is when the doctor kills the patient.

Death With Dignity or Murder?

Many people are strongly opposed to taking the life of even a person with a terminal illness. So the promoters of euthanasia coined the slogan "death with dignity" to soften the implications of what they are doing and to deceive the unwary. Now who does not want to die with dignity? But what do the mercy-killers mean by this phrase? They mean to bring about the death of a person so that he or she will no longer be a burden to others, will no longer interfere with the comfort and convenience of family or relatives, will no longer take up space in a hospital or institution that could be better utilized by someone else, and will no longer "waste" funds on care and therapy that could be better spent for more positive and constructive programs.

The Christian looks at "death with dignity" in a different light. We interpret the phrase to mean that the sick person is surrounded by relatives and other loved ones; is receiving excellent medical and nursing care in an attractive environment; can obtain the ordinary means of sustaining life and extraordinary means if they choose; and has access to a priest or minister who will provide religious and spiritual consolation.

The distinction between ordinary and extraordinary means is important. To preserve life we must take ordinary means, but usually we need not take extraordinary ones. Some things are quite clearly ordinary in most circumstances, such as the taking of food, water, or medicine, or a minor operation on one's foot. Others are quite clearly extraordinary, such as a liver or heart transplant. Traditional Catholic belief was long ago succinctly proclaimed to the world by Pope Pius XII:

Natural reason and Christian morality say that man (and whoever is entrusted with the task of taking care of his fellowman) has the right and the duty in case of serious illness to employ the measures necessary for the preservation of life and health. Normally one is held only to use ordinary means—according to circumstances of persons, places, times, and culture—that is to say, means that do not involve any grave burden for oneself or another. On the other hand, man is not forbidden to take more than the strictly necessary steps to preserve life and health.

The rights and duties of the doctor are correlative to those of the patient. The doctor, in fact, has no separate or independent right where the patient is concerned. In general he can take action only if the patient explicitly or implicitly, directly or indirectly, gives him permission. The rights and duties of the family generally depend upon the presumed will of the unconscious patient. Where the proper and independent duty of the family is concerned, they are usually bound only to the use of ordinary means. . . .

All forms of direct euthanasia, that is the administration of a drug in order to produce or hasten death, are unlawful because in that case one asserts the right to dispose directly of life (Address, February 14, 1957).

This teaching of Pius XII was incorporated into the Vatican's 1980 *Declaration on Euthanasia,* in which the Sacred Congregation for the Doctrine of the Faith offered some clarifications of the general principles because of "the rapid progress made in the treatment of sickness." The steps involved in reaching a correct judgment in these situations, the declaration said, must include "studying the type of treatment to be used, its degree of complexity or risk, its cost and the possibilities of using it, and comparing these elements with the result that can be expected, taking into account the state of the sick person and his or her physical and moral resources."

Pope John Paul II also spoke at some length about euthanasia in his encyclical on the "Gospel of Life" (*Evangelium Vitae*). Expressing concern about the attitude of those who see "the growing number of elderly and disabled people as intolerable and too burdensome," the Holy Father declared that "euthanasia is a grave violation of the law of God, since it is the deliberate and

morally unacceptable killing of a human person .... Depending on
the circumstances, this practice involves the malice proper to suicide or murder" (n. 65)

The Pope drew the distinction between euthanasia and
"medical procedures which no longer correspond to the real situation of the patient either because they are by now disproportion-
ate to any expected results or because they impose an excessive
burden on the patient and his family." He continued:

> In such situations, when death is clearly imminent and inevi-
> table, one can in conscience refuse forms of treatment that
> would only secure a precarious and burdensome prolonga-
> tion of life, so long as the normal care due to the sick person in
> similar cases is not interrupted. Certainly there is a moral
> obligation to care for oneself and to allow oneself to be cared
> for, but this duty must take account of concrete circum-
> stances. It needs to be determined whether the means of
> treatment available are objectively proportionate to the pros-
> pects for improvement. To forego extraordinary or dispropor-
> tionate means is not the equivalent of suicide or euthanasia;
> it rather expresses acceptance of the human condition in the
> face of death (n. 65).

In the same document, the Holy Father also condemned helping another person commit suicide, saying that this is "an injustice which can never be excused even it is requested." He called
euthanasia "a false mercy and indeed a disturbing 'perversion' of
mercy. True 'compassion' leads to sharing another's pain; it does
not kill the person whose suffering we cannot bear" (n. 66).

It is even worse, John Paul said, when the act of euthanasia
"is carried out by those like relatives, who are supposed to treat a
family member with patience and love, or by those such as doctors, who by virtue of their specific professions are supposed to
care for the sick person even in the most painful terminal stages"
(n. 66).

Opposing Unjust Laws

What is the Christian to do in the face of efforts to make legal
the killing of the old and the sick? "The real purpose of civil law,"
said Pope John Paul, "is to guarantee an ordered social coexist-

ence in true justice, so that all may 'lead a quiet and peaceable life, godly and respectful in every way' (1 Tm. 2:2) .... Consequently, laws which legitimize the direct killing of innocent human beings through abortion or euthanasia are in complete opposition to the inviolable right to life proper to every individual; they thus deny the equality of everyone before the law" (*Evangelium Vitae*, nn. 71-72).

Since "abortion and euthanasia are thus crimes which no human law can claim to legitimize," the Holy Father continued, "there is no obligation in conscience to obey such laws; instead there is a grave and clear obligation to oppose them by conscientious objection .... In the case of an intrinsically unjust law, such as a law permitting abortion or euthanasia, it is therefore never licit to obey it, or to take part in a propaganda campaign in favor of such a law or vote for it" (*Evangelium Vitae*, n. 73).

The time has come to reject the legalization of euthanasia, "death with dignity" statutes, and "living wills" which sanction euthanasia, not only because they are immoral, but also because they are unnecessary. The principles enunciated above are the only morally sound course of action for the seriously ill and dying. They also leave room for the Christian concept of redemptive suffering which, experience has shown, often brings out the finest qualities in people, both the person who is suffering and those who show love for the person by caring for him or her.

The Christian call to holiness has never been clearer. Ponder the words of Pope John Paul as he addressed an international congress on August 25, 1990:

> The Church demands a similar respect for the life of the person who is drawing near to death, and especially for those with terminal illnesses. We never celebrate and exalt life as much as we do in the nearness of death and in death itself. Life must be fully respected, protected, and assisted by those who are experiencing its natural conclusion as well. The sick person, even though he or she has been declared incurable by science, can never be considered untreatable.

> Our attitude to terminal illness is often the test of our sense of justice and charity, of our nobility of soul, of the responsibility and professional skill of health-care workers, beginning with the doctors. A positive understanding of suffering is often a decisive help for those who are bearing its weight and

becomes the greatest lesson about life for those who, gathered around the sick-bed, work to alleviate its effect....

Christ's death has conferred a new sacredness on every human death, and it has given a further reason for the prohibition against arbitrarily hastening its arrival by processes of euthanasia. You certainly know the Church's thinking on euthanasia. Her teaching cannot but find a confirmation in a science which sees human life in its unlimited richness and transcendent finality.

The Gospel of Life

The attack on innocent human life, and on the family structure, has reached frightening proportions today. While many people might not be directly affected by contraception and abortion, all are potential victims of the mercy-killers. No longer can you hide your head in the sand and say that you do not want to get involved. You are involved. And this time the life you save could be your own.

Christians must preach and practice the Gospel of Life which Pope John Paul summarized in *Evangelium Vitae* (n. 81):

Human life, as a gift of God, is sacred and inviolable. For this reason, procured abortion and euthanasia are absolutely unacceptable. Not only must human life not be taken, but it must be protected with loving concern. The meaning of life is found in giving and receiving love, and in this light human sexuality and procreation reach their true and full significance.

Love also gives meaning to suffering and death; despite the mystery which surrounds them, they can become saving events. Respect for life requires that science and technology should always be at the service of man and his integral development. Society as a whole must respect, defend, and promote the dignity of every human person, at every moment and in every condition of that person's life.

Chapter 8

Between Family and God

> Prayer needs to become a regular habit in the daily life of each family. Prayer is thanksgiving, praise of God, asking for forgiveness, supplication, and invocation. In all of these forms the prayer of the family has much to say to God. It also has much to say to others, beginning with the mutual commitment of persons joined together by family ties .... Families should pray for all of their members, in view of the good for which the family is for each individual and which each individual is for the whole family. — Pope John Paul II, *Letter to Families*, n. 10

On the wall of the research department of a large industrial firm, one visitor was surprised to see this sign in a prominent place: "The problem when solved will be simple."

We might apply those words to the present-day state of marriage and the family. Yes, there are many problems today eating away at the very foundations of the family. But the solution to those problems is not difficult; it is simply a return to Christ's blueprint for family life. God is the author of marriage and the family and, if we are wise, we will look to him for the design of the ideal family.

Today the spirit of paganism, hedonism, and selfishness has made serious inroads in the field of marriage. Sometimes it is due to ignorance, sometimes to malice. Christ's very explicit norms and ideals are being ignored and scoffed at on a widespread scale. Divorce, birth control, marital infidelity and unhappiness, abortion, euthanasia, rejection of the divine origin of marriage—all these elements are much too evident in our society.

Follow the Instructions

Whenever things deviate from their right order, as marriage and the family have done, difficulties will arise. When the manufacturer of an automobile gives a set of instructions with it, the wise thing is to obey the instructions; he who will not do so only causes trouble for himself. When God instituted the family, he gave a set of instructions to be obeyed. When the world cast them aside, problems began to occur. The basic answer to these problems today is a return to the divine plan.

God has laid down basic norms upon which the home must be based and our lives must be lived. Following these norms requires sacrifice and generosity. Families should try to carry out God's will and not their own because his way is the only sure way to true happiness. God blessed the first marriage in the Garden of Eden. God is the author and partner of every marriage today. If that fact were more widely acknowledged and accepted, families would be happier.

Help From God's Church

Families must know Christ's teachings in order to follow them. Back in 1930, Pope Pius XI, in his encyclical on Christian marriage, warned the world that the "subverters of marriage are entirely devoted to misleading the minds of men and corrupting their hearts, to making a mockery of matrimonial purity and extolling the filthiest of vices by means of books and pamphlets and other innumerable methods." The Holy Father said that we should, "by every fitting means, oppose error by truth, vice by the excellent dignity of chastity, the slavery of covetousness by the liberty of the sons of God, that disastrous ease in obtaining divorce by an enduring love in the bond of marriage and by the inviolate pledge of fidelity given even to death" (*Casti Connubii*, n. 106).

Nearly four decades later, Pope Paul VI echoed his predecessor in the pontificate, saying that the Church's teaching on the married life "will perhaps not be easily received by all. Too numerous are those voices amplified by the modern means of propaganda, which are contrary to the voice of the Church" (*Humanae Vitae*, n. 18). And like Pius XI, Pope Paul emphasized how "great indeed is the work of education, of progress, and of love to which we call you. . . . Truly a great work . . . since man cannot find true happiness . . . other than in respect of the laws written by God in his very nature, laws which he must observe with intelligence and love" (*Humanae Vitae*, n. 31).

The truth that we need to fight the "subverters of marriage" can be found in the consistent and coherent teaching of the Church over the centuries, particularly since 1930. Those seeking sound instruction on marriage and the family should consult the encyclicals *Casti Connubii* and *Humanae Vitae*, Sections 47-52 of the Second Vatican Council's *Pastoral Constitution on the Church in the Modern World*, the *Catechism of the Catholic Church*, and Pope John Paul's *The Role of the Christian Family in the Modern World* and his *Letter to Families*.

If there is to be a restoration of the divine plan with regard to the family, then the divine laws of marriage must be known with certainty and applied to our times. There must be an authoritative guide. That guide is the Holy Father, the successor of St. Peter, whom Christ himself commissioned to teach all nations "to carry out everything I have commanded you" and to whom Christ promised to be with "always, until the end of the world" (Matthew 28:20). The Pope and the bishops are responsible for guarding and interpreting the moral law handed to them by Christ and they deserve our wholehearted cooperation and obedience.

Those families who are trying to live up to the ideals of family life urged by Christ and the Catholic Church help not only themselves but act as a beacon of light to all those around them. Good, as well as bad, can spread like contagion or infection. One ideal family can have an influence it might never suspect. Such families must let their light shine before the world.

The Ideal Family

You recall the occasion when Christ was anointed with precious ointment and the question was asked: "What is the point of this extravagant waste?" (Mark 14:4). The same question has also been asked about the life of the Holy Family at Nazareth. Why did Christ spend thirty years of his life with Mary and Joseph, accomplishing apparently so little? Why did Christ, who came into this world on so sublime and important a mission, spend thirty years in just ordinary living? Why this "waste"?

It was through thirty hidden years that Christ sanctified and gave new meaning to "ordinary" family life. He spent those years with Mary and Joseph to teach the world the importance of family life and the sanctity of the home, that "ordinary" lives are enough if modeled on the Holy Family. Nazareth was meant to teach the world an important lesson.

If we could have observed that home two thousand years ago, we would have noticed that Jesus was liked by the people in the town and was obedient and devoted to his family. We would have seen Mary going about her tasks, going to the town well to draw water as was the woman's duty. We would have observed Mary as a woman devoted to her role as a mother, self-sacrificing, quick to help anyone in trouble. We would have noticed her modesty in dress and manner and would have sensed her strong character and virtue. We would have seen that the underlying motive of her life was complete submission to God's will in even the smallest events of her life, a principle of life expressed in her own words: "Let it be done to me as you say" (Luke 1:38).

We would have observed that Joseph was a man who knew his trade, did his job well, and was happy to be with his family when his work was done. In Joseph we have a concrete example of the new meaning which has been given to the dignity of labor. All of us cannot imitate the example of the saints who were great apostles or scholars or who devoted their entire lives to the care of the poor or sick. But the example of Joseph, the head of a family, is within reach of all. He worked no miracles that we know of; he did nothing outstanding. But what he did, he did for Christ.

Jesus attached great importance to just "ordinary" family life. He spent thirty years in such an environment. Nazareth is a concrete example of how the modern family might return to Christ's ideal of family life. Christ should be the head of every family, the witness of every deed, the reader of every thought. The family should speak to him daily in prayer. How can selfishness, or anger, or strife, or impurity, or drunkenness enter a household wherein there is a keen realization of Christ's presence? The home of the Holy Family at Nazareth is the ideal to which all Christian families should aspire.

Four Bonds of Family Life

Four strong bonds have traditionally held families together: the bond of affection, the bond of common work, the bond of common prayer, and the bond of common play. An observer of the modern family could not help but notice that these bonds, particularly the last three, have been greatly weakened. The bond of affection alone is not enough to keep a family stable. There must be something more. The restoration of the family might well come about sooner than we expect if more families would work together, pray together, and play together.

The Bond of Affection

We have already discussed love and affection as essential ingredients in any Christian family, but we might recapitulate. The family is, in the words of Pope John Paul, "the center and the heart of the civilization of love" (*Letter to Families*, n. 13). Any family who shuts out Christ shuts out love. In the book of Revelation, Christ says, "Here I stand, knocking at the door. If anyone hears me calling and opens the door, I will enter his house and have supper with him, and he with me" (3:20). Christian families who open the door to Christ will have him in their homes just as he was in the home of Martha and Mary.

Children learn of love early in life when mother or dad tucks them in at night, takes care of them when they are sick, gives them birthday parties, and cares for them in a thousand ways. This is the time to tell children that God loves them in the same way. Children who are really loved will respond with real love. In observing and sharing affection, kindness, and concern for others, the love of a family continues to grow and is a beautiful sight to behold. A happy and loving family is a foretaste of heaven.

The Bond of Work

A family should be like the oarsmen in a boat, with each member doing his or her share to keep the family functioning efficiently and smoothly. No one likes to do chores, but they are an unavoidable part of life and can be made less irksome if everyone pitches in. Parents should make chores a cooperative exercise so as to eliminate the drudgery. They should explain to the children about the operation and expense of maintaining a home and family and the consequent need for everyone's cooperation and assistance. Keeping the house and property clean, comfortable, and cozy should be the goal of every family. If all contribute enthusiastically to the realization of this goal, they will experience the satisfaction of a job well done and will be bound closer together.

Here are some tips for parents with regard to family chores and responsibilities:

1. Children can be paid allowances, but they should not be bribed to do chores. They must understand that chores are a normal and expected contribution to the well-being of the family.

2. Work well done should be praised. We all need encouragement and praise, especially when we have completed a task we would rather not have tackled in the first place. Frequent praise will inspire enthusiasm and a willingness to perform chores in the future.

3. Parents should not always insist on having chores done exactly as they would do them. Give children some flexibility.

4. When chores are completed, let the children go about their own activities. Children who are still restricted after chores are done will come to resent even minor tasks and minimal demands on their time.

5. Parents should watch their own attitudes toward household duties and responsibilities. If they treat a job as unpleasant, so will the children. But if parents undertake projects cheerfully, they will encourage a similar attitude in the children.

The Bond of Prayer

In years gone by, and among various religions, prayer was considered as essential in the home as in church. Morning and evening prayers in common were the rule. In one period of Protestantism, the family regularly assembled for family prayer, led by the father of the house. Family prayer played and still plays an important part in the Orthodox Jewish tradition. The family rosary must be marked down as a potent factor in the preservation of Catholic faith and Catholic family life.

Today, however, there is less emphasis on family prayer, which may explain in part the increasing breakup of families, as well as the tense and even hostile atmosphere that exists in some families. The time has come for a return to family prayer, for a reliving of the slogan, "The family that prays together stays together."

The Morning Offering, grace at meals, consecration of the family to the Sacred Heart, the family rosary, Bible reading, and night prayers in common are all powerful means of drawing the family closer together. From the very outset of their marriage, a husband and wife should make a practice of reciting their prayers in common. Any difficulties that may spring up in the course of the day will then tend to disappear. How can ill feeling or a grudge last for long with one who is praying by your side?

According to Pope John Paul, family prayer "is prayer offered in common, husband and wife together, parents and children together. Communion in prayer is both a consequence of and a requirement for the communion bestowed by the sacraments of Baptism and Matrimony. The words with which the Lord Jesus promises his presence can be applied to the members of the Christian family in a special way: 'Again I say to you, if two of you agree on earth about anything they ask, it will be done for them by my Father in heaven. For where two or three are gathered in my name, there am I in the midst of them'" (*The Role of the Christian Family in the Modern World*, n. 59).

Family prayer does not have to be restricted to a definite time every night, with every member of the house present under pain of excommunication. It can be flexible; it can be held at different times to accommodate family members who have other obligations; it can even be said with some members missing for good reasons. The important thing is that the family should pray together often. Common prayer can not only bring peace to troubled homes and be a means of solving difficulties, but also can solidify the foundation on which true Christian families are built. In the words of the Second Vatican Council:

> With their parents leading the way by example and family prayer, children and indeed everyone gathered around the family hearth will find a readier path to human maturity, salvation, and holiness (*Pastoral Constitution on the Church in the Modern World*, n. 48).

Another important feature of a Catholic home is the presence of religious articles, such as crucifixes, statues of Jesus and the Blessed Mother (perhaps even a shrine in your yard), holy pictures, a Bible, a sick call set for emergencies, a bottle of holy water, Catholic books, periodicals, and other literature. All of these are reminders of God's presence in our homes and in our lives. How can we expect children to grow up with a knowledge and love of Christ and his mother if their only exposure to their religion is one hour a week in a church building?

Is your home a Catholic home? Do Jesus and Mary have an important place in your family? Consider the following checklist and decide:

Are morning and night prayers a daily occurrence in your home?
Do you say grace before and thanks to God after meals?
Do you say a family rosary every night?
Do you carry a rosary at all times?
Do you wear a religious medal or a scapular?
Do you read and discuss the Bible often?
Is your home dedicated to the Sacred Heart of Jesus?
Is there a cross hanging in a prominent place?
Do you ask God's help in the solution of family problems?
Do you have a sick-call set for Communion or Anointing of the Sick?
Do you attend church as a family?
Do you go to Confession regularly?
Do the children attend a Catholic school or religious instruction program?
Do you have religious instruction at home?
Are there Catholic periodicals in your home?
Do you have a crib at Christmas?
Do you send out cards that indicate that Christmas is the birth of Christ?
Does Christmas mean the coming of Christ or a chance to get gifts?
Does Easter Sunday mean the resurrection of Christ or new clothes?
Do you ever invite lonesome or needy people to your home?
Do you ever provide a basket of food to a needy family, not just at Thanksgiving and Christmas but during the year?

In a nurse's lounge in a certain Catholic hospital, there is a chair with a silken cord tied across the arms. It is called "The Master's Chair," and represents the presence of Jesus in the home. It is a constant reminder that Christ has a place in the life of every nurse. That should be the spirit of every Christian home: The Master's Chair. Christ has a place. His presence is acknowledged.

In the famous painting of Christ knocking at the door, there is no handle to be seen. It is said that the artist made this omission purposely because Christ never forces his way in; he must be admitted by those inside. Is it possible that the Savior has been waiting outside your door all this time? Like the innkeeper of long ago, have you refused admission to Mary and Joseph? If so, you and your children have suffered a great loss.

Bring Jesus and Mary and Joseph into your home today. Once you really get to know them, you and your family will love them. And with that love will come the greatest happiness and confidence. All the temptations of modern life will hold no fear for you and your family because your help is in the name of the Lord, who made heaven and earth. The same Lord who promised that "where two or three are gathered in my name, there am I in their midst" (Matthew 18:20) will shower his blessings on your home.

The Bond of Play

One of the important tasks which faces families today is the restoration of family play or recreation. Families have almost lost the ability to enjoy each other. Dad goes off to one activity, mother to another, and the children to their pursuits. Thus, the family misses out on an opportunity to learn to enjoy and understand each other. Another obstacle is put in the way of family togetherness. What can be done to improve this situation?

First, we must get an idea of what recreation means. It is not just amusement or fun, but rather any activity apart from our regular work by which we re-create, that is, restore energy of mind and body. We have gotten far from this meaning today. Recreation as most of us know it has become very commercialized, involving the expenditure of money for sports events, movies with their flagrant sex and violence, and night clubs and resorts. It has also become almost exclusively passive, with no active participation by those in attendance, and escapist in character, that is, removed from real-life situations. Anyone who watches television often or goes to the movies frequently will know what we mean.

Many types of modern recreation are not evil in themselves. Television and the movies are not wrong until they begin to promote and glorify the evils we have been talking about in this book. But as a channel of recreation, they leave much to be desired. Recreation must become more creative. It must take on a more active character. It should become less commercialized. We must make an effort to bring a large part of family recreation back to the home. Family picnics and barbecues, a sing along, hobbies and crafts, dancing, games, making popcorn, coloring Easter eggs, making Christmas cards and tree ornaments, planting a garden, and countless other activities devised by imaginative parents and children can help greatly to strengthen the family bond. Do not neglect educational and cultural activities either. Reading, classes in religious and secular subjects, and discussions of current events can provide an intellectual challenge to members of the family.

Families might set aside at least one day, or night, each week to engage in some planned activity. It could be one of those mentioned above or could involve away-from-home activities, including swimming, skating, fishing, bicycling, hiking, camping, viewing historical sights, and visiting museums, zoos, farms, dairies, and amusement parks. Some of these outings are free, a significant factor for budget-conscious families. But whatever the activity, the spirit in which it is carried out is more important than the activity itself.

A word of caution: Organized activities for children are numerous today and begin at an early age. They not only take children away from the family and parental influence but often demand so much time of one or two members of the family that the rest of the household suffers as far as recreational and social activities are concerned. These organized outside activities are wholesome and healthy for children, but parents must be careful to balance the interests of individual members of the family with the unity and togetherness of the whole family.

Family recreation should be fun. It does not have to involve only special events; it can mean just a happy family atmosphere, with laughter at meals, romps at bedtime, and wrestling on the floor. Carried out properly, family play can ease tensions, relieve boredom, soften discipline, and promote affection.

Lastly, this most important advice: *Enjoy the family God gave you while you have them with you.*

The four great bonds of marriage and parenthood—affection, common work, common prayer, and common play—can be the foundation for a successful and happy family life. When the modern family learns once more to work together, pray together, and play together affectionately, under the guidance of Christ, the unseen head of the household, our families will be well on their way toward becoming again a vital force for God and country.

Prayer of a Married Couple

Almighty God, who has established and elevated the holy state of matrimony so that we, your creatures, might cooperate with you in fashioning citizens for heaven, and for our mutual help, consolation, and love, give us grace both thankfully to accept its blessings and faithfully to fulfill its duties. May your assistance continue in our union through our married life; help us to live together in love and peace, and aid us to fulfill faithfully our duties to you, to each other, and to our home.

Lord Jesus Christ, you gave a special dignity to family life by spending thirty years of your own life within a family; may the Holy Family of Nazareth be our model.

Accompany us, Lord, in all the daily actions of this life to which you have called us, and grant that the tie by which you have bound us together may ever grow stronger. Help us to be generous in giving ourselves for each other and making our home the best loved place of all. May you be our constant guide in the sacrifices we are called upon to make, and in the family responsibilities we must carry out.

And as you blessed the bridal couple at Cana by your presence, now bless our union and remain with us always; may we never forget you, the giver of all blessings. May our married life and home on earth lead us to our eternal home with you in heaven. Amen.

Prayer for Guidance in Choosing a State of Life

Almighty God, you know that in my heart I have a sincere desire of pleasing you and of doing your will in all things. Help me now through the intercession of Mary, my mother, to know what state of life I ought to choose. When I have determined it, grant me the grace and strength to follow it through, so that my life may be in accord with your divine plan, that I may work out my own salvation and bring others closer to you. Through Jesus Christ our Lord. Amen.

Prayer for Purity

Lord Jesus Christ, you who love to look upon a chaste soul and pure character, you who took upon yourself our human nature through the Immaculate Virgin Mary, look down mercifully upon my infirmity. Grant me a clean heart, O God, and renew a wholesome spirit to conquer every sinful desire. Grant me a filial fear and a devoted love of you and your immaculate Mother, so that this enemy may be overcome, and that I may serve you with a chaste body and please you with a pure heart. Amen. Immaculate Heart of Mary, pray for us.

Prayer for a Modern Parent

Lord Jesus Christ, you have seen fit to bless our marriage with children, and to entrust them to our care to raise them for you and prepare them for heaven. Give me your grace and help to be successful in carrying out this sacred trust. Teach me the right things to do; show me when to correct and when to praise or encourage; help me to be understanding, yet firm; considerate, yet watchful. Guide my actions from either being too indulgent or too severe. Help me to show my children by word and example the ways of wisdom, purity, holiness, and wholesomeness.

O Mary, stay close to our family and obtain for our children your Son's blessings, so that under our guidance they may grow in grace and love. Help us in guiding our children to keep the commandments more perfectly. Help us to fill our role worthily as God's partners in preparing souls for heaven, in so bringing up our children that they may be our joy in this world and our glory in the next. Amen.

The Prayer of a Young Bride on Her Wedding Day

This prayer was found among the personal effects of a young bride who died during an operation for appendicitis. She was only twenty-five years old, and had been married fourteen months.

O Father, my heart is filled with a happiness so wonderful I am almost afraid. This is my wedding day. I pray you that the beautiful joy of this morning may never grow dim with the tears of regret for the step I am about to take. Rather may its memories become more sweet and tender with each passing anniversary.

You have sent me the one who seems all worthy of my deepest regard. Grant me the power to keep him ever true and loving as now. May I prove indeed a helpmate, a sweetheart, a friend, a steadfast guiding star among all the temptations that beset this impulsive heart of mine.

Give me skill to make home the best loved place of all. Help me to make its light gleam. Let me, I pray you, meet the little misunderstandings and cares of life more bravely. Be with me as I start my mission of womanhood, and stay my path from failure all the way. Walk with us even to the end of our journey.

O Father, bless my wedding day, hallow my marriage night, sanctify my motherhood if you see fit to grant me that privilege. And when all my youthful charms are gone and cares and lessons have left their traces, let physical fascination give way to the greatest charm of companionship.

And so may we walk hand in hand down the highway of the valley of the shadow which we will be able to lighten with the sunshine of good and happy lives. Father, this is my prayer. Hear me, I beseech you. Amen.

Chapter 9

The Modern Woman

> The figure of Mary of Nazareth sheds light on womanhood as such by the very fact that God, in the sublime event of the Incarnation of his Son, entrusted himself to the ministry, the free and active ministry, of a woman. It can thus be said that women, by looking to Mary, find in her the secret of living their femininity with dignity and of achieving their own true advancement. —Pope John Paul II, *Mother of the Redeemer*, n. 46

If we turn back the pages of history to the days before Christ and Mary walked this earth of ours, we see that the position of women was indeed not an enviable one. The universal attitude was that a woman was a creature inferior to man, her purpose on earth being little more than a servant. She was completely excluded from public life, expected only to remain within the four walls of her own household and even there she was to hold an inferior place, indeed a degraded place. She received little or no education. Among pagans she was considered a chattel that could be bought and sold. She could not choose her own marriage partner, and in marriage she was not a companion but a servant whose life was little better than that of a slave. A woman wronged or mistreated by her husband had nowhere to turn for redress.

Even in the so-called cultured nations of Greece and Rome, women were for the most part looked upon as inferior. The world-renowned philosopher Aristotle referred to a woman as a subordinate creature. And Demosthenes frankly and brutally remarked: "We have woman friends for entertainment, but wives for children and household." Wives were given the place of servants in the household, while prostitutes held a prominent place in the social life of Greece and Rome. Such a philosophy of life dragged womanhood down to the depth of degradation.

This ancient pagan attitude toward women perseveres even in our own day when women are treated as objects to be used rather than as persons to be loved. Instead, said Pope John Paul, women should be seen for their important role "in transforming culture so that it supports life." He continued:

> Women occupy a place in thought and action which is unique and decisive. It depends on them to promote a "new feminism" which rejects the temptation of imitating models of "male domination" in order to acknowledge and affirm the true genius of women in every aspect of the life of society and overcome all discrimination, violence, and exploitation (*Evangelium Vitae*, n. 99).

Among the Jews

Even among the Jews of old, God's chosen people, whose moral outlook was on a much higher level, there was the idea that women should hold an inferior place. Women were considered less capable of spiritual development than men—an idea that strikes us as utterly ridiculous. As a result of this belief, they were not permitted to worship in the synagogues with men. They were put in a separate room reserved for them. It was considered an act of impiety to impart the words of the Law to a woman.

A Jewish man would not greet a woman on the streets. He would not even talk to his own wife or daughter on the street. There was a certain kind of fanatical Pharisee who went about with his eyes closed, lest he should see a woman. It was the woman alone who went to the well for water. A man considered himself disgraced if he should be seen carrying home water. In morning prayer, a Jewish man would thank God for not having made him "a gentile, a slave, or a woman."

Into such a world Mary was born and in a humble house at Nazareth one day there resounded the words: "Rejoice, O highly favored daughter! The Lord is with you. Blessed are you among women" (Luke 1:28). This greeting of the angel Gabriel to a simple teenage girl brought with it a revolutionary change and a singular lasting honor for womanhood. Christ chose a woman to be an indispensable instrument in the redemption of the world. He gave divine recognition to womanhood and signaled a change in the world's attitude toward women. Today every "Hail Mary" that is uttered is not only an expression of praise of her who is "blessed among women," but a reflected expression of honor, of divine recognition and esteem for every woman.

Christ's Concept of Womanhood

From Bethlehem to Calvary, our Lord paid Mary his personal tribute of reverence, love, and honor over a period of thirty-three years. This example of Christ united to the life of Mary, the model and exemplar for womanhood, gave a new meaning, a new place of importance to every woman. Christianity gave women their rightful place in the world. We are apt to take the role of women in the Gospel for granted, but when you consider the history of the world before the time of Christ, it can be seen that he revolutionized the position of women.

Remember the time when Christ was sitting by Jacob's Well in Samaria? The Apostles had gone into town to buy food, and our Lord was alone when a woman approached to draw water. She went about her task just as if no one were there—after all she was a woman and he a man and, in that land, at that time, there could be no question of a conversation or any friendliness between them.

Then almost as a clap of thunder out of the blue, Christ broke the silence by asking the woman for a drink of water. The answer of the woman reflects the revolutionary change Christ was introducing to the world: "How can you ask me, a Samaritan and a woman, for a drink?" (John 4:9). Our Lord then went on to manifest his divinity to this Samaritan woman. Jesus was throwing traditional attitudes aside; he was introducing to the world a new view toward women. Here was an entirely new concept of womanhood.

Picture to yourself a little town among the green hills in the southern part of Palestine. Off to one side of the town, a crooked path winds part way up the hill to a small, plain house surrounded by the bright scarlet flowers so common in the Holy Land. On the path a figure is seen making its way up the hill. It is a young Jewish girl, not yet twenty years of age. She walks quietly and thoughtfully, for she bears within her the body of a Child conceived only a few short weeks before by the miraculous power of God. The girl is Mary, the Mother of God, and the Child is Christ, the Son of the Eternal Father.

Mary enters the house, which is that of her cousin Elizabeth. The two women exchange a holy greeting, Elizabeth rejoicing with Mary because of the great favor that God has granted her, and Mary humbly speaking the praises of God. Mary remains with her cousin for three months and then returns to her home in Nazareth.

The story of the Visitation is as simple as that. It seems almost of no consequence. Certainly the Gospel story of the life of Christ would be complete without it. But St. Luke seems to include it because the days of Mary's pregnancy were such holy days. And so, year after year, the Church celebrates the feast of the Visitation of Mary to her cousin Elizabeth. It is not a feast that calls to mind some essential link in the chain of God's plan for our redemption. No, it is simply a day on which we are reminded of the tremendous honor that God showed to Mary and through her to all women.

In his statement on *The Role of the Christian Family in the Modern World,* Pope John Paul offered this summary of woman's lofty place in the plan of God:

In creating the human race "male and female," God gives man and woman an equal personal dignity, endowing them with the inalienable rights and responsibilities proper to the human person. God then manifests the dignity of women in the highest form possible, by assuming human flesh from the Virgin Mary, whom the Church honors as the Mother of God, calling her the new Eve and presenting her as the model of redeemed woman.

The sensitive respect of Jesus toward the women that he called to his following and his friendship, his appearing on Easter morning to a woman before the other disciples, the mission entrusted to women to carry the good news of the resurrection to the Apostles—these are all signs that confirm the special esteem of the Lord Jesus for women (n. 22).

The Unicorn and the Virgin

There is a fable almost two thousand years old about a certain unicorn that no hunters could ensnare. A unicorn is an imaginary animal, something like a horse, but with one horn in the center of its head. The unicorn of the fable was too strong and too swift for the best hunters. One day a young girl happened to be near when the hunters were trying to trap the animal and, strangely enough, the unicorn became tame and docile. The secret was this: The girl was a virgin, and the animal always became tame in the presence of a virgin.

Early Christians liked to express their thoughts in fables. This fable they interpreted by explaining that Christ was the unicorn, and that no human power could bring him down from heaven until Mary's perfect purity induced him to come and dwell with us. The fable shows clearly their high regard for womanhood.

One of the great boasts of communism was that it emancipated women. But it was Karl Marx who wrote: "Differences of age and sex have no longer any distinctive social validity. All are instruments of labor." The key word here is "instrument." Human beings are reduced to the dignity of a plumber's wrench. The communists "emancipated" women by forcing them to work in the mines and perform all manner of difficult and menial jobs.

A glance at history will show that it was not communism in modern times but Catholicism two thousand years ago which gave to women their rightful privileges, honor, and dignity.

Other Tributes to Women

One of the great tributes to Catholic womanhood was given by the pagan teacher of St. John Chrysostom. That pagan was so impressed with the influence on St. John by his mother that he exclaimed, "What wonderful women the Christians possess!"

Just a short time before he was taken prisoner by the communists and subjected to torture for his faith over a period of years, Jozsef Cardinal Mindszenty had written a book entitled *The Face of the Heavenly Mother*. The book in forceful language spoke out in praise of Mary and womanhood and the tremendous power of both in the modern world.

In one chapter, the Cardinal related the story of a mother in the Old Testament and her seven sons who were slain for refusing to deny a principle of their religion. The Cardinal's comment on the story was: "How well this mother had reared her sons." That comment proved to be a foreshadowing of Cardinal Mindszenty's own life, when through his own heroic imprisonment his mother continued to pray for him; when through his own torture for his faith his mother's influence shone forth.

For sixteen centuries women enjoyed their rightful place in Christ's plan, with the world looking up to them as models of devotion and love, models of virtue and the spirit of sacrifice. The husband was the head of the family but the wife was the heart. She was the molder of the character of the young. Women were the inspiration for so many great men and so many saints. But then things changed and the ideals of womanhood came under attack.

The Assault on Women

Four major factors in modern history have combined to undermine the ideals of Christian womanhood that had existed for some sixteen centuries since the time of Christ: the Industrial Revolution, secular humanism, communism, and the feminist movement.

We have already seen how Marxism and communism reduced women to mere spokes in the wheel of the state. The Industrial Revolution removed women from their place in the home—where they were models of devotion, love, and sacrifice and had earned the respect and honor of society—and put them to work in the factory. Economic necessity forced women to work outside the home and made it much more difficult for them to maintain their womanly ideals.

Also undermining the solid foundation of womanly virtue was the spread of secular humanism, the philosophy which seeks to exclude God and the Church from all areas of daily living. According to *Humanist Manifesto II,* which was issued in 1973 and signed by secular humanists throughout the world, there is no "prayer-hearing God," and "humans are responsible for what we are or will become. No deity will save us; we must save ourselves."

The *Manifesto,* among other things, also rejected "traditional moral codes," insisted on "the right to birth control, abortion, and divorce," and declared that "individuals should be permitted to express their sexual proclivities and pursue their lifestyles as they desire."

While some women thought they were being "liberated" from the attitudes and prejudices of the past, they found themselves exploited more than ever by abortionists, pornographers, and radical feminists. They were told that marriage, motherhood, and homemaking were forms of domestic slavery, but found themselves alone and lonely, without families or the career success they had been promised. They were told that they were gaining equality with men, but found themselves caught up in an agenda that included joining men in military combat.

Nowhere has the situation been more distorted than with regard to abortion.

Radical feminists argue that women's rights are more important than anyone else's rights; true feminists hold that an unborn baby has rights, too. Radical feminists promise women "reproductive freedom"; true feminists believe that means freedom to reproduce, not freedom to kill an unborn child. Radical feminists say that pregnant women have been oppressed and victimized by men into having unwanted babies; true feminists counter that women who have abortions are victimizing their unborn children. Radical feminists contend that opponents of abortion are trying to keep women from attaining social equality; true feminists respond that every individual can make an equally valuable contribution to society and that unborn babies are not second-class citizens.

Sexism Incarnate

Disagreeing vehemently with those who consider abortion a step forward for women's rights, Nancyjo Mann, founder of Women Exploited by Abortion, said that "legal abortion is the most destructive manifestation of discrimination against women today." She called the abortion mentality "sexism incarnate," and said that the sexism is apparent in four ways:

1. Easily available abortion makes it "easier than ever for men to sexually exploit women."

2. The abortion mentality "attacks the unique value of female sexuality" by separating women from their reproductive potential and eroding "the natural pride which women enjoy in

being able to conceive and bear children—a creative wonder which no man can duplicate."

3. Rather than receiving the love and support needed to cope with an unplanned pregnancy, "women are offered the easy way out, the 'quick-fix,' the cover-up—abortion. They are seen as second-rate citizens with second-rate problems, and so they are handed a makeshift solution."

4. The sexist abortion mentality says that "women are not 'strong' enough to survive an unplanned pregnancy, much less to raise an 'unwanted' child or endure giving it up for adoption. Instead of helping women to be strong, independent, and capable of handling their lives in spite of the social prejudices against 'problem' pregnancies, the expediency of abortion encourages women to be weak, dependent, and incapable of dealing with unexpected challenges."

Melissa Tulin, a true feminist, has said that "pro-life feminists are part of the women's movement, and we will no longer be content to stay at the back of the bus. Our goal is to create a world where no woman must have an abortion, and we hope that someday our pro-choice sisters will realize that women will never climb to equality over the dead bodies of their children."

To those women who have had an abortion, Pope John Paul offered these words of compassion:

The Church is aware of the many factors which may have influenced your decision, and she does not doubt that in many cases it was a painful and even shattering decision. The wound in your heart may not yet have healed. Certainly what happened was and remains terribly wrong. But do not give in to discouragement and do not lose hope. Try rather to understand what happened and face it honestly.

If you have not already done so, give yourselves over with humility and trust to repentance. The Father of mercies is ready to give you his forgiveness and his peace in the sacrament of Reconciliation. You will come to understand that nothing is definitively lost, and you will also be able to ask forgiveness from your child, who is now living in the Lord.

With the friendly and expert help and advice of other people and as a result of your own painful experience, you can be among the most eloquent defenders of everyone's right to life. Through your commitment to life, whether by accepting the birth of other children or by welcoming and caring for those most in need of someone to be close to them, you will become promoters of a new way of looking at human life (*Evangelium Vitae*, n. 99).

Advice from Another Pope

Today the world's attitude toward women is upside down. Women are praised for pursuing a career in the marketplace, but jeered for wanting a career as a mother. Both vocations are worthwhile as long as a woman remains faithful to herself and to the unsurpassed dignity that God gave her. Addressing a conference on Woman and Society on September 7, 1961, Pope John XXIII urged the modern woman, while holding to the ideals of true womanhood, to use her talents for the good of society:

> Modern social structures are still far from allowing woman, in the exercise of her professions, to achieve the fulfillment of her personality, and they do not allow her to make the contribution which the Church and society expect from her. Hence the urgency of finding new solutions, if we are to achieve an order and a balance more commensurate with woman's human and Christian dignity. Hence, too, the need for Catholic women to become aware of their obligations. Such obligations do not end, as they did once upon a time, within the confines of the family circle. Woman's gradual ascent to all the responsibilities of a shared life requires her active intervention on the social and political plane. Woman is as necessary as man to the progress of society, especially in all those fields which require tact, delicacy, and maternal intuition.

While urging women to take their proper place in society, John XXIII, in the same speech, also emphasized that women and men have different functions:

> Any consideration of a woman's occupation cannot disregard

the unmistakable characteristics with which God has marked her nature. It is true that living conditions tend to bring almost complete equality of the sexes. Nevertheless, while their justly-proclaimed equality of rights must extend to all the claims of personal and human dignity, it does not in any way imply equality of functions. The Creator endowed woman with the natural attributes, tendencies, and instincts which are strictly hers, or which she possesses to a different degree from man; this means that woman was also assigned specific tasks.

To overlook this difference in the respective functions of men and women, or the fact that they necessarily complement each other, would be tantamount to opposing nature: the result would be to debase woman and to remove the true foundations of her dignity.

We should also like to remind you that the end for which the Creator fashioned woman's entire being is motherhood. This vocation to motherhood is so proper to her and so much a part of her nature that it is operative even when actual generation of offspring does not occur. Therefore, if women are to be assisted in their choice of an occupation, and in preparing and perfecting their qualifications, it is necessary that, in the practice of their profession, there be some means for continuously developing a maternal spirit.

What a contribution to society it would be if she were given the opportunity to use these precious energies of hers to better advantage, especially in the fields of education, social work, and religious and apostolic activity, thereby transforming her occupations into various forms of spiritual motherhood! Today's world has need of maternal sensibilities to dispel the atmosphere of violence and grossness in which men are often struggling.

Partners, not Rivals

Men and women have an equal but distinct dignity. They have different vocations, but are partners in a common task with different responsibilities. Both have the obligation to live a useful life, but the woman's ordinary function is that of wife and mother, and this is always an engrossing task. Usually the man will devote his energies to his profession or occupation. The unmarried woman in the world has the right to live an independent life, but a life suited to her nature as a woman. By nature she is not meant to do whatever a man does, and when she attempts this she loses much of her feminine dignity.

In the Christian way of thinking, women and men are not rivals; they are partners. Each has a role to fill, a mission to perform, and neither the family nor the country will be properly served if the male and female roles are neglected or reversed (cf. Pope John Paul's *Letter to Families*, n. 6).

Echoing the thoughts of his predecessors in the pontificate, Pope John Paul II recognized in his apostolic exhortation *The Role of the Christian Family in the Modern World* that "women have the same right as men to perform various public functions." He added, however, that "society must be structured in such a way that wives and mothers are not in practice compelled to work outside the home, and that their families can live and prosper in a dignified way even when they themselves devote their full time to their own family" (n. 23).

The Holy Father criticized "the mentality which honors women more for their work outside the home than for their work within the family," and said that overcoming this mentality "requires that men should truly esteem and love women with total respect for their personal dignity, and that society should create and develop conditions favoring work in the home."

As for the different vocations of men and women, John Paul said that "the Church must in her own life promote as far as possible their equality of rights and dignity, and this for the good of all—the family, the Church, and society." He said that "this does not mean for women a renunciation of their femininity or an imitation of the male role, but the fullness of true feminine humanity which should be expressed in their activity, whether in the family or outside of it, without disregarding the differences of customs and cultures in this sphere" (n. 23).

Making Ideals a Reality

Just as the influence of the simple Jewish girl of Nazareth completely changed the condition of the world two thousand years ago and left its stamp on the world for all time, so today Catholic women hold a place of prime importance in making the ideals of Christ and Mary a reality. That can be done in proportion to the modern woman's devotion to and imitation of Mary.

First, in her own personal life the modern woman must know and practice the divine ideals of womanhood as exemplified by Mary. If women would in their own daily lives imitate the ideals that Mary gave the world in her life, then the world would begin to acknowledge and reverence once again the sublime dignity of womanhood.

Second, women must rebuild the Christian family, giving it its proper dignity and its full spiritual vitality as the basic unit of society. It is largely the woman—the wife and mother—who creates the true Christian spirit in the family. The writer Frederick Shannon has painted a vivid picture of the vital role that women play in the Christian family:

> No blocks of marble do they round into statues; no canvasses do they adorn with glowing colors; no books do they write with scholarly taste; no music do they compose with sweet strains; no platforms do they occupy with persuasive speech. Yet they are all these, and more, because they are God's disciples of the unexplored and the unexpressed.

> Sculptors, they chisel the veined marble of flesh and blood into living, breathing human statues; artists, they paint the colors of righteousness on undying souls; authors, they write the literature of godliness on the hearts of their sons; musicians, they sing the white song of chastity into the souls of their daughters; orators, their lives speak so eloquently of the invisible things of God that, after quitting the world, they being dead, speak on from the high places of eternity.

Thirdly, the modern woman, whether in religious life, living the single life, or in the married state, can have an influence she may never suspect, can become a powerful example of the spirit of dedication, devotion to duty, and self-sacrifice. The fewer sacrifices a woman is required to make, the less inclined she is to make even those few. But when a woman lives a life which is an example of self-sacrifice and generosity, she not only stimulates herself to further heights of virtue, but is an inspiration to all around her. Particularly is she an inspiration to her own family.

Where will the heroes of our nation come from, unless we have heroines in our homes? When the women of a nation become soft, then we have good cause for concern. History tells us that most of the nations that have fallen fell from within. Abraham Lincoln, with clear insight, remarked on one occasion that he was not afraid of America being conquered from without, but he was afraid of it decaying from within.

One of woman's essential functions in the divine plan is to be a living example of self-sacrifice, of wholehearted devotion—to family, to duty, to all the womanly ideals. Women will be successful in their task in proportion to their devotion to Mary, and to their imitation of her.

Mary's Place in Our Lives

The Blessed Virgin Mary is very much misunderstood these days. So many think of her as merely a sweet person, but she was much more than that. She was strong, courageous, self-sacrificing. She lived her life in the shadow of the cross—after all, she knew the prophecies concerning the death of her Son better than any other living person. She knew the suffering ahead, yet never once faltered, but unhesitatingly went about her daily tasks, completely devoted to her womanly mission. To imitate Mary is not to be merely a sweet person. To be like her means developing a strong character, being a tower of strength for all those around you.

One of the most glorious tributes to our Lady was given many years ago in New York City. The speaker was Alfred E. Smith, a former Governor of New York and the Democratic candidate for President in 1928:

> She brought him into the world under the most terrible conditions of childbirth—in a stable—because there was no room for her in the inn. She carried him over burning sands and under scorching skies into Egypt. She sought him sorrowing when he was lost and found him in the temple about his Father's business. She knew what happened in the Garden of

Gethsemani. She knew of the tragedy that was enacted on the porch of the palace of Pilate when he was scourged, spat upon, and crowned with thorns.

Remember—he was once her little boy. She loved him as only the perfect mother can love. What must have been the anguish that tore her heart when she met him on the road to Calvary just after he had fallen for the first time under the weight of the cross she was afterwards to see him nailed upon. She saw the soldier drive the spear into his Sacred Heart and she saw the last drop of his precious blood fall upon the soil of Calvary to the end that we may all have eternal life.

Men love her because she braved the battle all the way from the crib of Bethlehem to the cross on Calvary. No person aside from her divine Son ever suffered more than she, and that is why we call her the Queen of Martyrs. Men love her because she was brave. She did not collapse, for John, who was there, tells us that she stood.

Where were Peter, James, Andrew, and the other Apostles? The truth is man was weak, woman was strong, and because she was strong she rallied men to the banner of her divine Son, and on Pentecost Sunday we find her in the midst of the Apostles, abiding in prayer. It was around woman that the manhood of the Church gathered then, and it is so even to this hour.

Imitation of Mary

The world is filled with crime and sin. In the press, the theater, in books, on radio and television, the noble ideals of womanhood are being attacked. In a world which has such contempt for morality, today's women must defend the standards of Christ and Mary. Today's women must reject sinful fashions aimed at arousing the lusts of men; they must live so as to inspire men to look on womanhood with pure eyes; they must rebuild the ideals of marriage. By and large, women will set the moral standards of society. Today's women, if they are to fulfill their mission, must dare to be different.

In Catholic teaching, women hold a lofty and important place and have far-reaching responsibilities. A woman need not be in the public eye, in politics, or in business to influence the world. There is more truth than we might suspect in the adage, "The hand that rocks the cradle rules the world." Another adage says: "Not in the branches of a tree but in its roots do force and power reside." Women are a powerful influence at the roots of society. When those roots become strong, pure, and healthy, then society will manifest a new life.

The formula is simple. Mary, a humble girl, living in an obscure town, left a lasting imprint on womanhood, on family life, and on the world. Today the life of Catholic women can have a similar effect on the world if their actions are a reflection of Mary's. That ought to be the ideal of every woman.

"Woman has the awful choice of being Eve or Mary; she is rarely neutral," said Leo Cardinal Suenens. "Either she enobles and raises man up by her presence, by creating a climate of beauty and human nobility, or she drags him down with her to her own fall."

Women have had a tremendous power and influence for good throughout history and they can have a great impact in our own day. The Church has "always known women who have exercised an oftentimes decisive role in the Church herself and accomplished tasks of considerable value on her behalf," Pope John Paul said.

Writing in *Christifidelis Laici*, the Holy Father continued:

History is marked by grand works, quite often lowly and hidden, but not for this reason any less decisive to the growth and holiness of the Church. It is necessary that this history continue, indeed that it be expanded and intensified in the face of the growing and widespread awareness of the personal dignity of woman and her vocation, particularly in the light of the urgency of a 're-evangelization' and a major effort towards 'humanizing' social relations (n. 49).

Chapter 10

The Senior Citizen

I now address older people, oftentimes unjustly considered as unproductive if not directly an insupportable burden. I remind older people that the Church calls and expects them to continue to exercise their mission in the apostolic and missionary life. This is not only a possibility for them, but it is their duty even in this time in their life when age itself provides opportunities in some specific and basic way. — Pope John Paul II, *Christifideles Laici*, n. 48

In a day when the span of life is increasing and the number of older people is growing, our culture seems to be more and more focused on the needs and desires of young people. Whether it is movies and music, radio and television commercials, or newspaper and magazine advertising, the emphasis is on youthful pursuits and pleasures, on beautiful and healthy bodies, on the satisfactions of a materialistic and hedonistic culture. There is also a corresponding neglect of the elderly, an unwillingness to take care of those who worked so hard and sacrificed so much to provide the comforts that we take for granted today, and even a campaign to get rid of them through euthanasia and assisted suicide.

Other cultures are very different. Think of the Chinese. It would be considered a disgrace and socially reprehensible for a Chinese family to refuse to assume the responsibility of aging relatives. Indeed, the younger generation looks to the elderly to benefit from their wisdom and experience. Jewish and Italian family and social traditions have remained much the same as far as the elderly are concerned. It is this attitude that needs to be re-established again. Instead of shunting aside older people, the upcoming generation must help them see that their productive years are not over, that they are still capable of enjoying lives of fulfillment. Let us look at those on both sides of this issue.

Obligations Toward the Elderly

As we consider the senior citizen in today's society from two perspectives—the attitude of the younger and middle-aged toward the elderly and the attitude of the elderly toward their own lives—we need to remind ourselves of some important attitudes and obligations spelled out for us in the Bible and in the documents of the Second Vatican Council:

Stand up in the presence of the aged and show respect for the old.—Leviticus 19:32

Cast me not off in my old age; as my strength fails, forsake me not. —Psalm 71:9

And now that I am old and gray, O God, forsake me not till I proclaim your strength to every generation that is to come. —Psalm 71:18

Among the multiple activities of the family apostolate may be enumerated the following . . . help for the aged not only by providing them with the necessities of life but also by obtaining for them a fair share of the benefits of economic progress. —Vatican II, *Decree on the Apostolate of the Laity*, n. 11

With these thoughts as background, we appeal not just to the younger generation to show reverence and care for their elders. We also invite the older generation to deepen their incentive to enrich their own lives and ours by sharing what only they can give to the world and to the younger generation—experience, wisdom, and time for study, prayer, and apostolic work. All too often these assets are not utilized to the fullest degree.

The Challenge of Growing Old

Growing older ought to be looked upon not as a sentence to which one is consigned, but rather as a challenge. Older people usually have more time for study, thought, worthwhile reading, and helpful activity. The time-consuming task of bringing up a family is over, the hours of commitment to a job may be finished. It is unfortunate that so many waste these years just biding their time, sometimes in self-pity, or in passive television viewing when they could take advantage of interesting trips and outings sponsored by community organizations or otherwise occupy their time with fulfilling pursuits.

There is a massive supply of inexpensive books available, many of them in large print for easier reading by those whose eyesight is failing. In addition to secular books, there are also numerous religious and spiritual works.

Classes are offered in arts and crafts, giving retirees an opportunity to acquire new skills and satisfying hobbies or to resume old ones. Some of these may be utilized not only for self-enjoyment, but to help others. Production of ceramics, works of art and photography, knitted goods, or electronic items might be utilized to provide income for a senior citizens club.

Bookkeeping and clerical skills might be put to good use either on a voluntary basis or to bring a minimal income through one's own parish, school, or diocesan apostolic agency. The local home for the aged might use an older person's talents in almost any field, including painting, tailoring, carpentry, and electricity. Those who have developed some skills during their lives, or who are willing to acquire a new skill, can be of great use in their own local area by assisting a charitable or social service agency. There is no need for idleness.

Growth in Holiness

The retirement years can and should especially be used for growth in prayer and the spiritual life. Again, many books are available to deepen one's faith and bring a person closer to God. This can be particularly helpful to older persons with physical afflictions or feelings of loneliness. Both can be utilized in a spirit of sacrifice to grow spiritually. Priests, ministers, rabbis, and lay persons actively engaged in apostolic work often forget that a major powerhouse of spiritual help can come just through a request to the elderly. Ask them to back up your activity with their prayers and sacrifices; they will feel needed and you will feel the results.

With more available time, older people need not merely sit home and pray. There are unlimited apostolic activities in which they can set their own pace. Regular visits can be made to the sick and to those living alone right in one's own parish or city. Many nursing homes welcome regular visits to their patients. Baby-sitting can free young couples for active apostolic work or for needed relaxation. Census work and house visiting in a parish can help to ease the burden of the priests and sisters.

Another fruitful apostolate for older people is writing. Only some may have the talent for writing articles for publication, but almost all have the capability of letter-writing. This can be engaged in even by those who are confined either at home or in a home for the aged. The apostolate of the pen is largely overlooked these days, but think of the value of letters to legislators concerning desired laws; letters to television stations or sponsors commending good programs and protesting harmful or immoral ones; letters to city or town officials bringing to their attention needed reforms; or just letters to people who are sick or lonely. A person who has nothing to do might take on the project of "a letter a day to someone." In the course of a year, an enormous amount of good can be accomplished.

Get Involved with Others

Perhaps the most common and critical problem facing those in later years is loneliness. A particular effort should be made by the person and by friends and relatives to pursue contacts with others and to develop new contacts and continuing relationships. Regular visits and telephone calls to fellow-seniors who are living alone will be fruitful on both sides. Becoming involved in service to others either through organizations or on a person-to-person basis will be rewarding. Senior citizens clubs are an excellent vehicle for this social apostolate.

But even with all this, a person may still feel isolated. It is then one may finally realize that it is only by turning to God that true solace can be found. Christ knew loneliness in the Garden of Gethsemani and felt abandonment on the cross. A great sense of consolation, hope, optimism, and joy can be gained by the thought of God's loving presence. For a Catholic, this reaches its highest degree of perfection by spending time before the Blessed Sacrament. This might be in a nearby church or chapel; or, if one is fortunate, in a Catholic residence where there is a private chapel. Priests, deacons, and laity are only too happy to bring the Eucharist to shut-ins. In any case, a person should not wait to utilize this wonderful source of strength as a last resort, but should cultivate a closer relationship with Christ through the years.

It is not uncommon for a man or woman to reach a point in life which is by no means extreme old age and say: "My time for accomplishment is finished." We should remind them of those who made their greatest achievements in later life and who can serve as an inspiration to us. Verdi, Hayden, and Handel gave the world great music after the age of 70. Rembrandt painted some of his masterpieces toward the end of his life. Einstein and Schweitzer made their mark on the world at an advanced age.

Cardinal Farnese at 68 was bent double, walked with a cane, and appeared to be nearing the end of his life, but upon his election as Pope Paul III, he straightened up and reigned for fifteen years. Pope Leo XIII also was 68 when he was elected, and he sat in the Chair of Peter for twenty-five years, issuing eighty-six encyclicals, including the famous *Rerum Novarum* at the age of 81. Mother Teresa received the Nobel Peace Prize in her 70s and continued to serve the poor and dying, despite her own ill health, for many more years.

Another frequent plague of old age is worry. Many are concerned about past wrongdoings, they are worried about their present circumstances, and there is much anxiety about what the future will bring, particularly regarding security. These persons should take heart from the reminder of our Lord: "Do not worry about your livelihood, what you are to eat or drink or use for clothing. . . . Look at the birds in the sky. They do not sow or reap, they gather nothing into barns; yet your heavenly Father feeds them" (Matthew 6:25-26).

Christ does not want anxious or worried Christians. He looks for tranquil and joyous Christians. A deepened dependence upon Christ can bring peace to us. "Come to me, all you who are weary and find life burdensome," he said, "and I will refresh you" (Matthew 11:28). Remember, too, that the priest is Christ's representative; take your worries to him.

Two additional crises, often in combination, can beset the elderly: dealing with the unexpected and developing an attitude of resentment. It might be the move to a new place of residence, the death of a relative, or the abandonment of a friend. Age makes it more difficult to adjust to the unexpected, and both the older person and the people around him should realize this.

Sometimes this uncertainty develops into resentment directed at God: "I have tried to do right, but nothing seems to go right in my life." Or, "What have I done to deserve this?" A visit to hospitals or homes for the elderly will usually bring complaints that relatives, friends, and even God have "failed" the patient. While there is nothing that can restore the balance better than faith in God, a kind word or a willing ear can help.

The Need to Be Needed

Freud's opinion that people are primarily driven and influenced in their goals by the sexual drive has been called into question by many persons. Some psychologists today insist that the primary motivator is the search for meaning in life. Many an older person, having lost this sense of meaning, says, "I am of no use anymore." That person must discover again a sense of being needed, and those around him or her must help restore a sense of usefulness in life.

A nursing home with air conditioning, television, and every modern comfort, but without a staff that gives a sense of meaning and usefulness to the lives of its patients, is not fulfilling its purpose. An aging grandmother or grandfather whose baby-sitting is never asked for, whose help around the house is rejected, or to whom relatives or friends pay little attention can easily come to feel that life is without meaning. What a waste for such a person to withdraw from the world—or to be put on a shelf to vegetate by others—when there is so much love, wisdom, experience, and talent just waiting to be tapped.

Francois Mauriac was a famous novelist who died at the age of 84. In his own eulogy he wrote: "I believe as I did when I was a child, that life has meaning, direction, value; that no suffering is lost, that every tear counts, and each drop of blood; that the secret of the world is to be found in St. John's words, 'God is love.'"

May our country which values the vitality and idealism of youth come to recognize the experience, stability, devotion, and spiritual wellspring of age; may our youth in their zeal to accomplish good and restore social justice come to respect the wisdom that only age can give; may our senior citizens recognize what they have to offer society and, though they may have retired from a job, may they not retire from constructive living and activity.

As the youthful Mary of the Gospels visited the aging Elizabeth to honor her for giving a new life to the world, so may our society come to pay honor to our aging men and women as they by their lives give new vitality to our world.

No matter how old your parents or grandparents are, no matter how old you are, they need you and you need them. Presents, money, air conditioning, television sets, beautiful surroundings will not mean a thing without love for each other. It is love that makes the world go round, and that is true whether you are nine or 90.

Little Sisters of the Poor

Since 1839 the Little Sisters of the Poor have cared for tens of thousands of elderly persons throughout the world. The sisters, due in large part to the charisma of their foundress, Jeanne Jugan, view the elderly as God's "Anawim"—his "little" ones, his "poor" ones—regardless of their age, personality, or social status. They believe that the elderly are especially dear to God and are loved by him, and the sisters wish to communicate this message to them.

The goal of the Little Sister is to use existing conditions to create a spiritual atmosphere of peace, serenity, purposefulness, love, and understanding. She comes to read the heart of the elderly rather than the words they utter; to find the depth below the surface; to see the image of godliness masked by the forces which environment, heredity, grief, emotional deprivation, and insecurity have produced on the physiognomy. She comes to know that the person she sees has all the human needs of any other human being and, as the years advance, the "why" of life becomes more crucial than ever. But the solution also becomes simpler in that the elderly turn more readily to things spiritual and grasp their significance with an astounding ease.

The Little Sister tries to create a milieu that says this is home, that this home radiates the qualities of a Christian home—it has love, stability, mutual respect and concern, an air of "otherliness"—and that this home is a foretaste of our eternal home. Thus there is joy in the simple events of life—a birthday, a visit. There is meaningfulness to daily life, a feeling that "I can help" with some familiar chore, assisting a companion, praying for the needs of others, participating in the crafts programs.

The talents of early life have a usefulness: "I can still repair the plug, mend the dress, make a baby sweater for my neighbor's grandchild, reassure my companions, or just cheer them up with talking and listening about the 'old days.' "

The status of the elderly person as a decision-maker is respected. He or she plays a part in running the home and has a say in the programs to be carried out. Some need help to resume active lives; others prefer less social life. But each has a place and each is respected as an individual.

However, no home for the elderly will ever supplant the affection of loved ones, nor remove the ache of being forgotten or overlooked. The holidays are perhaps the hardest days for elderly residents. When memories abound, the absence of concern becomes acutely felt by the elderly. Not all are able to visit or return to their families at these times, and they cannot but feel neglected if the days pass and relatives are "too busy" to "squeeze in" a visit.

"Thank God for the nuns" or "Thank God for the staff" may be very complimentary to the nuns and the staff, but it is a sad reminder that something else was expected. The Little Sister tries to teach or recall to the resident the Christian value of such suffering when offered to God for some intention. However, there is nothing that makes it a good in itself.

Divine Providence is the mainstay of the Little Sister and all the more so must it be the mainstay of the elderly as well. Confidence in God's watchful care comes from a profound conviction of his love for the Anawim—the "remnant" of God's people. And as the situation becomes bleaker for the elderly, the dependence of the Little Sister on the power of God only becomes stronger. "If God wills it, it will be done"—this has long been her heritage and her belief.

Expert Advice from the Sisters

Based on more than a century and a half of experience, the Little Sisters of the Poor can give us valuable advice on what the elderly are like and how we can take care of them. The following information was provided for this book by the Little Sisters.

Elderly people, understood as those over 65, do think clearly, but a little more slowly. It takes time for them to grasp the full significance of something, but when they do their judgments are accurate and their suggestions are good.

Elderly people have a keen recall of the past, but have difficulty learning new things. However, they can learn them, and sometimes enjoy doing so.

Elderly people—at least those with religious sentiments—usually have a realistic attitude toward life and also toward death. They are not afraid of death and are glad when they can help others, by prayers and their presence, to die well. Relatives and staff in institutions have more difficulty with death than the elderly do.

Elderly people have the same human needs as other persons. They must have love, respect, recognition, and a sense of usefulness if their old age is to be positive and worthwhile.

Elderly people understand their limitations, but they are also quick to see through artifice. They will read the heart of what is said with the lips, and this is true of both good intentions which are perhaps expressed awkwardly, as well as of what amounts to only pretended interest.

The chief sufferings of the elderly are not physical. Yes, there are rough days for them because of physical ailments, but the chief sufferings are a sense of rejection, uselessness, loneliness, and grief. A small thought, a card, a visit, an expression of appreciation do more than a mountain of aspirin for ailing spirits. The finest surroundings are meaningless to the elderly, just as they are to children and adults, if they are void of love and concern.

Elderly people adjust to the most unusual conditions well and cheerfully if love and understanding are there. They especially need a peaceful and serene environment, which for many is found in religious expressions.

"Old" is a relative term and there are few elderly who really consider themselves old so long as life holds some purpose for them. And because the Christian elderly are Christian, there is no such thing as a useless human being. They can be the backbone of society and the support of the Church by the proper use of this time of their lives. In order to do this, however, many of them require the encouragement of religious leaders and persons who sincerely believe this to be true.

Reasons for Institutionalization

Only a small percentage of the elderly are institutionalized. The factors which require institutionalization are varied, and the adjustment of the individual to the process will be directly related to the reasons for which it is required. Here are some of the most common reasons for institutionalizing the elderly:

1. Concern on the part of the family.
   a) Old person lives alone and is becoming feeble or unable to carry out life functions (shopping, cooking).
   b) Parent will not live with children; parent incompatible with children due to personality clashes or changes due to advancing years; parent unable to live with children due to unavailable living quarters, size of family, or working child and marriage partner.
   c) No living relatives to assume responsibility.
   d) Desire for companionship of own age (usually as a means to combat depression and loneliness).
2. Lack of concern on the part of the family.
   a) Child and parent have been alienated over a long period of time (perhaps due to alcoholism, or a second marriage which was unfortunate for the child).
   b) Great distance separates them (not always real lack of concern, but has the same effect).
   c) Inability of the parent to accept the lifestyle of the child, giving rise to great unhappiness for both.

3. Self-determination of the elderly.

    a) They want to come to an institution for companionship, security, or religious motives.

4. The mental or physical state of the individual requires it.

    a) This factor is mentioned last deliberately. Nursing home institutionalization is often the result of this factor, but it is sometimes, if not frequently, only a contributing factor and not the primary one.

    b) Senility and Alzheimer's Disease are most difficult conditions and require special facilities to take care of individuals afflicted with them.

Adjusting to a New Lifestyle

1. The elderly person who is institutionalized goes through a "disengagement process" that is more or less severe depending upon several factors.

    a) Their personality structure.

    b) The willingness with which the transfer is made. Experience shows that the resident for whom the admission was misrepresented (that is, a visit, a vacation, a short stay, etc.), usually, if not always, will adjust poorly, even becoming agitated, disoriented, or psychotic. The same thing happens frequently when the individual has been living alone in a very nonstimulating environment, with few personal contacts, and has begun senile cerebral changes.

        Institutionalization seems to create severe orientation problems and, based on the basic strength of the individual's personality, may cause rapid disintegration and disorientation and produce senile psychotic symptoms. This has physical as well as mental and emotional manifestations.

2. Those do best in adjusting to a new lifestyle who:

    a) have been a part of the process of decision-making

    b) understand the reasons for it

    c) are assured of family concern and devotedness

d) want this living arrangement for any number of reasons (that is, they see it as a positive good)

e) have visited the facility, met some of the residents, and feel free in the new environment to continue at least some of the important (to them) lifestyle patterns to which they are accustomed.

3. In all honesty, it would seem that "disengagement" takes place in almost one hundred percent of those admitted and that this is the biggest factor in adjustment as well as survival. A cliché has it that if an elderly person survives the first year, his or her chances for adjustment are good. The death rate during the first year is highest for all deaths in a facility. Some are near this point physically on admission, but a large number become so due to the emotional drain and the inability to adapt. A sense of rejection by loved ones plays a crucial role in the death or deterioration process.

The *Catechism of the Catholic Church* summarizes our duties to the elderly:

The fourth commandment reminds grown children of their responsibilities toward their parents. As much as they can, they must give them material and moral support in old age and in times of illness, loneliness, or distress (n. 2218).

The *Catechism* also recalls the words of Sirach:

O son, help your father in his old age, and do not grieve him as long as he lives; even if he is lacking in understanding, show forebearance; in all your strength do not despise him .... Whoever forsakes his father is like a blasphemer, and whoever angers his mother is cursed by the Lord (3:12-13, 16).

Chapter 11

The Eighth Person

> Every form of social or cultural discrimination in fundamental personal rights on the grounds of sex, race, color, social conditions, language, or religion must be curbed and eradicated as incompatible with God's design. — *Catechism of the Catholic Church*, n. 1935

When we consider the racial makeup of the United States, we find that better than one person out of every eight in our country is a member of a minority group, and has human rights as inalienable as those of the other seven. Yet in this great country which proclaims equality and justice for all, is there anyone who can say in all sincerity that we have no racial problems?

In a conference with a high American diplomat just before the outbreak of World War II, Adolf Hitler defended his persecution of the Jews by pointing out American mistreatment of blacks. People today try to use the difficulties faced by blacks, Hispanics, Asians, and others to discredit America in the eyes of the world.

Racial problems in America, it can be demonstrated, have worldwide ramifications. Diplomats and politicians, sociologists and economists, educators and religious leaders are all studying this problem of "the eighth person in our midst." The day has passed when we can take a neutral stand on racial issues. Whether we are speaking about our country or our Church, we can no longer ignore the eighth person. If we truly believe that we are one nation under God, then we must pray and work for liberty and justice for all our brothers and sisters.

Racism Is a Sin

It was the Feast of Christ the King as the archbishop ascended his pulpit—an archbishop being threatened by his government with arrest and torture for his insistent presentation of Catholic principles. Slowly he began to speak:

> We assert that every people and every race which has been formed on earth today has the right to life and to treatment worthy of man. All of them without distinction, be they members of the Gypsy race or of another, be they Negroes or Europeans, be they Jews or Aryans, all have an equal right to say, "Our Father, who art in heaven." If God has granted this right to all human beings, what worldly power can deny it? Therefore the Catholic Church has always condemned and will always condemn every injustice and compulsion perpetrated in the name of social, racial, and national theories.

These words were spoken by the late Aloysius Cardinal Stepinac, who was shortly thereafter imprisoned by the communist powers in Yugoslavia. The Cardinal's statement seemed to re-echo that of another zealous priest who was also cast into prison. St. Paul preached these same teachings of the Lord in the simple words: "There does not exist among you Jew or Greek, slave or freeman, male or female. All are one in Christ Jesus" (Galatians 3:28). Yes, St. Paul knew that there were slave and free. He knew that there were different races. But he was saying that it makes no difference to God, that we are all his children, brothers and sisters under his fatherhood.

The same principle of love of neighbor, regardless of who that neighbor might be, has been preached just as vigorously by the Church in more recent times. In their 1980 pastoral letter *Brothers and Sisters to Us*, the Catholic Bishops of the United States stated unequivocally that "racism is a sin" because it "says some human beings are inherently superior and others essentially inferior because of race."

During a visit to New Orleans on September 12, 1987, Pope John Paul sounded very much like St. Paul when he told black

Catholic leaders that "there is no black church, no white church, no American church; but there is and must be, in the one Church of Jesus Christ, a home for blacks, whites, Americans, every culture and race."

The Holy Father expanded on this teaching a year later:

All forms of discrimination are totally unacceptable, especially those forms which unfortunately continue to divide and degrade the human family: from those based on race or economics to those social and cultural, from political to geographic, etc. Each discrimination constitutes an absolutely intolerable injustice, not so much for the tensions and the conflicts that can be generated in the social sphere, as much as for the dishonor inflicted on the dignity of the person—not only to the dignity of the individual who is the victim of the injustice, but still more to the one who commits the injustice (*Christifideles Laici*, n. 37).

Anti-Semitism Is a Sin

The same principle holds true with regard to those of other faiths, particularly the Jewish religion with whom we share a common spiritual heritage. At the height of the Nazi persecution of the Jews in 1938, Pope Pius XI declared on September 6th that "anti-Semitism cannot be admitted." On Christmas Day of that year, the Holy Father stated that the Nazi cross was an "enemy of the Cross of Christ."

His successor, Pope Pius XII, spearheaded an effort to rescue Jews from the Nazis that included hiding them in his own residence, as well as in Catholic convents and monasteries, and ordering sacred vessels at the Vatican melted down for gold to ransom Jews from their Nazi captors. In his book *Three Popes and the Jews*, former Israeli diplomat Pinchas Lapide estimated that Pius XII saved 860,000 Jews from death.

Yet detractors of the Holy Father continue to besmirch his name by charging that he failed to speak out against Hitler's annihilation of the Jews. Such charges are not supported by history. Following his Christmas message in 1941, for example, the *New York Times* praised Pius XII for being "about the only ruler on the continent of Europe who dares to raise his voice" against Nazism.

"In calling for a 'real new order' based on 'liberty, justice, and love,' to be attained only by a 'return to social and international principles capable of creating a barrier against the abuse of liberty and the abuse of power,' " said the *Times* editorial, "the Pope put himself squarely against Hitlerism."

These sentiments were reiterated after the Pope's death in 1958, when Golda Meir, then Israeli delegate to the United Nations and later to be Prime Minister of her country, delivered this eulogy:

> We share the grief of the world over the death of His Holiness Pope Pius XII. During a generation of wars and dissensions, he affirmed the high ideals of peace and compassion. During the ten years of the Nazi terror, when our people went through the horrors of martyrdom, the Pope raised his voice to condemn the persecutors and to commiserate with their victims.

The Second Vatican Council (1962-1965) made one the most definitive condemnations of hostility to the Jews when it stated that the Church "deplores the hatred, persecutions, and displays of anti-Semitism directed against the Jews at any time and from any source" (*Declaration on the Relationship of the Church to Non-Christian Religions*, n. 4).

The Council Fathers, in the same document, also rejected the notion that all Jews living at the time of Christ, and even those living today, could be collectively blamed for the crucifixion of our Lord:

> True, authorities of the Jews and those who followed their lead pressed for the death of Christ; still, what happened in his Passion cannot be blamed upon all the Jews then living, without distinction, nor upon the Jews of today. Although the Church is the new people of God, the Jews should not be presented as repudiated or cursed by God, as if such views followed from the holy Scriptures.
>
> All should take pains, then, lest in catechetical instruction and in the preaching of God's Word they teach anything out of harmony with the truth of the Gospel and the spirit of Christ.

The Least of Our Brothers

The good or evil done to another must be considered as good or evil done to Christ. Remember the story of Paul's persecution of the Church before his conversion? One day while on the road to Damascus, he was struck to the ground and heard the voice of Christ saying, "Saul, Saul, why do you persecute me?"(Acts 9:4). It was not Christ whom Paul was persecuting, but his followers—and yet those words rang in his ears: "Why do you persecute me?" He would later learn what Christ had said about the Last Judgment:

Come. You have my Father's blessing! Inherit the kingdom prepared for you from the creation of the world. For I was hungry and you gave me food, I was thirsty and you gave me drink. I was a stranger and you welcomed me, naked and you clothed me. I was ill and you comforted me, in prison and you came to visit me. Then the just will ask him: "Lord, when did we see you hungry and feed you or see you thirsty and give you drink? When did we welcome you away from home or clothe you in your nakedness? When did we visit you when you were ill and in prison?" The king will answer them: "I assure you, as often as you did it for one of my least brothers, you did it for me."

Then he will say to those on his left: "Out of my sight, you condemned, into that everlasting fire prepared for the devil and his angels! I was hungry and you gave me no food, I was thirsty and you gave me no drink. I was away from home and you gave me no welcome, naked and you gave me no clothing. I was ill and in prison and you did not come to comfort me." Then they in turn will ask: "Lord, when did we see you hungry or thirsty or away from home or naked or ill or in prison and not attend you in your needs?" He will answer them: "I assure you, as often as you neglected to do it to one of these least ones, you neglected to do it to me" (Matthew 25:34-45).

Of course there are people of all races and religions who do evil things. No matter what your racial or religious group may be, you must admit that some of your own people (and perhaps even yourself) have been guilty of bigotry and prejudice. The point to remember is that we must love the sinner while hating the sin. Bear in mind, too, that while we may not be particularly fond of everyone, we do have to love them, with the same sort of love that Jesus has for us. He knows that we are all sinners, and yet he loves us so much that he was willing to lay down his life for us.

What about the black person you did not want in the pew with you in Church? What about that Jewish fellow towards whom you were so uncharitable? What about that family you resented simply because they were white? What about the little Vietnamese girl you did not want in the same school with your children? What about the handicapped boy that you ridiculed? Weren't they made in the image and likeness of God, just as you were? Didn't Jesus die for them, too? Is it possible to call yourself a follower of Christ and not live up to his teachings on racial justice?

In working toward a Christian solution for the social problems of our day, we can often distinguish two groups of people. The first is made up of the overzealous and imprudent, those who want to dash ahead without really knowing what to expect. The second group is comprised of the overly timid and cautious, those who are satisfied with the status quo and who are not too anxious for improvement or change.

The two types may be compared to the accelerator and the brake of an automobile—neither one should be forgotten. Both are necessary if we hope to drive safely and to steer a straight course. That does not mean any compromising of principles, but it does necessitate building our strategy on a solid foundation. It does not mean that we are content with the application of Christ's principles of social justice in the world today; nor does it mean that we are satisfied with the racial and religious situation as it is. What it does mean is that if we are to bring about a lasting improvement, we ought to consider carefully the teachings of Christ and his Church and act in a prudent fashion in putting those teachings into practice.

Spiritual Schizophrenia

A couple vacationing in another state noticed a sign on a church lawn that asked the question: "If you were arrested as a Christian, would there be enough evidence to convict you?" It is not enough to profess to be a follower of Christ if we will not take a firm stand in applying his principles of social justice in the world today. We must never forget that Christianity is not simply a matter of avoiding sin. There are many positive things that we must do.

When a person on the last day finds himself standing before Christ, his Judge, and says, "I did not murder, steal, or commit adultery," Christ will ask, "But what *did* you do?" It is one thing to avoid injustice and uncharitableness in our own lives. It is quite another thing to do something about the violations of justice and charity taking place all around us.

There is a proverb that says, "The person who talks for both sides is not to be trusted by either." When we apply that axiom to the present-day bigot or racist, we can draw some interesting conclusions. The person who goes along with the tide of racial or national injustice and discrimination in his daily contacts, while professing to be a good Catholic or a follower of the teachings of Christ, is attempting something that is a contradiction. He has, so to speak, a religious split personality. Christianity, and in particular Christ's doctrine of love of God and neighbor, will when lived to the fullest end this "spiritual schizophrenia."

A person who finally comes to realize the shocking contradiction between racism and the social teachings of Christ sometimes asks, "Why doesn't the Catholic Church do something about it?" Actually, the Church is doing something about it. She speaks out daily in terms which are unmistakably clear in meaning. Yes, we use that word "daily" in its literal sense, for each day in the language of the liturgy, the Catholic Church eloquently proclaims lessons of interracial justice for Catholics to live.

How can a Catholic who really understands the Holy Sacrifice of the Mass and the doctrine of Christ's Mystical Body, and who applies that knowledge in his or her own life, ever consciously violate social justice?

Side by Side at Mass

Helen Caldwell Day was a black nurse who became a Catholic in her twenties. She had experienced the fears, anxieties, and sufferings of discriminatory practices. In these words, she told what the Catholic Faith and the Mass meant in her life:

When I went to chapel to Mass in the morning, I lost all my self-consciousness because I was no longer a stranger to these people but one with them. It was a wonderful thing to offer again with Christ and all the Christians of the world his perfect sacrifice to his Father. When the priest raised our Lord, that we might adore him in the Host, I would think that even while we gazed upon him, we were part of his Mystical Body, members of him and of each other.

Yes, the Mass and the Mystical Body of Christ can have far-reaching implications for us. As we kneel before the altar, side by side with our fellow Catholics and ready to assist at Mass, we must remember that what we are about to do is something much more important than kneeling down in our room for morning or night prayers. The Mass was given to us by Christ himself at the Last Supper and it is the official public and social prayer of the Catholic Church.

When we kneel for other prayers, they are merely our own prayers. When we assist at Mass, we are united to one billion other Catholics throughout the world. The priest who celebrates the Mass is not offering a private prayer. He is officially appointed and consecrated to act in the name of the community. The Mass, then, is the official prayer of the whole community, a sacrifice offered by all Catholics, with infinite social implications.

As we join with the priest at the Offertory of the Mass, we recall that the offering of the bread and wine is a symbol of our own offering to Christ. Can we put aside his almost stern reminder: "If you bring your gift to the altar and there recall that your brother has anything against you, leave your gift at the altar, go first to be reconciled with your brother, and then come and offer your gift" (Matthew 5:23-24)?

In light of those words, what about the "Sunday Catholic" who is guilty of violations of social justice during the other six days of the week? Can he in good conscience shut the door on his actions during the week and come on Sunday to offer his gift, his Mass, with the priest at the altar? It reminds us of a brief verse we first heard in grade school: "Mr. Jones went to church, he never missed a Sunday. But Mr. Jones went to hell for what he did on Monday."

As the priest holds aloft the chalice, offering to God the wine soon to become the Blood of Christ, he prays: "We have this wine to offer." Notice that the words are not "I have" but "we have." It is the offering of all those present. Perhaps we are joined in this part of the Mass with a Jewish convert on the other side of the church; the black college student facing exams that day; the old Italian woman who attends daily Mass; the Hispanic family that recently moved into our parish; the Chinese doctor who is on the staff of the nearby hospital. Do we really mean "we offer" or are there limits on the "we"? Are we coming to Mass filled with bigotry, prejudice, ideas of superiority and of "keeping those people in their places"? If so, then our Catholic life is a lie.

The heart of the Mass is the point at which, through the heaven-shaking words of the priest—"This is my Body"...."This is the cup of my Blood"—Christ's own Body and Blood become present upon the altar.

The Consecration is the climax of the Mass. It is a renewal of Calvary, where Christ's Blood was poured out to win the grace of salvation for every human soul. In the Mass, the merits won at the price of that Blood are channeled to us. And the Catholic Church will not have us forget that no one is excluded from the merits of that Blood.

Pope Pius XII, seeing the need of reminding the world, and particularly Catholics, of this fundamental truth, declared that "men may be separated by nationality and race, but our Savior poured out his blood to reconcile all men to God through the cross, and bid them all unite in one body" (*The Mystical Body of Christ*, n. 96).

In that same document, the Holy Father ruled out all spiritual schizophrenia by those who call themselves Catholics:

How can we claim to love the divine Redeemer if we hate those whom he has redeemed with his precious blood, so that he might make them members of his Mystical Body? For that reason the beloved disciple warns us: "If a man boasts of loving God, while he hates his own brother, he is a liar. He has seen his brother, and has no love for him; what love can he have for the God whom he has never seen? No, this is the divine command that has been given us: the man who loves God must be one who loves his brother as well" (n. 74).

All Children of One Father

We can never become individualistic about the Mass. When we kneel before the altar to join with the priest at Mass, we must realize that we are all members of one family. Every Catholic shares in the fruits of every Mass. No matter how unknown or obscure a Catholic may be, were he to die forgotten by friends and relatives, Christ and the Church will not forget him. He shares in the same benefits from Masses offered on thousands of altars as do we. Perhaps the graces from a Mass we have heard will contribute to his salvation. Perhaps the fruits of some Mass at which a few African natives or Chinese peasants are present will be the means of helping us toward heaven.

As we glance upwards at the Body of Christ and the chalice of his Blood raised aloft by the priest for our adoration, we cannot help but remember that his body was broken and his blood shed for everyone without exception. All Catholics—it matters not their race or nationality or shade of skin—are united in a larger family of brothers and sisters with Christ present on the altar as the head of that family.

The most familiar manifestation of that family of God is the local parish, which Pope John Paul has said "is founded on a theological reality because it is a Eucharistic community. This means that the parish is a community properly suited for celebrating the Eucharist, the living source for its upbuilding and the sacramental bond of its being in full communion with the whole Church" (*Christifideles Laici*, n. 26).

Shortly after the Consecration, the priest and the people recite the Our Father. Christ himself taught the world this prayer, and so it is fitting that it should find a place in the Mass. Without going any further than the opening phrase, our world can learn an important lesson. Every race , every creed, and every nation—Europeans or Asiatics, Africans or Americans, black or yellow or white, Jews or Gentiles—all have an equal right to say, "Our Father, who art in heaven." If Christ himself has reminded us of this right, and indeed commanded all equally to recite this prayer, then what power on earth has a right to reject the implications of those words?

The Catholic who receives Holy Communion on Saturday night or Sunday and maintains an attitude of discrimination the rest of the week is living a contradiction, a sham Catholicity. If we follow the life of Christ, we will notice that the two things which excited his just anger were duplicity and hypocrisy. It is bad enough for modern pagans to reject the doctrines of the universal Fatherhood of God, the brotherhood of man, and the Mystical Body of Christ, but it is infinitely worse for modern Christians who, while proclaiming belief in these truths, reject them in their daily lives. "Woe to . . . you frauds!" Jesus warned the hypocrites of his time (Matthew 23:27).

The social implications of the liturgy of the Catholic Church are not founded on pity for the common person. They are founded on reverence for him or her. This is not a plea for pity or sentiment. It is a prayer that the world may once more recognize the sublime dignity of human nature—all human nature.

The Catholic Church has for centuries been the champion and defender of every person, not because their state is at times so miserable, but because human nature is at all times so sublime.

Why Prejudice Makes No Sense

Prejudice (whether on the part of the majority against minorities or on the part of minority groups against the majority) is rooted in emotionalism. The way to overcome prejudice for a person of good will is based upon reason and fundamental moral principles. Here is an outline of those principles:

I. The unity of all persons

    A. Natural unity

        1. The soul of every person has the same spiritual origin; God created every human being.

2. The body of every person has the same physical origin: our first parents.

3. God has given all of us a common dwelling place with a natural right to share its resources.

4. All of us are interdependent economically and in society.

B. Supernatural unity

1. All persons have the same supernatural destiny, heaven. That is why each and every individual was created by God.

2. Christ died to redeem all of us. As Catholics are reminded at Mass: "This is the cup of my Blood, the blood of the new and everlasting covenant. It will be shed for you and for all."

3. All of us are united in a common bond of love with God. "How can we claim to love the divine Redeemer, if we hate those whom he has redeemed?" (Pope Pius XII, *The Mystical Body of Christ*).

4. All of us are called to a spirit of unity and fraternal charity in the Church established by Jesus Christ.

   a) "There is but one body and one Spirit. . . . There is one Lord, one faith, one baptism; one God and Father of all" (Ephesians 4:4-6).

   b) "If you bring your gift to the altar and there recall that your brother has anything against you, leave your gift at the altar, go first to be reconciled with your brother, and then come and offer your gift" (Matthew 5:23-24).

   c) The doctrine of the Mystical Body of Christ: "The body is one and has many members, but all the members, many though they are, are one body. . . . There are, indeed, many different members, but one body. The eye cannot say to the hand, 'I do not need you,' any more than the head can say to the feet, 'I do not need you.' Even those members of the body which seem less important are in fact indispensable. . . . God has so constructed the body as to give greater honor to the lowly members, that there may be no dissension in the body, but that all the members may be concerned for one another. If one member suffers, all the members suffer with it; if one member is honored, all the members share its joy. You, then, are the body of Christ. Every one of you is a member of it" (1 Corinthians 12:12, 20-27).

II. The natural equality of all persons

   A. Founded upon the very nature of man and woman

      1. All persons have been endowed by their Creator with the same essential faculties of intellect and free will.

      2. Human rights spring from human nature; they are not conferred by other humans. "At the basis of all human rights is the dignity of the human person created in the image and likeness of God. A recognition of this human dignity is also a part of your civil tradition in the United States, and is expressed in the declaration of your nation's independence: all people are created equal in their human dignity and are endowed by their Creator with inalienable rights to life, liberty, and the pursuit of happiness. All other rights, too, are rooted in human dignity" (Pope John Paul II in Los Angeles, September 15, 1987).

      3. Pope John Paul has called this dignity "the indestructible property of every human being. The force of this affirmation is based on the uniqueness and irrepeatability of every person. . . . As an individual, a person is not a number or simply a link in a chain, nor even less an impersonal element in some system. The most radical and elevating affirmation of the value of every human being was made by the Son of God in his becoming man in the womb

of a woman, as we continue to be reminded each Christmas" (*Christifideles Laici*, n. 37).

B. The right to human life implies other rights to carry on life as a human being: the right to work, to enjoy a reasonable livelihood, to education, to decent housing, to esteem and honor, to worship God.

    1. One cannot own anything until he is already alive. Life is a prerequisite of ownership. Therefore, no one owns even his own life. The owner of human life is not man or woman but God, who gave life to them.

    2. Interference with life, or denial of rights inherent in carrying on human life, is not within the province of another human being.

III.   Relative to prejudice giving rise to acts of discrimination, hatred, or the demeaning of an individual, legal, sociological, or good-will considerations are secondary. Basic to the problem is the fact that the law of God and the natural law are flouted, for which violators will one day answer to God. "Every form of discrimination based on race, whether occasionally or systematically practiced and whether it is aimed at individuals or whole racial groups, is absolutely unacceptable" —(Pope John Paul II, Weekly Audience, July 7, 1984).

For a good summary of these principles, see the *Catechism of the Catholic Church*, nn. 1928-1948.

Chapter 12

Christian Stewardship

All that we have received from God—life itself as well as material goods—does not belong to us but is given to us for our use. Generosity in giving must always be enlightened and inspired by faith: then we will truly be more blessed in giving than in receiving. — Pope John Paul II, *Redemptoris Missio*, n. 81

There is a story of a man who went to heaven and was greeted by St. Peter. Before entering heaven, the man asked if he could see what hell was like. So Peter whisked him to the regions of hell where he observed rows and rows of banquet tables, covered with fine linen and laden with every kind of food and drink imaginable. The people seated at the tables were nicely dressed and held in their hands forks that were three feet long. They were able to pick up the food in front of them, but were not able to feed themselves, so the atmosphere was one of anger, frustration, and hatred.

Relieved that he would not have to spend an eternity in hell, the man asked St. Peter to return him to heaven. But as he walked through the gates he was startled to see what appeared to be the same scene he had witnessed in hell. There were rows and rows of banquet tables, covered with fine linen and laden with every kind of food and drink imaginable. The people seated at the tables also were nicely dressed and held in their hands forks that were three feet long. But there was one major difference in heaven: here the people were not trying the impossible task of feeding themselves; they were feeding each other, and the atmosphere was one of serenity, contentment, and love.

The story is not true, of course, but the lesson it teaches is true. Our salvation depends on how we respond to the cries of our neighbors for help. The road to heaven is paved with acts of charity, kindness, and generosity. True love and happiness in this life come from giving of ourselves and our material goods to others. We all know from experience the wonderful feeling we have when we do something good for another person.

That is what Christian stewardship is all about—sharing our time, talents, and treasure with those who are less fortunate. Showing love for the needy is the same as showing love for Christ, who has told us that whatever we do for the least of our brothers and sisters, we do for him (Matthew 25:40). Stewardship is not something we can ignore if we want to attain eternal life. Jesus is very explicit when he warns us that failure to feed the hungry, give drink to the thirsty, clothe the naked, and visit the sick and imprisoned will keep a person out of heaven.

There is another story of a woman whose car stalled at a traffic light. The driver behind her began honking his horn impatiently. Finally, the woman got out of her car, walked back to the restless motorist leaning on his horn, and said quietly, "I'll tell you what. If you'll fix my car, I'll be glad to sit in your car and keep blowing the horn." Too many Christians, seeing others in need of assistance, stand by and honk instead of helping. They fail to act upon their obligation of stewardship or to influence others to lend a hand.

Every Catholic has rights and duties. Our rights include a special claim to the means of grace supplied by the Church. In turn, we also have the duty to obey our ecclesiastical superiors in spiritual matters, and to work with them in serving God and neighbor. This latter duty is a very broad obligation. Some people think that they have done their share by giving money, but that might be the least of all the things they could do. God may want their talents much more than their money. When a swimmer is drowning, a donation to the lifeguard's fund will not do him much good.

St. Paul gave a stark reminder of the *esprit de corps* that Christians should have when he said, "You are strangers and aliens no longer" (Ephesians 2:19). In certain languages the word for "stranger" and the word for "enemy" is the same. Among the Greeks and Romans the stranger was looked upon as a barbarian and an enemy. In English the word stranger originally meant foreigner, one who does not belong. This implies a gap between people. Stewardship is the catalyst which can narrow such a gap because stewardship is based upon love—of God and neighbor—and implies service to others. It can be summed up in three words: Know, Love, and Serve.

Our life is not entirely our own. It has been entrusted to us by God and is the instrument by which we are to work out our own salvation while at the same time helping others to do the same. The Christian is to be in the world, but not of the world. The Vatican Council spoke repeatedly of self-renewal, knowing that if enough people truly renew themselves, they will begin to renew the face of the earth. Stewardship, the voluntary and proportionate sharing of time, talent, and material resources, can with the right motivation be a true act of worship of God.

Christ and Stewardship

Read the teaching of Christ in the New Testament. There is scarcely a duty which is referred to implicitly or explicitly more often than stewardship. Most of the parables our Lord used to teach the people make the following three points: All the things that we possess and did not bring into existence ourselves are gifts of God; we must not use them selfishly, but rather for the glory of God and the good of others; we must be prepared to give an account of our stewardship of these possessions (Luke 16:2).

To see what we mean, read and ponder such parables of Christ as the Sower and the Seed (Matthew 13:4-9, 18-23), the Good Samaritan (Luke 10:25-37), the Rich Man and Lazarus (Luke 16:19-31), and the Ten Virgins (Matthew 25:1-13). Or recall in particular the parable of the Silver Pieces, which compels us to use our talents and treasure as God intended:

> The case of a man who was going on a journey is similar. He called in his servants and handed his funds over to them according to each man's abilities. To one he disbursed five thousand silver pieces, to a second two thousand, and to a third a thousand. Then he went away. Immediately the man who received the five thousand went to invest it and made another five. In the same way, the man who received the two thousand doubled his figure. The man who received the thousand went off instead and dug a hole in the ground, where he buried his master's money.
>
> After a long absence, the master of those servants came home and settled accounts with them. The man who had re-

ceived the five thousand came forward bringing the additional five. "My lord," he said, "you let me have five thousand. See, I have made five thousand more." His master said to him, "Well done! You are an industrious and reliable servant. Since you were dependable in a small matter I will put you in charge of larger affairs. Come, share your master's joy!" The man who had received the two thousand then stepped forward. "My lord," he said, "you entrusted me with two thousand and I have made two thousand more." His master said to him. "Cleverly done! You too are an industrious and reliable servant. Since you were dependable in a small matter I will put you in charge of larger affairs. Come, share your master's joy!"

Finally the man who had received the thousand stepped forward. "My lord," he said, "I knew you were a hard man. You reap where you did not sow and gather where you did not scatter, so out of fear I went off and buried your thousand silver pieces in the ground. Here is your money back." His master exclaimed: "You worthless, lazy lout! You know I reap where I did not sow and gather where I did not scatter. All the more reason to deposit my money with the bankers, so that on my return I could have it back with interest. You, there! Take the thousand away from him and give it to the man with the ten thousand. Those who have will get more until they grow rich, while those who have not will lose even the little they have. Throw this worthless servant into the darkness outside, where he can wail and grind his teeth" (Matthew 25:14-30).

Stewardship in Today's World

When we speak of people in any generation, we must recognize them for what they are, and one of the most obvious of our qualities is that we are dependent. The poet Francis Thompson tells us that "we are born in another's pain, and we perish in our own," which is only to say that even for life itself we are in debt to others. We need others for companionship, for love, for sociability, for our education, for all the amenities that contribute to what we call living. "No man is an island" is a phrase that has become part of our language because it represents a fact that is basic to a proper understanding of human beings.

But as each person has a relationship of dependence with others, so too do we relate to the source of all life, the God of creation. For all that we are, and for all that we have, we must thank a wise and generous God and acknowledge a dependence on his creative power and on his grace and goodness. This is usually done— we might even say instinctively done—in prayer, which recognizes the Lord's dominion over us and expresses our grateful thoughts for his enduring and loving providence.

Both of these relationships of dependence—with God and with our fellow human beings—tell us something immensely significant about ourselves. They remind us that our lives reach out in two directions—vertically to the Creator and horizontally to others. These facts must be expressed in our lives if we are to be genuine and not phony. And the word that best describes this human situation is stewardship.

A steward is one who is in charge of things which in reality belong to another. He is responsible for them and for their good management. What we must remember about ourselves is that, for the years of our life, we are stewards of all that has been given us—all that is ours in time, ability, opportunity, special talent, and material goods. These things are held by us for our use, and we are responsible for their good management—not as their creator, not even as their owner, but precisely as their steward. And like the servants in the parable of the Silver Pieces, we will one day be called upon to give an account of our stewardship.

What Can We Share?

There are many things that we can share with other people. There is, first of all and best of all, ourselves. We can share our happiness and joy, our fun and laughter; we can share our love and our affection, our strength and our vitality. To those whose lives lack all or some of these elements, there are no greater gifts to give. We can share a gift of song, a sense of beauty, a kindly phrase, a helping hand, a warm heart. All of these should be part of every person's living experience, and where they are absent we must make them present.

Each one of us in a special way can give of talent and ability, even when these appear to be of a humble sort. It is not the size of the gift that counts, it is the willingness of the giver. We must share with others not just in proportion to what we have, but rather in proportion to the other's need. To promote this human situation is to promote human development and generate peace among individuals and nations.

We must of course apply the rule of stewardship to our possessions as well as to ourselves. We are required not only to share with the needy from our abundance, but also from our normal resources if the needs of others are greater than ours. Unhappily, the temptation too often is to make some routine donation and avoid as much as possible any real involvement. The most precious thing to give is ourselves, and if this is held back our stewardship is incomplete.

Christians are particularly called upon to demonstrate what Pope John Paul has called "the option or love of preference for the poor." Considering the worldwide dimensions of the problem, the Holy Father said: "This love of preference for the poor, and the decisions which it inspires in us, cannot but embrace the immense multitudes of the hungry, the needy, the homeless, those without medical care, and, above all, those without hope of a better future. It is impossible not to take account of the existence of these realities. To ignore them would mean becoming like the 'rich man' who pretended not to know the beggar Lazarus lying at his gate" (*On Social Concern,* n. 42).

Church Support and Virtue

We do not hear much these days about the virtues, specifically the theological virtues of faith, hope, and charity, or the cardinal virtues of prudence, justice, fortitude, and temperance. Nor is there enough emphasis on the virtue of giving financial support to the Church, which remains one of the Commandments or Precepts of the Church: "To strengthen and support the Church: one's own parish community and parish priests; the worldwide Church and the Holy Father."

The Catholic Church is not wealthy, as some critics have charged. Yes, the Church does have a worldwide network of churches, schools, convents, monasteries, hospitals, orphanages, and homes for the aged, the troubled, and the dying. But these physical structures are not used to make anyone rich; they are used to bring the love and mercy and teachings of God to people of every nation. It costs a huge amount of money to maintain these buildings and operate the agencies and programs they house, but the universal Church exists to save souls, not to make a profit.

Critics of the Catholic Church have also argued that the Church should sell the many valuable books, works of art, and historical treasures it has preserved over the centuries and give the money to the poor. But even if the Church were to sell all those priceless artifacts, the proceeds would provide hardly more than a day's food to the millions of hungry people around the world. They would be hungry again the next day, but the marvelous treasures of our civilization would no longer be available to the public.

This is not to say that some of the Church's possessions could not be sold to help the poor. Pope John Paul, in his encyclical *On Social Concern*, urged the sale of "superfluous church ornaments and costly furnishings for divine worship . . . in order to provide food, drink, clothing, and shelter for those who lack these things." He said that there is a "hierarchy of values—in the framework of the right to property—between 'having' and 'being,' especially when the 'having' of a few can be to the detriment of the 'being' of many others" (n. 31).

The financial support of the church involves two virtues, the virtue of justice and the virtue of generosity. Priests must not fail to remind the people of these virtues as they apply to the support of the church. Priests must not hesitate to talk straight talk about parish financing because parishioners must understand that the expenses of running a parish are not unlike those of running a home. Pastors must not allow a parish to deteriorate, or the educational mission of the parish to slip, because a homily about parish financial needs might offend some of those in the congregation. In short, pastors of souls must talk about money in parish life. And parishioners must respond with generosity.

The weekly collection involves the virtue of justice because we owe God a debt. Justice is a precise virtue which obligates us to give everyone what is due to them. We do not pay the cashier at the supermarket some vague amount; we pay exactly for the groceries we have put in our cart. We do not owe God a vague amount either, and we must try to be precise about the amount owed in support of our parish. This precise amount is based on the needs of the parish, the needs of the Church in our diocese and throughout the world, and our own financial resources.

Justice is not an appealing virtue when we are the one who owes the debt. It is unpopular to the debtor because it seems to squeeze him. Justice can also be an unpopular virtue because the parishioner is the debtor to God, and priests do not usually discuss justice in connection with church support.

Generosity is a more appealing and popular virtue. You are appealing to a person's noble sense when you ask him to be generous. The priest usually speaks of generosity in connection with the weekly offering. If $7 per Sunday is what you owe in justice, and you give $10, then the extra $3 represents your generosity. These amounts vary with the income of the parishioner and the condition of the economy, and they have been selected to illustrate that you cannot be generous until you have been just.

All virtues are good habits, that is, fixed tendencies which result from the same repeated acts. There is no virtue that is not a good habit. You are virtuous in regard to your parish when you make a habit of responding regularly, justly, and generously. Make your church support a good habit. Make your offering a regular part of your weekly budget. Prepare your offering ahead of time. Get in the habit of using your envelope regularly and your reward will be great.

The Weekly Parish Offering

Our weekly parish offering or contribution can be a cold and meaningless gesture, or it can be an event of beautiful significance among the religious acts of our lives. For some, the weekly collection is devoid of meaning: reach into your pocket, toss a coin, avoid being embarrassed by looking cheap in front of others. For others, the collection seems an undignified racket—ushers bustling, baskets passing, coins clanking, people shuffling—all so earthly and materialistic against the backdrop of the Mass being celebrated.

But the Offertory collection exists at Mass because it fits at Mass. The collection is not a racket but an expression of faith. The Mass renews the death of Christ on the cross. As Christ offers his very life for us, the follower of Christ feels moved to offer something in return. We symbolically seal our relationship with him in his moment of offertory. The collection dramatizes our offertory.

The collection fits in another way into the scheme of our religious worship. As we pause to note that all we have is from God— our talents, our health, opportunity, freedom, faith—we are moved to give to him in return. The collection dramatizes our gratitude. Sometimes we might choose to give money to God as an act of penance for our sins. Because I used the money to buy sin, or as the instrument of sin, I now part from my money in atonement for sin. Our donation could dramatize penance. Sometimes we give money to God as a prayer of petition: "I give to you, O Lord, please give to me, or to my son, or to my daughter, or wife, or husband." The collection dramatizes prayerful petition.

Therefore, the next time I reach into my pocket or purse for my offering, it will not be an empty gesture to avoid being embarrassed before those around me; it will be a meaningful gesture so that God will not be ashamed of me. The collection will not seem a racket, but religion. The bustling ushers will be my messengers to God, the clanking of the coins will be the bell sounds of my gratitude, the clicking of purses will be the clatter of acclaim to our God, the people shuffling will be the stirring of community response to God's presence among us.

I cannot offer a trifle to God when he has given me everything. I am not very grateful if God has given me hundreds and I give him ones. I am not very penitent if my sin cost me fifty dollars and my atonement is fifty cents. I am not very strong in petitioning when I ask for a miracle and give a mite.

Recall Jesus' praise for the widow who gave to the temple only two small coins while the wealthy were contributing large amounts of money. "This poor widow contributed more than all the others who donated to the treasury," said Jesus. "They gave from their surplus wealth, but she gave from her want, all that she had to live on" (Mark 12:41-44). The weekly collection is a significant religious act. It is God challenging me to honest offertory, generous gratitude, sincere penance, and powerful petition.

You Are God's Steward

Stewardship implies the practical recognition that we are not exclusive masters of our talents, energies, and possessions. These are gifts of God and we must use them according to God's plan. Whether it's money, artistic ability or other skills, mental acumen, education, an abundance of grace—all must be used not only for our own salvation but for the spread of God's kingdom on earth and for the temporal and eternal welfare of others. We are our brother's keeper. The Beatitudes enunciated in the Sermon on the Mount were not "self-centered" but "other-centered."

In our day we have a special obligation to make ourselves the neighbor of absolutely every person, and of actively helping that person when he or she crosses our path. Whether it is an old person without family or friends, a teenager looking for love and affection, a refugee struggling in a new land, a woman faced with a problem pregnancy, a child born out of wedlock and in need of a loving environment, or a hungry and homeless person who disturbs our conscience, we must remember the words of the Lord: "As often as you did it for one of my least brothers, you did it for me" (Matthew 25:40).

One of the reasons for our existence on earth is to be a worthy steward, a just and generous administrator of all that we are and all that we have. "When much has been given a man," our Lord said, "much will be required of him. More will be asked of a man to whom more has been entrusted" (Luke 12:48). St. Paul said that "the first requirement of an administrator is that he prove trustworthy" (1 Corinthians 4:2). Loyalty and trustworthiness are indispensable in a steward or an administrator. The constant search for pleasure, amusement, and superficial materialistic acquisitions leads individuals to neglect their duty to be administrators for Christ. It is not just talk but action that Jesus expects from us. "What good is it to profess faith without practicing it?" (James 2:14).

Give an Account of Your Stewardship

As one
in public life
or business—   Are you serving the people justly and acting as a living example of Christian service? "The lay faithful are never to relinquish their participation in 'public life,' that is, in the many different economic, social, legislative, administrative, and cultural areas which are intended to promote organically and institutionally the common good" (Pope John Paul II).

As a
Christian—   Are you guilty of racial prejudice or intolerance? "Racism is the sin that says some human beings are inherently superior and others essentially inferior because of race" (U.S. Catholic Bishops).

As an
able-bodied
citizen—

Are you conscious of and working toward the dignity of senior citizens? "Among the multiple activities of the family apostolate may be enumerated . . . help for the aged not only by providing them with the necessities of life but also by obtaining for them a fair share of the benefits of economic progress" (Vatican II).

As a
woman—

Are you serving the cause of furthering the ideals of Christian womanhood? "Women, by looking to Mary, find in her the secret of living their femininity with dignity and of achieving their own true advancement. In the light of Mary, the Church sees in the face of women the reflection of a beauty which mirrors the loftiest sentiments of which the human heart is capable: the self-offering totality of love; the strength that is capable of bearing the greatest sorrows; limitless fidelity and tireless devotion to work; the ability to combine penetrating intuition with words of support and encouragement" (Pope John Paul II).

As a
husband
or wife—

Are you truly faithful to and working toward the furtherance of the ideals of Christian marriage? "Christian families give priceless testimony to Christ before the world by remaining faithful to the Gospel and by providing a model of Christian marriage throughout their lives" (Vatican II).

As a declared
follower of
Jesus Christ—

Are you doing anything to combat the forces of atheism and secularism? "The remedy which must be applied to atheism, however, is to be sought in a proper presentation of the Church's teaching as well as in the integral life of the Church and her members" (Vatican II).

As one who
has been given
talents by God– Are you truthfully using them for God, the Church, and others? "When much has been given a man, much will be required of him. More will be asked of a man to whom more has been entrusted" (Luke 12:48).

As a
parishioner— What are you doing in your parish? "In the present circumstances the lay faithful have the ability to do very much and, therefore, ought to do very much towards the growth of an authentic ecclesial communion in their parishes in order to reawaken missionary zeal towards nonbelievers and believers themselves who have abandoned the faith or grown lax in the Christian life" (Pope John Paul II).

As a
Catholic
lay person— What are you doing for the Church and others? "It is within the everyday world that you the laity must bear witness to God's Kingdom; through you the Church's mission is fulfilled by the power of the Holy Spirit. . . . You are called to live in the world, to engage in secular professions and occupations, to live in those ordinary circumstances of family life and life in society from which is woven the very web of your existence. You are called by God himself to exercise your proper functions according to the spirit of the Gospel, and to work for the sanctification of the world from within, in the manner of leaven. In this way you can make Christ known to others, especially by the witness of your lives" (Pope John Paul II).

Chapter 13

Morality in Public Life

> Authority is exercised legitimately if it is committed to the common good of society. To attain this it must employ morally acceptable means .... The common good consists of three essential elements: respect for and promotion of the fundamental rights of the person; prosperity, or the development of the spiritual and temporal goods of society; the peace and security of the group and of its members. — *Catechism of the Catholic Church*, nn. 1921, 1925

Just after his last presidential election, Abraham Lincoln declared: "Being only mortal, after all, I should have been a little mortified if I had been beaten . . . but that sting would have been more than compensated by the thought that the people had notified me that all my official responsibilities were soon to be lifted off my back." When someone commented that Lincoln was remembered daily in prayer by many people, the President replied: "I have been a good deal helped by just that thought."

He then said that he "should be the most presumptuous blockhead upon this footstool if for one day I thought that I could discharge the duties which have come upon me since I came into this place without the aid and enlightenment of One who is stronger and wiser than all others."

Abraham Lincoln, like many other occupants of high offices, recognized the awesome reponsibilities of public service, along with the necessity of divine assistance if one is to discharge one's duties faithfully and withstand the sometimes harsh and unforgiving criticisms of the citizenry. An unfortunate sign of our times is that many Catholics have failed to see the relationship between their Faith and their daily activity, between the principles of their religion and the way of life which is the source of their livelihood. This has become particularly true of many in public life, in government, in politics.

The principles we shall discuss are applicable not only to those who actually hold public office but also to any Catholic man or woman who works for a public official and can exercise a moral influence on that person, or who casts a conscientious vote at the polls on election day. This constitutional right to vote must be exercised in accordance with certain moral and ethical principles if we are to remain truly "one nation under God."

The prevailing situation today can be illustrated by the example of the young boy who asked his father, "Dad, what does the expression 'practical Catholic' mean?" To which his father replied: "Son, that means that a person does not let his religion interfere with his life." Many Catholics in public life follow that false standard, insisting that they can separate their "private morality" from their "public morality," particularly on such crucial issues as the protection of innocent human life against abortion and euthanasia. What the nation really needs, however, is principled Catholics, not "practical" ones.

Principles for Politicians

There are three major prerequisites to be looked for in a person aspiring to or holding political office. These essential qualities that make a person suitable for public service are: required knowledge, moral integrity, and willingness to accept the office. It is regrettable that so often today many candidates have only the third of these qualifications, and that so many voters utterly discount the first two.

The knowledge necessary for a public officeholder, and the knowledge which Catholics as citizens must demand of those whom they support, is easily available to any Catholic. We have the guidance of the Second Vatican Council, the encyclicals of the Popes, the writings of the Catholic Bishops of the United States, and the *Catechism of the Catholic Church*, as well as the clear teachings on right and wrong that the Church has enunciated over the centuries. Any Catholic in public life who has not availed himself or herself of the Church's teachings on social justice, human rights, labor, secularism, organized atheism, and other moral and ethical issues is not worthy to hold office; and Catholic citizens may not in conscience vote for a candidate who is lacking this knowledge.

If a friend of ours is in need of medical attention, we would not think of sending him to a person who is very willing to help but who never went to medical school. Such a person would be utterly lacking in knowledge for the job at hand. Unfortunately, we have no such training school for those in public office. We must leave it up to their conscience to obtain the required knowledge for their job, but we do have the moral obligation to refrain from voting for an incompetent candidate.

To retain one's moral integrity in a culture of ethical relativism, a Catholic public official must adhere to the words of Scripture: "Better for us to obey God than men!" (Acts 5:29), and to the teachings of the Church. In his encyclical *Pacem in Terris*, Pope John XXIII offered this guideline:

> It is generally accepted today that the common good is best safeguarded when personal rights and duties are guaranteed. The chief concern of civil authorities must therefore be to ensure that these rights are recognized, respected, coordinated, defended, and promoted, and that each individual is enabled to perform his duties more easily.

> For to safeguard the inviolable rights of the human person and to facilitate the performance of his duties is the principal duty of every public authority. Thus any government which refused to recognize human rights or acted in violation of them would not only fail in its duty; its decrees would be wholly lacking in binding force.

The absence of moral integrity in the lives of many in public life, both Catholic and non-Catholic, cannot be denied. There are even those who falsely assert that there is hardly an honest Catholic politician. This is indeed untrue. There are many Catholic officials whose activities are beyond reproach in private and public life but, sadly, it is those who act contrary to the teachings and morality of the Church who seem to get the most publicity.

Here is a challenge for those who have the first two qualities—the required knowledge and the moral integrity—to cultivate the third, willingness to accept public office. We cannot expect to improve the present lamentable situation unless we have many capable and honest persons in public office.

Here is a challenge for those engaged in political activities of any sort, though not holding an office, to support only people who are capable and whose practices are beyond reproach.

Here also is a challenge to voters to seek out the best candidate and to renounce candidates who are incompetent, or whose principles are questionable. It is a challenge to those voters not to support a person simply because he or she is the candidate of a particular party, or because of the favors that might be gained. Sufficient knowledge, competency, honesty, moral integrity, and a willingness to serve in public office—these are the qualities we want to see in our public officials. These are the qualities that the conscientious voter must take into consideration.

Exercising political power in a spirit of service, Pope John Paul said, "requires a full-scale battle and a determination to overcome every temptation, such as the recourse to disloyalty and to falsehood; the waste of public funds for the advantage of a few and those with special interests; and the use of ambiguous and illicit means for acquiring, maintaining, and increasing power at any cost" (*Christifideles Laici*, n. 42).

You Shall Not Take Graft

When we speak of the seventh commandment, "You shall not steal," Catholics often brush it aside lightly with the thought that stealing from anyone is about the last sin they would think of committing. But there is one violation of this commandment that we seem to have forgotten. That is the problem of graft, bribes, and other forms of dishonesty in public life, some of which are almost considered socially acceptable practices in some political circles.

Those may be harsh words, but hardly a day goes by that we don't read about some political figure who has been caught with a hand in the taxpayer's pocket. To banish these evils is the direct concern of those in public office and the indirect, but nonetheless very real, concern of all citizens and voters.

It must be admitted that not a few Catholics are guilty of these dishonest practices so common in our day, even though their Church has spoken out so often and so clearly against them.

Nor does it solve the problem to say that's the way things are, or that everybody is doing it, or that many non-Catholics are guilty as well. First of all, we have every right to expect more of Catholics, for they belong to the Church established by Christ himself, have at their fingertips the light of truth and the guidance of their Church, and have available the grace and strength of the sacraments. And second, right is still right no matter how many others are in the wrong.

Dishonesty in public life is at times used to gain higher office or greater power, but more often than not it is simply a means to obtain more money. The love of money is indeed the root of all evil (1 Timothy 6:10). The graft and bribery so widely practiced in political life may take many forms, but all of them are violations of the seventh commandment and all render the violator, whether a private or public official, a Catholic or a non-Catholic, guilty of serious sin.

Sometimes an individual is rewarded with a soft job or a useless job, or is given an office created just for him in return for votes or for party loyalty, rather than because of a community or social need. To take a salary for such a job is nothing less than stealing.

The "spoils system" which dates back to the time of Andrew Jackson, and by which public offices are distributed to supporters of a particular political party, may be allowed under certain definite conditions. Only applicants who are worthy and capable may be rewarded with a government job. Certainly no office may be bestowed in return for a bribe. Any public official who rejects a qualified job-seeker simply because he will not pay the required bribe is guilty of sin. This sin is further aggravated if the individual appointed is not only less capable than another, but is positively unworthy and incapable of performing the duties of the office. In this case, there is a double sin of injustice—against the worthy candidates and against the community.

No matter how acceptable the practice has become, we cannot escape the fact that in the eyes of God it is sinful to demand payment in return for an appointment to the police department, the fire department, or any other city, state, or national position, no matter on how high or low a level. When two hundred applicants apply for a job on the police force or clerical work at City Hall, and it becomes known that a certain amount of money will secure the appointment, the official guilty of this injustice must restore any money gained. To answer that the candidates are willing to pay for the job is no argument. A parent whose child is kidnapped is willing in the same way to pay, but that does not give the kidnapper a right to the money. Bribery and graft are essentially no different from robbery.

Sometimes we hear the expression "honest graft." This phrase is a contradiction in terms. No matter how innocuous it appears, no matter how acceptable a practice of bribery might be to some persons, it is still wrong. The fire inspector who okays a building in return for a consideration, the police official who in return for regular payment closes his eyes to illegal activity, the building inspector who approves a building that should be condemned, the electrical inspector who overlooks bad wiring, the assessor who puts the wrong value on a piece of property—all may get away with their dishonesty for now, but they must one day answer to Christ their judge.

The same is true for the person who receives payment in return for secret official information; who pads the budget with fictitious expenses; who creates unnecessary jobs for his friends and supporters; who takes money in return for awarding a contract for public work; who sends government employees to work on his private home; or who takes public property for his own use. Every one of these persons has sinned against justice and will one day have to answer to God for transgressing the seventh commandment.

The Art of Being Honest

Thomas Jefferson once summed up the basis of good government when he said that "the whole of government consists in the art of being honest." Somehow or other, by some strange reasoning, people who may consider themselves honorable and upright in their private life often feel quite free to engage in corruption and graft in public life.

We concede that it is indeed difficult at times for a public official to be perfectly honest in carrying out his or her tasks. There are so many temptations and opportunities that it sometimes requires almost heroic efforts to do the right thing. Even a basically good person can rationalize that some dishonesty is all right if the majority of his actions are for the common good.

Any moral compromise, however small it may seem at first,

can only lead to bigger compromises until the basically good person becomes barely distinguishable from the thoroughly corrupt rascal. For this reason, the sincere and honest person must be willing to go to any length, to make any sacrifice, to preserve his moral integrity. And voters must support honest government officials and denounce those who betray the public trust.

Those in public office have an obligation in conscience before God to use their authority for the good of society, not for their own gain or advancement. To do otherwise would be a sin. Thus a person holding an office, and being paid by the taxpayers, who uses a large part of his time working for next year's election, shrewdly organizing his political machine, or buying the favor of others with his services, instead of devoting his time and energies to the job for which he was chosen, is guilty of a grave moral infraction.

The same is true for those public officials who grant pardons in return for favors, use their office and even force to break strikes for a friendly employer, bow to the unjust demands of some labor unions, use the power of their veto to defeat legislation unfavorable to their friends or benefactors, or bow to pressure groups opposed to any restrictions on such evils as abortion.

The task of the laity in such positions, said Pope John Paul, is to "bear witness to those human and gospel values that are intimately connected with political activity itself, such as liberty and justice, solidarity, faithful and unselfish dedication for the good of all, a simple lifestyle, and a preferential love for the poor and the least" (*Christifideles Laici*, n. 42).

Politics and the Eighth Commandment

Today there is also a widespread violation of the eighth commandment of God by the use of slander and detraction during political campaigns. There is no suspension of this commandment for politicians and those working for them. A person commits the sin of slander when by lying he injures the good name of another. A person commits the sin of detraction when, without a good reason, he makes known the hidden faults of another.

Detraction does not cease to be detraction when uttered by a politician. Slander does not cease to be slander because it issues forth from the lips of a political adviser or a campaign committee. And the obligation to repair the harm done is still on the conscience of the person violating this commandment, whether he or she is a private individual or someone already holding public office.

The eighth commandment also covers the obligation of not making official information known when it would be contrary to the public good or if it would give one person an unfair advantage over another. Take the example of a public official who knows that a piece of property will soon become very valuable because of a public building to be erected in the vicinity. He transmits this information to a friend so that the friend can purchase the property for a much lower price than it will be worth when the word gets out about the planned public building nearby. This is an unjust and illegal revelation of an official secret.

Challenge to Conscientious Catholics

We do not mean to imply that sincere politicians cannot fulfill their tasks morally and conscientiously. It can be done, but it is not easy. Nor do we mean to denigrate political and governmental service. Both are essential for a well-ordered society, and the Catholic Church has long encouraged her sons and daughters to enter this domain.

"Let those who are suited for it, or can become so, prepare themselves for the difficult but most honorable art of politics," said the Second Vatican Council. "Let them work to exercise this art without thought of personal convenience and without benefit of bribery. Prudently and honorably let them fight against injustice and oppression, the arbitrary rule of one man or one party, and lack of tolerance. Let them devote themselves to the welfare of all sincerely and fairly, indeed with charity and political courage" (*Pastoral Constitution on the Church in the Modern World*, n. 75).

The challenge has been issued. It is now incumbent upon truly Catholic politicians, Catholic voters, and Catholic citizens to work to restore Christian social teaching and the principles of Christ to modern society through the political process.

Chapter 14

Cults and the New Age Movement

> Man commits idolatry whenever he honors and reveres a creature in place of God, whether this be gods or demons (for example, satanism), power, pleasure, race, ancestors, the state, money, etc. Jesus says, "You cannot serve God and mammon."— *Catechism of the Catholic Church*, n. 2113

Recent history has witnessed a rising phenomenon of cults and new religious movements. By some estimates, there are more than 5,000 of these entities in the United States, with up to five million members. Perhaps one-half of those who belong to these cults are thought to be former Catholics.

There is quite a bit of reliable information about this phenomenon, and we would recommend four books in particular — *Cults, Sects, and the New Age* by Rev. James J. LeBar, *Today's Cults and Destructive Movements* by Rev. Lawrence J. Gesy, *Satanism: Is It Real?* by Fr. Jeffrey J. Steffon, and *Catholics and the New Age* by Mitch Pacwa, S.J.

Because the word "cult" can mean any group involved in religious worship, even in adoration of the one, true God, it needs to be emphasized that we will talking about *destructive* religious cults. They are usually characterized by a charismatic leader who demands total obedience, a quick initiation process that prevents the recruit from analyzing what is really happening, use of mind-control techniques, isolation from family and friends, hatred of anyone outside the group, and threats of spiritual or bodily harm if members attempt to leave the group.

Definition of a Destructive Cult

"A destructive cult or sect is a highly manipulative group which exploits and sometimes physically and/or psychologically damages members and recruits," says the American Family Foundation, an organization that promotes cult awareness. The foundation explains further:

A destructive cult:

a) dictates — sometimes in great detail — how members should think, feel, and act;

b) claims a special exalted status (e.g., occult powers, a mission to save humanity) for itself and/or its leaders – which usually sets it in opposition to mainline society and/or the family;

c) exploits its members psychologically, financially, and/or physically;

d) utilizes manipulative or "mind-control" techniques, especially the denigration of independent critical thinking, to recruit prospects and make members loyal, obedient, and subservient; and

e) causes considerable psychological harm to many of its members and to its members' families.

Fr. Lawrence Gesy says that our beliefs provide the yardstick by which we can judge what is right or wrong in contemporary religious movements. He says that if a religious movement does not measure up to or violates natural law, the Sacred Scriptures, the Traditions of the Church, the Constitution of the United States and the civil laws implementing it, our personal conscience, and our freedom of will to choose in accordance with that conscience, that movement is destructive.

Why Do People Join Cults?

Those who can look objectively at the definition above have difficulty imagining why any person would join such a group. But those who are attracted to new religious movements are not usually thinking objectively or looking at life realistically. Perhaps they are particularly vulnerable because of some crisis in their lives — the death of a loved one, the end of a romantic relationship, graduation from high school or college, loss of a job, relocation to another town, low self-esteem, loneliness or depression, a desire to belong or to participate in something worthwhile, a need for love and acceptance, a search for answers to the problems of society, lack of a strong religious faith, and so forth.

But whatever the reason, whatever the person is searching for, there are groups that will take advantage of this vulnerability. The potential recruit doesn't have to go looking for a cult; its disciples will find their way to him. The recruiter might be a friend or an acquaintance who is already a member of the group. Or it might be a professional cultist who roams college campuses, libraries, and dorms looking for recruits, zeroing in on those young men and women who seem susceptible.

According to many former cult members, the initial appeal will likely be emotional, not intellectual. There may be an invitation to a workshop, or a party, or a vacation trip, or a Bible study where other members of the group will overwhelm the unsuspecting initiate with friendship and flattery (the technique is known as "love-bombing") and ready-made answers to whatever questions may be asked.

Before the convert can evaluate what is taking place, he or she will be whisked into a process that includes isolation from outside friends or influences, focus on past problems and hangups in the person's life, a barrage of new information, use of behavior modification and consciousness-altering techniques, whirlwind activity and even sleep deprivation to keep the recruit too tired to evaluate what's going on, constant supervision so that he or she has no privacy, and imposition of guilt feelings for expressing doubts about the group, its leader, or its mission.

Having seen some characteristics of cults, and some of the reasons why people join them, we need to look more closely at these psuedo-religious movements, particularly the New Age Movement, which actually is an umbrella-type designation for many groups. The four books mentioned previously offer details about certain cults, and Church leaders have divided them into several general categories.

Four Types of Movements

Speaking to a consistory of the world's Cardinals at the Vatican on April 5, 1991, Francis Cardinal Arinze, prefect of the Vatican Council for Interreligious Dialogue, addressed the challenge of the new religious movements that have arisen throughout the world since the end of World War II. He said that he preferred to use the term "new religious movements" for these groups because it is "more neutral than that of sects." He continued:

> They are called new not only because they showed themselves in their present form after the Second World War, but also because they present themselves as alternatives to the institutional official religions and the prevailing culture. They are called religious because they profess to offer a vision of the religious or sacred world, or means to reach other objectives, such as transcendental knowledge, spiritual illumination, or self-realization, or because they offer to members their answers to fundamental questions.

The Cardinal said that four types of these new religious movements can be distinguished:

> There are movements based on Holy Scripture. These are therefore Christian or they are derived from Christianity.

> A second group of NRMs are those derived from other religions, such as Hinduism. Buddhism, or traditional religions. Some of them assume in a syncretistic way elements coming from Christianity.

> A third group of sects shows signs of a decomposition of the genuine idea of religion and of a return to paganism.

> A fourth set of sects are gnostic.

The prelate did not identify any specific groups that belonged in each category, but Fr. Gesy speculates that the Jehovah's Witnesses and Seventh Day Adventists could be included in the first category; Hare Krishnas, practitioners of transcendental meditation, Shintoism, Santeria, and Voodoo in the second; Wicca, or witchcraft, and possibly satanism in the third; and the "human potential" or "religious therapeutic groups," such as est (now called The Forum), the Esalen Institute, Christian Science, and New Age practitioners in the fourth.

Gnosticism (*gnosis* in Greek) was an ancient heresy whose disciples believed that they were godlike and that they possessed a special kind of secret knowledge, unavailable to ordinary humans, that would enable them to escape this evil universe and flee to a new and better world.

The authors mentioned earlier discuss particular groups in their books, and they also recommend many other sources that the inquiring reader may consult. But it might be useful to discuss three general categories of cults: witchcraft, satanism, and New Age.

Wicca or Witchcraft

Wicca is an old English term for witchcraft. It is preferred by modern-day witches, many of whom whom put their emphasis on worshiping the "Mother Goddess," because it does not carry the sinister connotations associated with witchcraft in the past. If their powers are used for good purposes, it is called "white witchcraft"; if for evil purposes, it is called "black witchcraft." They are organized into groups of thirteen called covens and they practice a variety of rituals on their "holy days," which are called sabbats.

Their eight sabbats are February 2nd (Feast of Lights), March 21st (Solar Festival), April 30th (Fire Festival), June 22nd (Fire and Water Festival), July 31st (Solar Festival), September 21st (Solar Festival), October 31st (Fire Festival), and December 22nd (Death and Rebirth of Sun God).

The Wiccan belief system was agreed upon in 1974 when the Council of American Witches met in Minnesota. Some of the thirteen tenets they approved are:

> We recognize that our intelligence gives us a unique responsibility toward our environment.We seek to live in harmony with Nature, in ecological balance offering fulfillment to life and consciousness within an evolutionary concept....

> We see religion, magic, and wisdom-in-living as being united in the way one views the world and lives within it — a world view and philosophy of life which we identify as Witchcraft, the Wiccan Way....

Our only animosity toward Christianity, or toward any other religion or philosophy of life, is to the extent that its institutions have claimed to be "the one true right and only way" and have sought to deny freedom to others and to suppress other ways of religious practices and belief.

We do not accept the concept of "absolute evil," nor do we worship any entity known as "Satan" or "the Devil" as defined by Christian Tradition....

Modern Wiccans, who not infrequently appear on television talk shows, insist that they are not disciples of Satan, although it should be noted that the late British satanist Aleister Crowley was largely responsible for the revival of interest in witchcraft in the twentieth century. They do practice clairvoyance and divination, using tarot cards, crystal balls, and black mirrors, in an effort to tap into the spirit world of the universe.

Such actions certainly leave even the best-intentioned Wiccans open to evil influences. As Donna Steichen said in her important book *Ungodly Rage*, "Any spirits encountered in neo-pagan rites are unlikely to be holy." Mrs. Steichen then quoted a repentant former Wiccan describing her experience with rites that were anything but harmless:

When I was a witch, I performed rituals. I invoked spirits. I called entities. I cast spells, burned candles, concocted brews. The only thing I didn't do was fly on a broom, but I probably would have figured it out if given time. But where did it lead to? Into darkness, depression, and the creation of an aura of gloom around me.

I was frequently under demon attack. The house where I lived was alive with poltergeist activity ... due to residual "guests" from rituals. My friends and family were afraid of me. I knew I had no future; all I had was a dark present. I was locked in by oaths and "destiny." But I had *power*, something I'd always wanted.

It wasn't Satan's fault. He didn't exist — or so I thought. I gave it all up, and came to Jesus on my knees .... He freed me from the oppression and gave me back my soul — the one I had so foolishly given to evil in exchange for power .... Our salvation was bought at a great price and all we have to do is reach out for it. But we cannot serve two masters.

Satanism

The thought of selling one's soul to Satan, or of worshiping the leader of the fallen angels seems like something out of a sensational horror film concocted by some imaginative screenwriter in Hollywood. But hardly a week goes by, as police forces throughout the land will attest, without the discovery of another satanic cult or ritual involving spray-painting satanic symbols on buildings, mutilation, sexual orgies, stealing of corpses from cemeteries, and the slaying of animals, and sometimes humans, in a brutal, gruesome, and bloody manner.

Young people who start out fooling with ouija boards or seances, getting hooked on "Dungeons & Dragons" and other fantasy role-playing games that flirt with the occult, or immersing themselves in "heavy metal" music, with its pounding beat and satanic message (cf. the band Black Sabbath, one of whose albums shows a nude satanic ritual on the cover) suddenly find themselves in the clutches of the powers of hell.

Pat Pulling, an expert on occult activity in the United States, became involved after her 16-year-old son killed himself following a brief and terrifying journey into the occult. He had become obsessed with "Dungeons & Dragons," a game that is set in the Middle Ages and sometimes moves from fantasy to reality as the players become the characters in the game.

These characters are expected to commit murder, rape, robbery, and mutilation in order to survive and to attain power and wealth. "There is no doubt in my mind," said Dr. Thomas Radecki, chairman of the National Coalition on Television Violence, "that the game 'Dungeons & Dragons' is causing young men to kill themselves and others."

Mrs. Pulling agrees, saying that "the vast majority of the information in the D&D manuals is violence-oriented. It consists of detailed descriptions of killing, including occultic human sacrifice, assassination, and premeditated murder as well as sadism and curses of insanity which include suicidal and homicidal mania. Much of the material draws upon ancient systems of demonology" (*The Devil's Web*, p. 83).

The aforementioned Aleister Crowley helped to spread satanism in England in the 1920s and 1930s. One of its major promoters in America has been Anton Levey, who established the Church of Satan in San Francisco in 1966 and subsequently published *The Satanic Bible* and *The Satanic Rituals*. Both are widely available in bookstores and libraries, and Levey's writings have influenced many teenagers to engage in satanic rites.

According to Fr. Jeffrey Steffon, there are five levels of satanism: (1) those who engage in divination, mild forms of witchcraft, and contact with the spirit world (channeling); (2) those who dabble with "Dungeons & Dragons," heavy metal music, drugs, and seances; (3) self-styled satanic groups who follow the belief systems of Crowley and Levey; (4) those who belong to such official groups as the Church of Satan, whose principal rite is the "Black Mass," a blasphemous parody of the Catholic Mass that features praise of Satan instead of God, prayers said backwards, sexual orgies, and, if possible, desecration of a consecrated Host stolen from a Catholic Church; and (5) hard-core satanists who truly worship Satan and carry out human sacrifice.

Some observers place the number of satanic covens in the United States at around eight thousand, with a membership of perhaps one hundred thousand, but there is no way of corroborating such figures. Those who get involved with these cults do so in varying degrees; very few go beyond the third or fourth step, although there is a sixth degree called an *adept* or *illuminati*. These are said to have the power to see and talk with Satan.

People are attracted to satanism in much the same way as to any cult or new religious movement. Some enter through curiosity and some because of a tragedy in their lives. Others are recruited at schools, churches, rock concerts, bus and train stations, and through "Dungeons & Dragons" clubs, often with promises of all the drugs, power, sex, and wealth they could want. Still others are brought in by their parents, who are already involved in the world of cults.

Parents, and teenagers themselves, can help young people stay away from satanism by educating themselves about its evil nature, watching for signs of satanic involvement (withdrawal from family or friends, wearing black clothing with occult jewelry, fascination with death, interest in occult movies and literature, collection of such occult items as skulls, bones, ritual knives, and candles, and threats of suicide), encouraging recourse to the sacraments of Penance/Reconciliation and the Holy Eucharist — in short, putting one's life completely in the hands of Jesus, who has already triumphed over Satan.

Prayer to our guardian angel and also to St. Michael the Archangel, who drove Satan and his minions out of heaven, is also essential. Recite every day this prayer to St. Michael:

St. Michael, the Archangel, defend us in the battle. Be our protection against the malice and snares of the devil. Rebuke him, O God, we humbly beseech you, and do you, O prince of the heavenly hosts, by the divine power, drive into hell Satan and the other evil spirits who wander through the world seeking the ruin of souls. Amen.

New Age Movement

Although it is called the "New Age Movement," there really is nothing new about it. The many-faceted movement is a blend of some Eastern religions (Buddhism and Hinduism) and ancient heresies (gnosticism, monism, and pantheism) with modern Western occultism and mind-control techniques to bring about altered states of consciousness, a reliving of one's birth (rebirthing), and imaginary travel to other places (astral projection).

It worships the creature instead of the Creator, the environment instead of the One who made it. It rejects the Christian concept of a loving, personal God and says that God is some kind of impersonal energy force that is in everything (pantheism), that God and all beings are one (monism), and that all religions are one (syncretism). Actress Shirley MacLaine, a New Age guru, puts it this way in her book *Dancing in the Light*:

Each soul is its own God. You must never worship anyone or anything other than self. For *you* are God. To love self is to love God.

The NAM says that Jesus is not the Son of God and Savior of the world, but just another spiritual guide, or "ascended master," like Buddha or Krishna. It says that there are no absolute truths or binding moral codes (so much for the Ten Commandments!) and that each person can decide for himself what is right and wrong. They teach the law of karma, which says that whatever good or evil a person does will be repaid either in this life or in another life. They contend that the pain and suffering in the world is the result of bad karma on the part of those afflicted and that we have no responsibility for helping them.

This is quite different from the command of Jesus to reach out to those in need because whatever we do for the least of our brothers and sisters, we do for him (Matthew 25:40).

The NAM offers reincarnation for those who want to escape responsibility for their sins in this life and come back to do things better in another life, even though St. Paul rejected reincarnation in his letter to the Hebrews: "It is appointed that men die once, and after death be judged" (9:27).

Jesus died on the cross for our sins, and it is only by sincerely seeking his forgiveness that we can attain what the New Agers call nirvana or paradise, and what we call heaven.

The NAM also promotes the use of colored glass crystals that allegedly act as channels of healing energy through the power of the occult, not through the power of God. But there is no scientific evidence that crystals can heal anything. True healing, whether of the body or the spirit, can only come through the power of Jesus and his Church, particularly through such sacraments as Penance and the Anointing of the Sick.

New Agers also engage in spiritism or channeling to put themselves in touch with spirits and entities from another world, thus exposing themselves to the power of Satan and other evil spirits. This is condemned by God in the Bible (cf. Leviticus 20:27 and Deuteronomy 18:9-14), and reiterated in the *Catechism of the Catholic Church*:

> All forms of divination are to be rejected: recourse to Satan or demons, conjuring up the dead or other practices falsely supposed to "unveil" the future. Consulting horoscopes, astrology, palm reading, interpretation of omens and lots, the phenomena of clairvoyance, and recourse to mediums all conceal a desire for power over time, history, and, in the last analysis, other human beings, as well as a wish to conciliate hidden powers. They contradict the honor, respect, and loving fear that we owe to God alone (n. 2116).

Enneagrams

An increasingly popular New Age fad in some parishes and retreat houses are workshops on the Enneagram. The Enneagram is a circular diagram on which nine personality types are represented at equidistant points around the circumference. The personality types are perfectionist, caregiver, achiever, artist, observer, team player, optimist, competitor, and peacemaker, and study of the diagram under the guidance of a leader is supposed to help identify one's own psychological personality, or that of others participating in the exercise.

The premise that there are only nine personality types has never been proven. According to one observer, the Enneagram resembles more a "college-educated horoscope" than a reliable tool for spiritual direction. Furthermore, says Fr. Mitch Pacwa in his book *Catholics and the New Age*, the roots of the Enneagram are in the occult world (cf. pages 111-124), and there are so many non-Christian elements mixed into it that he recommends that Catholics not patronize workshops or seminars promoting the Enneagram.

Fr. Pacwa reminds us of St. Paul's advice to "test everything; retain what is good. Avoid any semblance of evil" (1Thessalonians 5:21-22).

A Warning from the Holy Father

A similar warning was issued by Pope John Paul II. Speaking to the Bishops of the United States on May 28, 1993, the Holy Father said:

New Age ideas sometimes find their way into preaching, catechesis, workshops, and retreats, and influence even practicing Catholics, who perhaps are unaware of the incompatibility of those ideas with the Church's faith. In their syncretistic and immanent outlook, these pararreligious movements pay little heed to Revelation, and instead try to come to God through knowledge and experience based on elements borrowed from Eastern spirituality or from psychological techniques. They tend to relativize religious doctrine in favor of a vague worldview expressed as a system of myths and symbols dressed in religious language.

Combatting the New Age Movement

How are we to deal with New Agers in our families, schools, parishes, and communities? Fr. Mitch Pacwa offers several suggestions in his book (cf. pages 191-204) and also lists organizations and materials that can help combat cults and the NAM.

His suggestions include strengthening one's own spiritual life through prayer, the sacraments, and reading Scripture; reflection on the moral code that we find in the Bible; devotion to the Blessed Virgin Mary, particularly by praying the rosary; an active ministry to the poor, the helpless, and the sick; study of the Faith so that we can explain and defend it; bringing in speakers or literature that counter the effects of a New Age presentation; and, finally, praying for New Agers with the confidence that the love and power of Christ will change their minds and hearts.

Chapter 15

Advocates of Atheism

> Atheism must be accounted among the most serious problems of this age, and is deserving of closer examination. — Vatican II, *Pastoral Constitution on the Church in the Modern World*, n. 19

Although the Second Vatican Council did not specifically mention atheistic communism, the Council Fathers did say that "the Church has already repudiated and cannot cease repudiating, sorrowfully but as firmly as possible, those poisonous doctrines and actions which contradict reason and the common experience of humanity, and dethrone man from his native excellence" (*Pastoral Constitution on the Church in the Modern World*, n. 21).

An official footnote to this paragraph cited clear condemnations of atheistic communism in the papal encyclicals of Pius XI (*Divini Redemptoris*), Pius XII (*Ad Apostolorum Principis*), John XXIII (*Mater et Magistra*), and Paul VI (*Ecclesiam Suam*).

Similiar pronouncements have been made by more recent successors of Peter and will continue to be made as long as atheism remains, in the words of Pope John Paul II, "the striking phenomenon of our time." The system that has carried atheism to its extreme form, the Holy Father said, "is dialectical and historical materialism, which is still recognized as the essential core of Marxism" (*Dominum et Vivificantem*, n. 56).

He said the basic problem of materialism is that it "radically excludes the presence and action of God, who is spirit, in the world and above all in man. Fundamentally this is because it does not accept God's existence, being a system that is essentially and systematically atheistic" (*Ibid.*). The *Catechism of the Catholic Church* adds these comments:

> The name "atheism" covers many different phenomena. One common form is the practical materialism which restricts its needs and aspirations to space and time. Atheistic humanism falsely considers man to be an end to himself, and the sole maker, with supreme control, of his own history.
>
> Another form of contemporary atheism looks for the liberation of man through economic and social liberation. It holds that religion, of its very nature, thwarts such emancipation by raising man's hopes in a future life, thus both deceiving him and discouraging him from working for a better form of life on earth (n. 2124).

Whether this materialistic and atheistic movement that has had such a profoundly evil effect on the world is called communism or Marxism or totalitarian socialism, it is the direct antithesis of Christianity. A true follower of Jesus Christ cannot, of course, subscribe or adhere to Marxism, but he can—and should—learn its principles in order to understand this phenomenon of the twentieth century and be able to apply the teachings of Christ to the problems that it has presented to the world.

Like it or not, we can learn some practical things from Marx and his followers because, as Christ pointed out, worldly-minded people take more initiative in their pursuits than religious people do (Luke 16:8).

The nature of communism and the structure of the Communist Party appear to have changed in recent years, and many believe that "communism is dead," that the "Cold War" between the forces of freedom and totalitarianism has ended, and that an era of peace and progress is on the horizon. There are others, however, who are not so sure.

But no matter who is right in this crucial matter, it is worth looking more closely at the principles and practices of Marxism and communism and reviewing briefly the lives of some of the key personalities involved in this atheistic movement that so radically altered the history of the twentieth century. For if we do not learn from history, as one philosopher remarked, we may be condemned to repeat it.

We will first profile the theoreticians—Marx and Engels—and then those who put the theory into bloody practice—Lenin and Gorbachev—before discussing the philosophy of Marxism-Leninism itself.

Karl Marx

Born in the Rhine Province of Prussia in 1818, Karl Marx was baptized at the age of six after his father, a successful lawyer, converted to the Evangelical Established Church. He showed himself to be an intelligent child in school and, as he grew up, displayed a capacity for work that was to be a keynote of his life. He also demonstrated early in life an arrogance and rebelliousness that were very much an integral part of his character. Although he attended universities in Bonn and Berlin, Karl seldom went to classes; he was more interested in the socialistic and materialistic philosophies of the day, and soon became an atheist. He had met Jenny von Westphalen, the daughter of a government official, his first year at Bonn University, and they married in 1843.

Although Marx spent several years at German universities, he was never graduated. Nor did he ever hold a regular job. He depended mostly on the generosity of the few friends he made, the most important of whom was Friedrich Engels, also a German, whom he first met in 1842. Engels became a close associate and benefactor of Marx. It is ironic that the founder of modern communism was to a large extent supported and financed by a relatively wealthy man. Marx moved to Paris in 1843 and, in 1849, took his family to London, where he continued writing, usually in the British Museum, until his death in 1883.

His key works on communism, such as *Das Kapital* (*Capital*), were written in an atmosphere of poverty, which really was the fault of Marx himself since he had little desire to obtain any steady employment. There was seldom enough money even to live in frugal but respectable circumstances. When his daughter died before the age of one, there was not enough money for a funeral. Sometimes Marx lacked sufficient clothes to go out of the house. When his wife was sick, no doctor could be called because there was no money. Yet Marx persisted in his writing and continued neglecting his family. It has been reported that on one occasion his mother said that Karl might do better to stop writing *Capital* and begin trying to make some.

Karl Marx was a revolutionary without a revolution. The theories that he proposed were put into action by others long after his death. But he set the tone for revolution with *The Communist Manifesto*, a collaborative effort with Friedrich Engels that appeared in 1848. "A spectre is haunting Europe—the spectre of Communism," Marx wrote in the first line of the *Manifesto*.

He then proceeded to outline a philosophy that talked about the struggle between the wealthy, ruling class "bourgeoisie" and the poor, working class "proletariat," and said that the aim of the communists was "formation of the proletariat into a class, overthrow of the bourgeois supremacy, conquest of political power by the proletariat."

The *Manifesto* called for abolition of private property and abolition of the family, and concluded with this revolutionary battle cry:

> The communists disdain to conceal their views and aims. They openly declare that their ends can be attained only by the forcible overthrow of all existing social conditions. Let the ruling classes tremble at a communist revolution. The proletarians have nothing to lose but their chains. They have a world to win. Working men of all countries, unite!

Friedrich Engels

Friedrich Engels was born in the Rhine Province of Prussia in 1820, son of a wealthy textile manufacturer. He was raised in a Protestant family but, like Karl Marx, became an atheist. While serving in the military, Engels attended lectures at the University of Berlin and was exposed to the same materialistic philosophies that had infected Marx. He moved to Manchester, England, made contact with socialists and communists there, and began the research that led to his first book, *The Conditions of the Working Class in England*. Engels later wrote *Socialism: Utopian and Scientific*, and he edited and had published the last two volumes of *Das Kapital*. He spent most of his life in England and died there in 1895.

Unlike Marx, who was morose and slow to make friends, Engels was what we would call today a playboy. He was a lover of horses and women and, for twenty years, lived with a woman named Mary Burns, a worker in one of his father's factories, but never married her. When she died, he took up with her sister Elizabeth, but did not finally marry her until she was on her deathbed.

While Marx lived in utter poverty and suffered constantly from headaches and rheumatism, Engels lived rather well and enjoyed good health. It is one of the oddities of history that these two men who were so different in personalities and lifestyles should have been so drawn together and should have remained intimate friends for forty years. The common denominator was their atheism and revolutionary fervor. Engels had a brilliant mind, a fine memory, and a knowledge of industry and the military. He was a better organized and more facile writer than Marx, but together they produced an ideology that changed the course of history.

V. I. Lenin

Born Vladimir Ilyich Ulyanov in 1870, the man who became known to the world as Lenin was one of six children of a middle-class family. Lenin's father was a school inspector with an earned title of nobility and a member of the Russian Orthodox Church. As with Marx and Engels, Lenin drifted into atheism at an early age and was a revolutionary by the time he was graduated from high school in 1887, shortly after his brother Alexander had been executed for conspiring to assassinate Tsar Alexander III.

Lenin was expelled from Kazan University in December 1887 for his part in student demonstrations and spent the next six years studying the writings of Marx, Engels, and other revolutionaries. In his first political pamphlet, written in 1894, Lenin concluded that "the Russian worker, rising at the head of all democratic elements, will overthrow absolutism and lead the Russian proletariat (together with the proletariat of all countries) along the direct road of open political struggle to the victorious Communist Revolution."

He was arrested for revolutionary activities in 1895 and exiled to Siberia from 1897 to 1900. After spending the next five years out of the country, during which time he published a leftwing newspaper whose name in English was translated *The Spark*, Lenin returned to Russia in 1905. He left again not long after that and remained in exile from 1908 to 1917 in Finland,

France, Austria, and Switzerland. He contributed articles to the Russian newspaper *Pravda* during those years and guided its editorial policy until the paper was suppressed at the start of World War I.

Lenin's historical greatness is attributable to several character traits, said William Henry Chamberlin in his two-volume work *The Russian Revolution*. Those traits included "absolute dogmatic faith in his cause," the "bold sweep of tactical imagination, combined with an abiding layer of shrewd common sense which was lacking in many of his lieutenants," a "keen sense for the breaking point in popular endurance," and the ability to be "quite pitiless and ruthless when the occasion demanded."

A series of coalition governments had tried to bring order to Russia after Tsar Nicholas abdicated in March 1917, but worker unrest, economic chaos, and the devastating toll of at least six to eight million dead and wounded Russian men in World War I had provided the ingredients for revolution. Lenin had been smuggled into Petrograd in April of that year and he was joined in May by fellow revolutionary Leon Trotsky. Conditions continued to deteriorate and the socialist government of Alexander Kerensky was unable to retain control of the situation.

There were no more than twenty-five thousand of Lenin's disciples—they were known as Bolsheviks, which means the majority—among the one hundred fifty million people living in Russia when the Kerensky government was toppled in November 1917 (October according to the Russian calendar then in effect), but they were concentrated in the country's two centers of power, the capital city of Petrograd (formerly St. Petersburg, then Leningrad, and now St. Petersburg again) and Moscow.

The anti-Bolshevik forces were never able to produce leaders with Lenin's organizational and tactical brilliance, nor were they able to formulate a cause or an idea around which the people could rally. The communists captured Russia almost by default and that nation's atheistic rulers subsequently brought death and destruction to hundreds of millions of people, not only within the borders of Russia, but in various nations around the globe.

From 1917 until his death in 1924, a ruthless consolidation of power took place under Lenin. He imposed not a dictatorship of the proletariat, but a dictatorship of the party, saying that "the scientific concept of dictatorship means nothing else but this:

power without limit, resting directly upon force, restrained by no laws, absolutely unrestricted by rules." He first abolished the freely elected Constituent Assembly and then wiped out organized religion. A bloody civil war that lasted from 1918 to 1920 resulted in the deaths of more than ten million people before the Bolsheviks finally crushed all major opposition to their dictatorial rule.

Life in Russia during that Civil War, said William Henry Chamberlin, featured "unparalleled physical suffering of all classes of the population," the "prodigious uprooting of innumerable human existences," and "one of the greatest explosions of hatred, or rather hatreds, old and new, organized and instinctive, some of them causes, some of them results of the Revolution, ever witnessed in history. There was hatred of man against man, of class against class, of race against race." This hatred against individuals, classes, and races was encouraged by Lenin and his comrades because it focused hostility away from them.

Under Lenin a ruthless disregard for human life was common practice. On one occasion, Lenin asked Felix Dzerzhinsky, head of the secret police network known as the Cheka, how many traitors were then in prison. On being told that there were fifteen hundred, Lenin asked for the list so he could see how many he had known previously as friends. He put a cross at the top of the list to indicate that he had seen it. Dzerzhinsky took the list and, within forty-four hours, all had been executed, and he so informed Lenin. But the Bolshevik ruler was unmoved by the fact that a mere doodle on a sheet of paper had been mistaken for an execution order, and that fifteen hundred men had died on that account.

Lenin not only created the dreaded secret police unit that until recently went by the initials KGB, but he also pioneered the policy of mass terror. With reference to the French Revolution, Lenin once said that "the guillotine only terrorized *active* resistance. . . . We have to break down *passive* resistance, which doubtless is the most harmful and dangerous of all." He said that "we shall be ruthless toward our enemies, as well as toward all hesitant and noxious elements"—thus including virtually the entire population of Russia.

In March 1919, Lenin established the Third International, also known as the Communist International or Comintern, as the means by which communism could be spread throughout the world. The revolution in Russia was only the beginning.

Mikhail Gorbachev

Shortly after being named head of the Soviet Communist Party and ruler of the Soviet Union in 1985, Mikhail Gorbachev declared that "we will firmly follow the Leninist course of peace and peaceful coexistence." To the naive, that sounded wonderful; to those who knew something about Lenin, who knew that peace, in the communist lexicon, means the elimination of all opposition to communism, it sounded ominous. Two years later, in November 1987, Gorbachev said, "In October 1917, we parted with the Old World, rejecting it once and for all. We are moving toward a new world, the world of communism. We shall never turn off that road."

But statements like these never seemed to get as much publicity as the Soviet ruler's cheerful demeanor during visits to the United States and other countries, his smiles and waves and greetings, his promises of *perestroika* or a restructuring of the Soviet system. He was *Time* magazine's "Man of the Decade" and the winner of the Nobel Peace Prize in 1990. Those who called attention to the other side of Gorbachev, to a series of statements and actions that were all too reminiscent of his Marxist-Leninist predecessors, were barely heard. Those who urged caution and prudence were brushed aside by people who wanted to believe that the communist leopard had changed its spots and that a new era of peace was upon us. Unfortunately, this wishful thinking did not conform with reality, as a review of Gorbachev's background and policies will indicate.

Mikhail Sergeyevich Gorbachev was born in Stavropol in 1931. After becoming a top official of the Young Communist League there, he went to Moscow and was graduated from Moscow State University in 1955. While advancing through the ranks of the Communist Party in Stavropol, Gorbachev became friendly with Yuri Andropov, who frequently vacationed there while he was head of the Soviet KGB and who would become ruler of the Soviet Union from 1982 to 1984. When the post of Central Committee Secretary of Agriculture became available in 1978, Gorbachev got the job.

He was promoted to full membership in the ruling Politburo in 1980, acted as point man for Andropov's purge of top-ranking communist leaders in 1983, and was elected in 1984 as chairman of the Foreign Affairs Committee of the Supreme Soviet. When

Konstantin Chernenko, who had succeeded Andropov in 1984, died in 1985, the Politburo chose Gorbachev to be General Secretary of the Communist Party of the Soviet Union, which made him undisputed ruler of the far-flung Union of Soviet Socialist Republics.

Over the next few years, Gorbachev issued statements and implemented policies that would not have disappointed Lenin. Herewith some examples of his commitment to Leninism and totalitarian socialism:

- November 1987—"In our work and worries, we are motivated by those Leninist ideals and noble endeavors and goals which mobilized the workers of Russia seven decades ago to fight for the new and happy world of socialism. Perestroika is a continuation of the October Revolution."
- December 1989—"I am a communist, a convinced communist. For some that may be a fantasy. But for me it is my main goal."
- April 1990—"The Bolshevik art of convincing the people of one's correctness needs to be revived." (That "art," you may recall, resulted in the deaths of ten million Russians.)
- November 1990—"I can't accept private ownership of land, whatever you do with me."
- January 1991—"The events of recent days [the killing by Soviet soldiers of Lithuanians and Latvians seeking freedom from communist oppression] were used by certain circles to aggravate the situation under the pretext of a purported turn to the right and the danger of dictatorship. I resolutely rebuff these allegations. The achievements of perestroika, democratization, and glasnost were and remain eternal values which presidential power will protect."

By presidential power, Gorbachev meant the use of tanks and troops to kill people who thought that perestroika meant more freedom for themselves. It became obvious that perestroika was only a euphemism for maintaining the state's domination over the people. Gorbachev made this quite clear in his book *Perestroika*, when he said, "We are not going to change Soviet power, of course, or abandon its fundamental principles, but we acknowledge the need for changes that will strengthen socialism and make it more dynamic and politically meaningful."

If Mikhail Gorbachev's words echoed those of Lenin, his deeds mirrored those of Stalin. After ascending to power in 1985, Gorbachev directed the massacre of half a million Afghan civilians—men, women, and children—using such barbaric methods as disguising bombs as toys. He maintained some two thousand labor camps in the USSR with an estimated population of ten million prisoners (see Avraham Shifrin's *First Guidebook to Prisons and Concentration Camps of the Soviet Union* for details). His forces used troops, tanks, and even poison gas to crush protesters seeking more freedom in Kazakhstan in 1986, in Georgia and Uzbekistan in 1989, in Azerbaijan and Tadzhikistan in 1990, and in Lithuania and Latvia in 1991.

Those were not the actions of a man of peace. Nor was the provision of tens of billions of dollars in war materials to his clients in Afghanistan, Angola, Cuba, Libya, Nicaragua, North Korea, Syria, and Iraq during the same period a sign of peaceful intentions.

Despite the fall of the Berlin Wall in 1989 and the later removal of Gorbachev from power, the main elements of a totalitarian society were still in place in Russia, and in some other countries, at the end of 1996. Those elements included the army, the secret police, the slave labor camps, the socialist system, and a huge bureaucracy (*nomenklatura*) run by many of the same people who had long been committed to Marxism-Leninism.

Whether all the talk of reform, disarmament, and more freedom for the citizens of the former USSR will be translated into concrete actions by Gorbachev's successors remains to be seen. But until the main elements of a totalitarian society are abolished, the Russian people will not truly be free.

CHAPTER 16

A Movement That Changed the World

The atheism which Marxism professes and promotes is a blindness which man and society will have to pay for in the end with the gravest consequences. . . . Class struggle raised to a system harms and impedes social peace and inevitably ends in violence and oppression, leading to the abolition of freedom. —Pope Paul VI, Address on the 75th anniversary of the encyclical *Rerum Novarum*, May 22, 1966

On July 13, 1917, three months before Lenin seized power in Russia, the Blessed Mother appeared to three shepherd children in the Portuguese village of Fatima and made a startling prediction. She said that if people did not stop sinning and turn back to God, "Russia will spread her errors throughout the world, promoting wars and persecution of the Church. The good will be martyred, the Holy Father will have much to suffer, and various nations will be annihilated."

The prediction was astounding primarily because Russia was then in the throes of economic, social, and political chaos and was about the last nation on earth that one might expect to become a world power. But we now know from history that the Blessed Virgin was absolutely correct. Russia, which became the Soviet Union in 1922, did indeed spread the errors of Marxism-Leninism throughout the world, promoting wars, persecution, martyrdom, suffering, and the deaths of over one hundred million people.

But we can take comfort in the promise of our Lady that "in the end, my Immaculate Heart will triumph. The Holy Father will consecrate Russia to me and it will be converted, and a time of peace will be conceded to the world." When that promised conversion will happen, and when true peace will come to a troubled world, we do not know. What we do know is that this will not occur until more people heed the Blessed Mother's appeal at Fatima to pray, do penance, and make reparation for sin.

Twenty years after the Bolshevik Revolution, Pope Pius XI asked how it was possible that the Marxist-Leninist system—"long since rejected scientifically and now proved erroneous by experience . . . could spread so rapidly in all parts of the world?" He answered his own question in the encyclical on atheistic communism (*Divini Redemptoris*) in these words: "The explanation lies in the fact that too few have been able to grasp the nature of communism. The majority instead succumb to its deception, skillfully concealed by the most extravagant promises" (n. 15).

The Pontiff went on to suggest two other reasons for the rapid diffusion of the communist ideology: (1) "a propaganda so truly diabolical that the world has perhaps never witnessed its like before" (n. 17), and (2) "the conspiracy of silence on the part of a large section of the non-Catholic press of the world. We say conspiracy because it is impossible otherwise to explain how a press usually so eager to exploit even the little daily incidents of life has been able to remain silent for so long about the horrors perpetrated in Russia, in Mexico, and even in a great part of Spain; and that it should have relatively so little to say concerning a world organization as vast as Russian communism" (n. 18).

Pope's Warning Still True

Although these words were written in 1937, many people today still do not understand the nature of communism or, more accurately, the totalitarian socialist system that was imposed on the people of Russia and the many surrounding republics that were forcibly incorporated into the Soviet slave empire. There is still a great deal of false information and diabolical propaganda emanating from the disciples and sympathizers of Lenin, and the media continue their conspiracy of silence about the horrors that were perpetrated in the Soviet Union and other parts of the world.

For example, it took decades to learn the full truth about Stalin's slaughter of more than fourteen million Russian peasants in the early 1930s, and the execution by Soviet troops of up to fifteen thousand Polish prisoners of war, many of them priests, medical doctors, lawyers, and teachers, in the Katyn Forest region of Poland in 1940. How many more recent communist atrocities have been concealed from the world, and how long will it take before those atrocities become known?

But even when communist barbarism was widely publicized, many people thought it was only an aberration and that the barbarians could still be trusted. How much lasting damage was done to the Marxist-Leninist movement by the terrible plight of the "boat people" who fled South Vietnam after the communist takeover in 1975; by the communist Khmer Rouge's genocidal murder of more than two million Cambodians in the mid-1970s; by the devastation wreaked on Afghanistan by the Soviet Union during the decade of the eighties, a devastation that saw more than half of the country's fifteen million people killed or turned into refugees; and by the Red Chinese massacre of thousands of students and workers demonstrating for more freedom in Beijing's Tiananmen Square in June 1989?

These massive abuses of human rights were not aberrations; they were the historical and typical response of Marxist-Leninist regimes to those who threatened their domination of a country. Communism is not merely an ideology. It is also a grab for power, a way of imposing a dictatorship on a nation and maintaining total control over the people. It was not Hitler, but Lenin and Stalin, who pioneered all-powerful and all-pervasive government, widespread terror, mass starvation, slave labor camps, forced confessions, brainwashing, and all the other trappings of a totalitarian system. They provided the bloody blueprint for all those seeking to impose tyranny on their fellow human beings.

If communism were to throw out this blueprint, it would no longer be communism. And that is the ultimate test of whether communism has really changed: Have the communists changed only the name of their system and the names of the ruling elite, while keeping in effect the Marxist-Leninist structure and practices, or have they truly abandoned both?

Have they removed their troops from foreign countries, abolished the labor camps, eliminated the secret police, held free elections, and guaranteed genuine freedom of religion, speech, press, assembly, and other civil rights. Never mind what they have *said* they would do; it is deeds, not words, that really matter.

The communists were for many decades master strategists and tacticians who used, in the words of Pope Pius XI, "trickery of various forms" to hide their "real designs behind ideas that in themselves are good and attractive." The Holy Father gave us these examples:

> Aware of the universal desire for peace, the leaders of communism pretend to be the most zealous promoters and propagandists in the movement for world amity. Yet at the same time they stir up a class warfare which causes rivers of blood to flow and, realizing that their system offers no internal guarantee of peace, they have recourse to unlimited armaments. Under various names which do not suggest communism, they establish organizations and periodicals with the sole purpose of carrying their ideas into quarters otherwise inaccessible.
>
> They try perfidiously to worm their way even into professedly Catholic and religious organizations. Again, without receding an inch from their subversive principles, they invite Catholics to collaborate with them in the realm of so-called humanitarianism and charity; and at times even make proposals that are in perfect harmony with the Christian spirit and the doctrine of the Church.
>
> Elsewhere they carry their hypocrisy so far as to encourage the belief that communism, in countries where faith and culture are more strongly entrenched, will assume another and much milder form. It will not interfere with the practice of religion. It will respect liberty of conscience. There are some even who refer to certain changes recently introduced into Soviet legislation as a proof that communism is about to abandon its program of war against God (*Divini Redemptoris*, n. 57).

The Holy Father's warning in that long-ago encyclical bears repeating today:

> See to it, Venerable Brethren, that the Faithful do not allow themselves to be deceived! Communism is intrinsically wrong, and no one who would save Christian civilization may collaborate with it in any undertaking whatsoever. Those

who permit themselves to be deceived into lending their aid toward the triumph of communism in their own country will be the first to fall victims of their error. And the greater the antiquity and grandeur of the Christian civilization in the regions where communism successfully penetrates, so much more devastating will be the hatred displayed by the godless (n. 58).

What Is Communism?

It is virtually impossible to define or explain the concept of Marxism or communism in a paragraph or two. It is an ideology, a power theory that seeks to dominate every aspect of the lives of the people under its control. Put simply, *communism means the state ownership of all material goods, with no private or individual ownership of wealth or property*. It is based on the doctrine of dialectical materialism, which contends that the world came into being without God and which rejects the idea that God exists. Communism, therefore, is diametrically opposed to all religion. It rejects all other philosophies, political systems, and beliefs and seeks the overthrow, by force and violence if necessary, of all existing societies and governments in the world.

However appealing the way by which communists try to present their doctrines, their basic beliefs can be summarized as follows:

- God does not exist.
- Everything is in motion; nothing is at rest.
- Humans are nothing more than animals.
- We are headed inevitably toward a classless society, the first step of which is socialism and the final step is communism.
- This can be achieved only by force and violence, bloodshed and revolution. It is not possible to achieve the aims of communism by peaceful means.

While the complete philosophy of Marxism-Leninism in all its details is most complicated and difficult to grasp, the fundamental goals and beliefs are not at all difficult to understand. We don't have to search very far either to find them clearly stated. *The Communist Manifesto* itself openly declared that the goal to be achieved is the "forcible overthrow of all existing social condi-

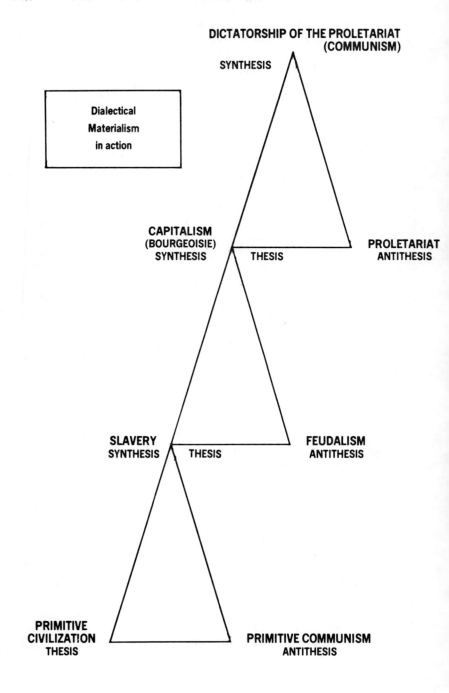

tions." That goal was restated by communist leaders in this century and was put into bloody practice in more than one-third of the world, all but annihilating some nations and sending more than one hundred million people to their graves.

Dialectical Materialism

Marx and Lenin developed this fundamental communist doctrine by combining two concepts: first, they said, everything in the universe is in a constant state of change as well as in a state of conflict—this is dialectics; second, they argued, there is no God and the world is composed only of matter—this is atheistic materialism. Picture a triangle that represents motion. The left corner is the status quo. The right corner is the opposing force which inevitably rises to strike down the status quo. The uppermost corner represents the emergence of a third state resulting from the interaction of the other two forces. This new status quo now becomes the left base of a new triangle and the entire process of violent change begins all over again.

Another way of saying this is that every idea contains within itself its opposite—a thesis in conflict with its antithesis that results in a synthesis of the two ideas. This synthesis in turn becomes a thesis in struggle with a new antithesis. As the diagram on page 210 shows, exploiters (thesis) and the exploited (antithesis) will emerge from their struggle as an entirely new class. Thus, capitalism emerged from feudalism; the bourgeoisie emerged from the feudal landlords; and communism, or the dictatorship of the proletariat, will emerge from the struggle between the wage earners (workers or proletariat) and the capitalists (bourgeoisie).

The theory is interesting, but there are two things wrong with it. First of all, neither Marx nor Engels, nor any of their followers, were able to explain where the alleged motion came from. They have never been able to answer the argument of St. Thomas Aquinas that the existence of motion in matter proves the existence of a First Mover, whom we call God.

Second, the theory will never work because people in power do not want to give up that power. As Lord Acton said, "Power tends to corrupt and absolute power corrupts absolutely." The dialectic ends with the dictatorship of the party. No communist ruler has ever voluntarily relinquished control of a nation. The communist/socialist elite in the Soviet Union always lived like wealthy capitalists, with their fancy cars, special stores, and dachas in the country. They never showed any desire to give up their privileged status or to let their power wither away in the interests of the proletariat or some classless society.

Economic Determinism

Another key doctrine of Marxism is economic determinism, which says that economic conditions and conflicts determine the way in which a society develops. It holds that those who control the means of production (natural resources, farms, factories, machinery, tools, money, transportation, and communications) control the progress of society. It falsely contends that religion, law, and other spiritual developments are actually the outcome of the way in which goods are produced and distributed. Economic conflicts, the Marxists believe, are the driving force in the class struggle.

This theory is partially true in that economic conditions do have an influence on society. But the great religious, cultural, legal, and other factors in world history did not arise from economic influences. Even the history of communism itself disproves this theory. As historian Christopher Dawson pointed out in his *Essays in Order*, Marxism-Leninism had its origins in the mind of "that arch-individualist, Karl Marx, and the forces that inspired him were neither of the economic nor of the material order."

Ten Steps to Communism

Communists never made a secret of their intentions. Marx and Engels proclaimed in *The Communist Manifesto* the ways to prepare a country for domination by communism:

1. Abolition of property in land and application of all rents of land to public purposes.
2. A heavy progressive or graduated income tax.
3. Abolition of all right of inheritance.
4. Confiscation of the property of all emigrants and rebels.
5. Centralization of credit in the hands of the State by

means of a national bank with State capital and an exclusive monopoly.

6. Centralization of the means of communication and transport in the hands of the State.

7. Extension of factories and instruments of production owned by the State, the bringing into cultivation of waste lands, and the improvement of soil generally in accordance with a common plan.

8. Equal liability of all to labor. Establishment of industrial armies, especially for agriculture.

9. Combination of agriculture with manufacturing industries; gradual abolition of the distinction between town and country by a more equitable distribution of the population over the country.

10. Free education for all children in public schools.

The first of the ten points, abolition of private property, is one of the most fundamental tenets of Marxism and communism. Marx said so in 1848 and Mikhail Gorbachev said so in 1990 ("I can't accept private ownership of land"). Such a doctrine is completely opposed to the teaching of the Catholic Church.

"Private property, including that of productive goods," said Pope John XXIII, "is a natural right possessed by all, which the state may by no means suppress." The Holy Father emphasized, however, that "there is from nature a social aspect to private property," meaning that "he who uses his right in this regard must take into account not merely his own welfare but that of others as well" (*Mater et Magistra*, n. 19). Later in the same encyclical, he called the right of private property "permanently valid" and explained why it is so important:

It is rooted in the very nature of things, whereby we learn that individual men are prior to civil society and, hence, that civil society is to be directed toward man as its end. Indeed, the right of private individuals to act freely in economic affairs is recognized in vain, unless they are at the same time given an opportunity of freely selecting and using things necessary for the exercise of this right.

Moreover, experience and history testify that where political regimes do not allow to private individuals the possession also of productive goods, the exercise of human liberty is violated or completely destroyed in matters of primary importance. Thus it becomes clear that in the right of property, the exercise of liberty finds both a safeguard and a stimulus (n. 109).

It should be clear by now that communism is intrinsically wrong because it is atheistic and materialistic and because it denies to people everywhere human dignity, human rights, and human freedom.

As early as 1846, two years before the publication of *The Communist Manifesto*, Pope Pius IX solemnly condemned "that infamous doctrine of so-called communism, which is absolutely contrary to the natural law and, if once adopted, would utterly destroy the rights, property, and possessions of all men, and even society itself." Communism is radically opposed to Christianity, and no Catholic may adhere to its evil principles or practices.

The same is true of socialism, communism's evil twin, which also considers the individual to be nothing more than a spoke in the wheel of the state and which would bring about the same results as communism, only by evolution rather than revolution.

Remember that USSR meant the Union of Soviet *Socialist* Republics, that it is revolutionary socialism that Lenin and his followers imposed on Russia and other nations, and that a country which merely changes the name of its system from communism to socialism, without changing the corrupt system itself, has not moved any closer toward recognizing the dignity of each of its citizens or toward allowing them to live in an atmosphere of liberty, economic opportunity, and justice for all.

Pope John XXIII expressed the Catholic teaching on socialism in *Mater et Magistra*:

> Nor may Catholics, in any way, give approbation to the teachings of socialists who seemingly profess more moderate views [than communists]. From their basic outlook it follows that, inasmuch as the order of social life is confined to time, it is directed solely to temporal welfare; that since the social relationships of men pertain merely to the production of goods, human liberty is excessively restricted and the true concept of social authority is overlooked (n. 34).

He was echoed in the *Catechism of the Catholic Church*:

Excessive intervention by the state can threaten personal freedom and initiative. The teaching of the Church has elaborated the principle of subsidiarity, according to which a community of a higher order should not interfere in the internal life of a community of a lower order, depriving the latter of its functions, but rather should support it in case of need and help to coordinate its activity with the activities of the rest of society, always with a view to the common good (n. 1883).

"The principle of subsidiarity," the *Catechism* said, "is opposed to all forms of collectivism. It sets limits for state intervention. It aims at harmonizing the relationships between individuals and societies. It tends toward the establishment of true international order" (n. 1885).

How different the past century would have been had this principle been promulgated and implemented by governments instead of the precepts of Marxism-Leninism!

Chapter 17

Marxism and Religion

> The right to religious liberty is neither a moral license to adhere to error, nor a supposed right to error, but rather a natural right of the human person to civil liberty, i.e., immunity, within just limits, from external constraint in religious matters by political authorities. — *Catechism of the Catholic Church*, n. 2108

It was May 13, 1981, the 64th anniversary of the Blessed Mother's first appearance to the children in Fatima. Tens of thousands of people were waiting in St. Peter's Square in Rome to see the Pope who had dedicated his papacy to the Blessed Virgin. As John Paul II moved through the crowd in a vehicle nicknamed the "Popemobile," a man with a gun stepped forward and shot the Pontiff three times, in the arm, in the hand, and in the stomach. Though gravely wounded in the attack, the Holy Father survived and attributed his survival to the intervention of the Blessed Mother. He traveled to Fatima a year later, on May 13, 1982, and publicly thanked our Lady for saving his life.

The man arrested and convicted of the assassination attempt on John Paul was Mehmet Ali Agca, a Turkish terrorist who had been given the murder assignment by the Bulgarian Security Service, which had long functioned as an arm of the Soviet KGB. Experts on terrorism, such as Claire Sterling (author of *The Terror Network* and *The Time of the Assassins*), produced convincing evidence that the plot to kill the Pope had been hatched in the Soviet Union, perhaps by then-KGB chief Yuri Andropov, because Kremlin rulers saw him as a threat to their continued domination of Poland.

Just a few months before the attempt on his life, John Paul had sent a letter to Soviet Communist Party boss Leonid Brezhnev, telling him that if Soviet troops invaded Poland, the Pontiff would return home to stand up against the invaders with his people. There was no Soviet invasion of Poland.

Three years after the Communists failed to kill a Polish Pope, they brutally murdered a Polish priest, Fr. Jerzy Popieluszko, the spiritual patron of Solidarity, the trade union founded in Poland in 1980. When the communist regime outlawed Solidarity in December 1981 and jailed its leaders and thousands of its supporters, Father Jerzy gathered money, food, and clothing for the families of those arrested and made his church a rallying place for Polish patriots. His Masses for the homeland on the last Sunday of each month were attended by thousands who heard the priest pray for the victims of martial law, criticize the government, and urge the people to "overcome evil with good."

Father Jerzy became one of the best-known priests in the country. His sermons were reprinted in the underground press and broadcast back into Poland by the BBC, the Voice of America, and Radio Free Europe. When the Catholic Primate of Poland tried to silence the young priest, he received a message from Pope John Paul endorsing Father Jerzy's work and warning: "Today it is Popieluszko, tomorrow another priest, and the day after tomorrow a bishop, and that is how they will deal with the Church."

After shadowing Father Jerzy, summoning him for interrogations more than a dozen times, and planting explosives and revolutionary literature in his apartment, the Polish secret police made their first attempt to kill the priest on October 13, 1984, but his driver skillfully avoided the ambush on a remote road in northern Poland. Six nights later, however, as Father Jerzy was returning from a rosary vigil, he was arrested, savagely beaten, stuffed in the trunk of a car, driven to a reservoir about 80 miles northwest of Warsaw, beaten again, and thrown into the water with bags of stones tied to his feet.

His horribly tortured body was recovered eleven days later when an accomplice of one of the secret policemen led authorities to the reservoir. Father Jerzy's brother was able to identify the terribly disfigured body only by a birthmark on the chest. The full autopsy report was suppressed because both government and Church officials feared that it would cause an explosion of outrage against the communist regime. Jerzy Popieluszko has since become Poland's greatest martyr since Fr. Maximilian Kolbe gave his life for a fellow prisoner in the Nazi death camp at Auschwitz in 1941. Father Kolbe was elevated to sainthood in 1982.

Hatred of Religion

If there is one thing that even poorly informed people know, it is the violent hatred which communists have for religion and religious people. "Religion is the sigh of the oppressed creature, the sentiment of a heartless world. . . . It is the opiate of the people," said Marx. "Every religious idea, every idea of a god, even every flirtation with the idea of a god is unutterable vileness of the most dangerous kind, disease of the most abominable kind," said Lenin. "Millions of sins, filthy deeds, acts of violence, and physical contagions are far less dangerous than the subtle, spiritual idea of a god decked out in the smartest 'ideological' costumes."

These beliefs of Marx and Lenin were put into practice with a vengeance in many countries of the world. Because allegiance to God precluded total allegiance to the communist state, Marxist-Leninist regimes historically sought to destroy churches, to subvert them by replacing the clergy with communist sympathizers and even secret police, or to suppress them with atheistic regulations and laws forbidding religious worship. Aleksandr Solzhenitsyn, the exiled Russian author who wrote eloquently of life under communism in his monumental three-volume work *The Gulag Archipelago*, has explained the unrelenting communist hostility toward God this way:

> Within the philosophical system of Marx and Lenin, and at the heart of their psychology, hatred of God is the principal driving force, more fundamental than their political and economic pretensions. Militant atheism is not merely incidental or marginal to communist policy; it is not a side effect, but the central pivot. To achieve its diabolical ends, communism needs to control a population devoid of religious and national feeling, and this entails the destruction of faith and nationhood. Communists proclaim both of these objectives openly, and just as openly go about carrying them out.

Solzhenitsyn's wife, Natalia, has described the effects of this hatred on the Russian Orthodox Church. "We had three hundred thousand priests in Russia at the end of the nineteenth century; there are now only thirteen thousand," she said in a speech at Dartmouth College in 1978. "Church bells are not ringing any longer in Russia. There used to be sixty thousand churches, twenty-five thousand chapels, approximately eight hundred monasteries; today there are less than ten monasteries and the churches are sixty-five hundred. People travel several hundred miles to go to church."

Bear in mind that during the years referred to by Mrs. Solzhenitsyn, Article 124 of the Soviet constitution stated that "freedom of religious worship and freedom of anti-religious propaganda is recognized for all citizens." The reality, of course, was quite different from what Article 124 promised. Those churches that were allowed to remain open were under the control of the State Council for Religious Affairs and followed communist policy subserviently. Those who attended church were monitored by the KGB and were subject to reprisals or denial of such things as a job or housing.

After the upheaval in communist Europe and the Soviet Union in 1989, churches were reopened in those countries and thousands of believers flocked to attend the services. The communist attempt to destroy religious belief had not been successful. Faith in God had not died out despite decades of persecution.

That the Catholic Church was able to persevere behind the "Iron Curtain" through those terrible years of persecution was due in part to the courageous leadership of such valiant shepherds as Archbishop Josef Beran of Czechoslovakia, Aloysius Cardinal Stepinac of Yugoslavia, Joszef Cardinal Mindszenty of Hungary, Stefan Cardinal Wyszynski of Poland, and a Polish bishop named Karol Wojtyla, who took the name John Paul II in 1978.

Cardinal Mindszenty, who was subjected to thirty-nine consecutive days of diabolical interrogation and torture before a three-day show trial in 1949 that led to nearly eight years in solitary confinement, described in his *Memoirs* one of the torture sessions:

> The tormentor raged, roared, and in response to my silence took the implements of torture into his hands. This time he held the truncheon in one hand, a long, sharp knife in the other. And then he drove me like a horse in training, forcing me to trot and gallop. The truncheon lashed down on my back

repeatedly—for some time without a pause. Then we stood still and he brutally threatened: "I'll kill you; by morning I'll tear you to pieces and throw the remains of your corpse to the dogs or into the canal. We are the masters here now." Then he forced me to begin running again. Although I was gasping for breath and the splinters of the wooden floor stabbed painfully into my bare feet, I ran as fast as I could to escape his blows.

The horror inflicted by the communists on the Catholic Church in Spain, its clergy, religious, and laity, during the Spanish Civil War (1936-1939) virtually defies description.

"Every vestige of the Christian religion was eradicated," said Pope Pius XI. Not only was there "indiscriminate slaughter" of bishops and thousands of priests and religious, he said, but also of "all those who have been devoting their lives to the welfare of the working classes and the poor," as well as "laymen of all conditions and classes. . . . And this fearful destruction has been carried out with a hatred and a savage barbarity one would not have believed possible in our age" (*Divini Redemptoris*, n. 20).

Sir Arnold Lunn, in his eyewitness account of the slaughter (*Spanish Rehearsal*), gives this summary:

> The national [Catholic] Church in Spain, on the evidence of the *Manchester Guardian* correspondent, was the victim of a persecution more ruthless, more violent, and more thorough than any religious persecution in modern times. . . . Not one parish priest is alive in the four Catalan provinces. Eleven bishops have been martyred, some of them burnt alive. According to the highest ecclesiastical authority in Spain, more than ten thousand priests and monks have been murdered. Thousands of nuns have been assassinated and outraged."

The same war on religion was waged by communists in the Western Hemisphere, particularly in Cuba, where there were one thousand priests and twenty-seven hundred nuns before Fidel Castro seized power in 1959 but only about one hundred of each ten years later. Castro, who was a nominal Catholic before he became a communist, closed churches, interrupted religious services, persecuted the Catholic hierarchy, and seized all Catholic hospitals, asylums, social centers, and educational institutions.

Armando Valladares, who spent twenty-two years in Castro's prisons for opposing the communist regime, tells in his book, *Against All Hope*, about a fellow prisoner named Gerardo, a Protestant minister whom the men called the "Brother of the Faith" because he was always exhorting them to pray, to help one another, and to forgive their captors. One day, said Valladares, when the guards were furiously beating the prisoners,

> . . . Suddenly one prisoner, as the guards rained blows on his back, raised his arms and face to the sky and shouted, "Forgive them, Lord, for they know not what they do!" There was not a trace of pain, not a tremble in his voice; it was as though it were not his back the machete was lashing over and over again, shredding his skin. The brilliant eyes of the "Brother of the Faith" seemed to burn; his arms open to the sky seemed to draw down pardon for his executioners. He was at that instant an incredible, supernatural, marvelous man. His hat fell off his head and the wind ruffled his white hair. Very few men knew his real name, but they knew that he was an inexhaustible store of faith. He managed somehow to transmit that faith to his companions, even in the hardest, most desperate circumstances.

Liberation Theology

In Nicaragua, during the 1980s, the communists tried to undermine the Catholic Church by creating what they called "the People's Church," a church that was subservient to the Sandinista communist regime. This so-called church was made up of base communities, neighborhood groups of Catholics which ostensibly met for prayer and religious services, but which were combined with and controlled by Sandinista Defense Committees under the supervision of Interior Minister Tomas Borge, a communist. The doctrine of the "People's Church" was known as "liberation theology." It portrayed Jesus as a Marxist revolutionary and interpreted the Bible from a Marxist perspective.

During a visit to Mexico in 1979, Pope John Paul had told Latin American bishops that it was wrong "to depict Jesus as a political activist, as a fighter against Roman domination and the authorities, and even as someone involved in the class struggle." The Pontiff said that "this conception of Christ . . . as the subversive from Nazareth does not tally with the Church's catechesis."

The Holy Father repeated his opposition to the "People's Church" during a visit to Nicaragua in 1983, saying that it was "absurd and dangerous to imagine that outside—if not to say against—the church built around the bishop there should be another church, conceived only as 'charismatic' and not institutional, 'new' and not traditional, alternative and as it has been called recently, a people's church."

The Sandinistas used the occasion of a papal Mass in Managua to stage a demonstration against John Paul. They shouted slogans during the Pope's homily and, when he started to consecrate the bread and wine, the communists began to make speeches over microphones controlled by the same Sandinista technicians controlling the Holy Father's microphone. They were angry at the Pontiff for having criticized five Catholic priests for holding top posts in the Sandinista government.

The position of the Church on "liberation theology" was clearly stated by the Vatican's Sacred Congregation for the Doctrine of the Faith in August 1984. An instruction signed by Joseph Cardinal Ratzinger, prefect of the congregation, and approved by Pope John Paul, said that "an authentic theology of liberation will be one which is rooted in the Word of God, correctly interpreted," and not in a Marxist analysis "which seriously departs from the faith of the Church and, in fact, actually constitutes a practical negation."

The instruction also declared that "the class struggle as a road toward a classless society is a myth which slows reform and aggravates poverty and injustice." The instruction further called attention to the millions of people who have been deprived of their basic freedoms "by totalitarian and atheistic regimes which came to power by violent and revolutionary means, precisely in the name of the liberation of the people. . . . Those who, perhaps inadvertently, make themselves accomplices of similar enslavements betray the very poor they mean to help."

Communism and Morality

Essential to any understanding of communists is the realization that they have different moral standards than we do. Whatever helps to bring about a communist dictatorship is good in their eyes, and whatever interferes with that goal is bad. Does that mean that murder, lying, cheating, and injustice are seen by the communists as morally good? Yes, if they advance the cause of communism; if they retard that cause, they are immoral. In his pamphlet on *The Young Generation*, Lenin said:

> We repudiate all morality derived from non-human and non-class concepts. We say that it is a deception, a fraud, a befogging of the minds of the workers and peasants in the interests of the landlords and capitalists .... When people talk to us about morality, we say: for the communist, morality lies entirely in this compact, united, disciplined, and conscious mass struggle against the exploiters. We do not believe in an eternal morality, and we expose all the lying fables about morality.

The brutal history of Marxism-Leninism showed precisely this disregard for the moral standards exemplified in the Ten Commandments and the Sermon on the Mount, and especially for the two basic commandments to love God and neighbor.

Over one hundred million people murdered, hundreds of millions more subjected to terrible abuses of fundamental human rights, promotion of wars and insurrections, support for sabotage and terrorism, violations of literally thousands of solemn agreements and accords, and countless examples of what Lenin called "all sorts of stratagems, artifices, illegal methods ... evasions, and subterfuges" to infiltrate and gain control of trade unions, organizations, and even governments — this is the immoral legacy of communism, and those who fail to learn from this well-documented record of death and duplicity could be doomed to repeat it.

Chapter 18

The Christian Response

The remedy which must be applied to atheism, however, is to be sought in a proper presentation of the Church's teaching as well as in the integral life of the Church and her members. For it is the function of the Church, led by the Holy Spirit who renews and purifies her ceaselessly, to make God the Father and his Incarnate Son present and in a sense visible. —Vatican II, *Pastoral Constitution on the Church in the Modern World*, n. 21

Two powerful movements stood side by side in the world during the twentieth century: communism and Christianity. They were diametrically opposed to each other; what one held to be true, the other considered false. Yet the false ideology of Marxism-Leninism enslaved hundreds of millions of people. It did not convert these hundreds of millions to its beliefs; it conquered them by force or deception.

Pope Paul VI, at a general audience on April 1, 1973, described the plight of believers in those countries:

There still is a Church obliged to live, rather survive, in the shadow of fear and in the asphyxiating and paralyzing darkness of an artificial and oppressing legality. It is a Church of silence, of patience, of agony because of its lack of the legitimate and natural right to profess, in perfect civic loyalty, its religious faith and carry out its mission of spiritual and moral education, as well as its function of social charity.

Seventeen years later, an article appeared in the June 1990 *Reader's Digest* that was based on interviews with survivors of prison camps in Communist China and friends and relatives of those who had disappeared since the massacre in Tiananmen Square a year earlier. The article gave this chilling account of life in the "Bamboo Gulag":

> Welcome to your new home. You live in a room with forty other prisoners. You're not allowed private possessions: no books, no photographs, no keepsakes, no clothes, nothing.
>
> You dig irrigation ditches from sunrise to sunset, seven days a week. When there is a full moon, you work at night too. You come to hate the moon.
>
> Guards don't wait for an infraction to punish you. They tie your elbows behind your back with a wet thong that tightens as it dries. After an hour, you go numb.
>
> The next time, guards push wires through the flesh of your ankles, put an iron band around your skull, and tighten it until your head cracks. Then they handcuff your arms underneath one leg, raising it tight against your chest. They leave you like that for days, sometimes weeks.
>
> No one escapes from the camp. There's nowhere to go, just sand in every direction for hundreds of miles.

This was not an account of the "old days," when most people knew communism was bad. It was an accurate description of life under Chinese Communist rule as recently as 1990, when things were supposed to have changed for the better, when the communists were supposed to have "mellowed" and forsaken the atrocities of the past. We can be sure that that dictatorship, and others like it, will eventually crumble and die. Christianity will preside at their burial. But how much more suffering, how much more martyrdom, how much more contempt for human freedom and dignity will occur? And for how long?

The answer may depend on how many of us are inspired to engage in fervent prayer and vigorous action. Because communism and like-minded atheistic ideologies are based upon hatred and are anti-Christ, anti-religion, and satanic in concept and execution, the weapons most efficacious in bringing about their demise will be "the sword of the spirit, the word of God" (Ephesians 6:17).

Let us take the time to review once again the differences between communism and Christianity so that we may understand clearly what the struggle was about.

Communism Versus Christianity

Communism on the one hand and Christianity on the other are diametrically opposed on several fundamental points:

1. Christianity teaches belief in God and the divinity of Jesus Christ; communism denies the existence of God and hates Christ.

2. Christianity teaches the inherent dignity and importance of the individual; communism denies the worth of an individual and teaches that he is only an instrument of the state in the class struggle.

3. Christianity teaches a responsibility toward those in need—the corporal works of mercy; communism would exploit anyone to gain power. Its fine words concerning help for the workers are contradicted by its ruthless and oppressive actions.

4. Christianity teaches that life has a meaning and purpose beyond the here and now; the materialism of communism teaches that the only goal of humanity is an earthly "paradise."

5. Christianity teaches the existence of a moral law which must be obeyed; communism teaches no right and wrong except the norm of what will further its own interest.

6. Christianity teaches a doctrine based upon love; communism is based upon hate.

Communist leaders declared that they followed the teaching of Lenin on religion and morality. Therefore, their attitude was one of unremitting hatred and hostility toward God, religious institutions and beliefs, and Judeo-Christian morality. Christianity could no more coexist peacefully with communism than Christ could coexist with Satan.

As these lines are written, there are still millions of our fellow human beings living in hopelessness and despair in countries ruled by Marxist-Leninists and other atheists or totalitarians who are hostile to religion, and who refuse to grant fundamental human rights to their citizens. Until that situation is reversed, we still have a moral obligation to pray and work for peace, freedom, and justice for our suffering brothers and sisters.

Carrying out this obligation will be difficult, especially when so many seem not to recognize it as an obligation, but the Christian response to the problems of the world has always been difficult to implement. Jesus never said that his followers would have an easy time. He said that they would have their own crosses to carry, that they would be persecuted just as he was persecuted.

The important thing to remember, though, is that our Lord said, "Blest are those persecuted for holiness' sake; the reign of God is theirs. Blest are you when they insult you and persecute you and utter every kind of slander against you because of me. Be glad and rejoice, for your reward is great in heaven" (Matthew 5:10-12).

Christians Have Been Indifferent

The forces of atheism should pose no mystery to us. There has never been a lack of knowledge of their plans. Their aims and the means to achieve those aims have been repeatedly and publicly stated, and acted upon, by them. But our opposition to those plans, strangely enough, has only been half-hearted and sporadic; the atheistic threat has largely been met with indifference.

We are in general a peace-loving and tolerant people. It is very difficult for us to realize fully that there are others whose policies are based upon hatred, conflict, bloody revolution, and suffering. Furthermore, the leaders of these movements often stated their goals in a jargon which had a very specific meaning to them but was sometimes hard for us to understand unless we were willing to do some reading and studying. Few have been willing to take the time and energy to do this.

But if we expect to win the battle against organized atheism, or Marxism-Leninism, or whatever future scourges afflict our world,we must grasp the true nature and goals of the enemy, educate others about these threats to peace and freedom and justice, courageously and persistently support ways of combatting them, and revitalize and spread the principles of Christianity in both public and private life. The foes of all that is good and right are counting on our apathy and indifference. We must wake up our fellow citizens and enlist them in the fight. We have the information; now we need the dedication and perspiration.

There are many people suffering under totalitarianism today who perhaps have said to themselves: "If only I had known what was happening, there isn't anything I wouldn't have done to protect my family, to defend my church, to save my country."

If you have read this far, you know what is happening to your brothers and sisters in other lands. Will you stand by and let this continue to happen? Doesn't each one of us have an obligation to help the least of our brothers and sisters? Recall the words of our Lord: "I assure you, as often as you did it for one of my least brothers, you did it for me" (Matthew 25:40).

One of the fifty-six signers of the Declaration of Independence was Joseph Hewes of North Carolina, who died in 1779, a lonely man whose strong belief in independence had led to estrangement from his family and friends.

"My country is entitled to my services," he declared, "and I shall not shrink from the cause, even though it should cost me my life." Are you willing to fight for those same freedoms for which Joseph Hewes and his fellow patriots pledged their lives, their fortunes, and their sacred honor?

What You Can Do

The following are some thoughts on what an individual Christian can do for Christ in the light of today's challenge.

1. **Study, work, and be willing to sacrifice** for your convictions with as much dedication and perseverance as Marxist-Leninists devoted to theirs. Karl Marx used to divide his time between looking for enough money to survive and doing research at the library of the British Museum. He often stayed there from nine a.m. until it closed in the evening. Then he would write at his desk most of the night.

2. **Be willing to practice self-denial.** Lenin, as a schoolboy, gave up skating to devote more time to studying the cause he believed in. His complete giving of self to the spread of communism from his earliest years gave him added vigor

and force in later life. He told his followers: "We must train people who will devote to the revolution not only their spare evenings but the whole of their lives."

3. **Don't procrastinate.** A sense of urgency has contributed much to the spread of atheism. Be motivated by a consuming desire to bring the love and truth of Christ to all the world as soon as possible.

4. **Help others to understand atheism** and its uncompromising objective to impose on others godless beliefs and governments under which the individual would have no rights. Make it widely known that atheism seeks to degrade and debase all human and spiritual values.

5. **Insist that your political representatives acquire an understanding of atheistic movements and take enlightened action.** Do not allow their deceptions to go unchallenged. Be as resourceful for truth as others are for falsehood. "You must be clever as snakes and innocent as doves" (Matthew 10:16).

6. **Make your voice heard.** Letters stating the truth and requesting action should be sent to public officials and all those who mold public opinion (newspapers and magazines, radio and television stations). **Be fair and objective, unemotional but firm. Avoid extreme or intemperate language.** State the facts, but do not go beyond the evidence; do not attempt to draw conclusions that are not supported by the evidence; do not engage in name-calling or in trying to guess a person's motives.

7. **These are not political problems but spiritual and moral problems, so do not neglect prayer.** Our Lady in her appearances at Fatima urged prayer, particularly the recitation of the rosary, penance, and reparation for sin. The world will neglect this solution at its peril.

8. **Any step, however small, to restore religion is a step in the right direction.** The number one goal of the atheists in any country is to weaken and eliminate any reminder that we derive our basic human rights from a personal

God, not from the state. Since their number one goal is to eliminate religion, it is basic common sense to restore and strengthen what they would try to destroy.

9. **Keep first things first**. Be on guard against overlooking the primary spiritual values while seeking solutions for the social, racial, and economic problems that beset our nation and the world. Only when we recognize the spiritual worth of our fellow human beings do we show true reverence and respect for their human dignity.

10. **Deepen our own spiritual roots**. "Put on the armor of God so that you may be able to stand firm against the tactics of the devil. Our battle is not against human forces but against the principalities and powers, the rulers of this world of darkness. . . . You must put on the armor of God if you are to resist on the evil day" (Ephesians 6:11-13).

11. **Warn the irreligious**. Those who are indifferent to God and religion are unwittingly aiding the forces of atheism. Jesus said, "He who is not with me is against me" (Matthew 12:30).

12. **Take a positive stand and encourage others to do the same.** Do more than just oppose atheism. Take constructive action to strengthen weaknesses and correct abuses wherever they are. Recall that one Marxist theorist, Nicolai Bukharin, recognized the dynamism of love that proves itself in action when he wrote: "Christian love, which applies to all, even to one's enemies, is the worst adversary of communism."

13. **Fulfill your responsibilities as a citizen**. Study the issues and vote intelligently. Take an active part in organizations to which you belong. Help raise the moral tone in public life and in the communications media. Urge family, friends, and associates to right wrongs they know exist in their neighborhood, community, and nation.

14. **Prove your love for the underprivileged**. Those living in poverty and misery, those who are objects of racial intolerance, are not impressed when Christians wait until it is

fashionable or popular to come to their assistance. They interpret this more as self-interest than as a desire to help Christ's poor.

15. **Overcome evil by doing good**. "Do not be conquered by evil but conquer evil with good" (Romans 12:21).

16. **Take heart**. Communism, Marxism-Leninism, and other forms of atheism must eventually fail because they are diametrically opposed to the plan of God and human nature. The have within themselves the seeds of their own destruction. But instead of causing us to let down our guard, this fact should spur each one of us to take reasonable and effective steps to overcome these forces before they can do any more harm.

17. **Restore elementary principles** to the mainstream of life: The existence of a personal God. The redeeming death of Jesus Christ on the cross. The Ten Commandments. The sacred dignity and divine worth of each individual made in the image and likeness of God. The permanence of the marriage bond. The sanctity of the home and the family as the basic unit of society. The human rights of every person from God, not from the state. The right to possess private property. Due respect for domestic, civil, and religious authority. Judgment after death.

18. **Champion the rights of the persecuted peoples**. In the world at the end of 1998, according to Fides, the news agency of the Vatican's Congregation for the Evangelization of Peoples, "there are more than 200 million Christians persecuted and more than 400 million discriminated against because of their faith. At fault are about 70 countries ruled by an atheistic regime — [Red] China, Vietnam, Cuba, Laos, North Korea — or by a growing fundamentalism — Sudan, Pakistan, Egypt, India, Indonesia, Saudi Arabia, etc." As Catholics, we must recognize that there are fellow Christians who cannot practice their religion and are deprived of such fundamental human rights as life, liberty, and the pursuit of happiness. Please pray daily for all of our persecuted brothers and sisters.

Chapter 19

The Perfect Prayer

"The Lord's Prayer is truly the summary of the whole Gospel," the "most perfect of prayers." It is at the center of the Scriptures. — *Catechism of the Catholic Church*, n. 2774

In the years following the Second Vatican Council, there was considerable confusion among Catholics about changes in the Church. The confusion was partly due to individuals making statements and inaugurating changes on the grounds that they were sanctioned by the "spirit of Vatican II." In point of fact, however, there was nothing in the official record of the Council, as expressed in its 16 documents, to justify some of the statements made or some of the changes introduced.

The confusion was particularly prevalent in the field of religious education, and catechists involved in teaching the Faith in those days can surely recall hearing some rather bizarre pronouncements from persons who were presumed to be speaking accurately about what the Council had said. One of the authors of this book, for example, remembers being told at a training session for catechists that there was no reason to require children to memorize the Our Father since that prayer really wasn't all that important. This about the only prayer that Jesus taught us!

Fortunately, that kind of foolishness did not last long and, with the issuance of the *Catechism of the Catholic Church* in 1992, the Our Father was given the prominence it deserves in the life of every Catholic. In the fourth and last pillar of the *Catechism*, which deals with "Christian Prayer," there are 107 para-

233

graphs about the Lord's Prayer, which St. Thomas Aquinas called the "most perfect of prayers." What else could one expect from the most perfect Person who ever prayed?

The first Christian communities recognized the significance of the Our Father, praying it three times a day in place of the "Eighteen Benedictions" that pious Jews were accustomed to praying. If we will say this prayer as devoutly and live it as fervently as our predecessors in the Faith, we will also have a holy and wholesome effect on society as we respond enthusiastically to our Christian call to holiness.

The Lord's Prayer

St. Luke tells us that one day when Jesus had finished praying in a certain place, "one of his disciples asked him, 'Lord, teach us to pray, as John taught his disciples' " (Luke 11:1). Jesus responded by giving the disciples, and us, these familiar words:

Our Father who art in heaven, hallowed be thy name. Thy kingdom come. Thy will be done on earth, as it is in heaven. Give us this day our daily bread, and forgive us our trespasses, as we forgive those who trespass against us, and lead us not into temptation, but deliver us from evil. Amen.

Luke has given us only five petitions of the Our Father, while St. Matthew (6:9-13) has given us a more developed version of seven petitions, but the liturgical tradition of the Church has retained Matthew's text. There are only 56 words in the prayer, but as we shall see, those words are packed with meaning for us.

One can even see a parallel with the Ten Commandments. Just as the first three commandments are about putting God first, so the first three petitions of the Our Father are about loving God. They carry us away from ourselves and toward the Father as we focus on *thy* name, *thy* kingdom, *thy* will. And just as the last seven commandments concern love of neighbor, so too the last four petitions of the Our Father cause us to think about others as we ask, "give *us*, forgive *us*, lead *us* not, and deliver *us*."

The *Catechism* offers this summary of the seven petitions:

In the Our Father, the object of the first three petitions is the glory of the Father: the sanctification of his name, the coming of the kingdom, and the fulfillment of his will. The four others present our wants to him: they ask that our lives be nourished, healed of sin, and made victorious in the struggle of good over evil (n. 2857).

Praying the Our Father sincerely, the *Catechism* says, leaves all individualism behind because "the 'our' at the beginning of the Lord's Prayer, like the 'us' of the last four petitions, excludes no one. If we are to say it truthfully, our divisions and oppositions have to be overcome. The baptized cannot pray to 'our' Father without bringing before him all those for whom he gave his beloved Son. God's love has no bounds, neither should our prayer" (nn. 2792-2793).

Our Father

It is said that St. Teresa had great difficulty getting beyond these first two words in the Lord's Prayer because saying them was like being transported to a beautiful country and never wanting to leave. Perhaps we would feel the same way if we said these words slowly and reflectively, instead of rushing through them and giving little or no thought to their meaning.

For the God whom we personally address really is "our" Father and we are "his" children. In calling him by name, we do not divide the Godhead or confuse the Persons of the Holy Trinity. Rather, we declare that our communion is with the Father and his Son, Jesus Christ, in their one Holy Spirit. Since the Trinity is indivisible, the *Catechism* tells us, "when we pray to the Father, we adore and glorify him together with the Son and the Holy Spirit" (n. 2789).

Praying to our Father should dispose us to become like him and to behave as one would expect God's children to behave. As St. John Chrysostom put it: "You cannot call the God of all kindness your Father if you preserve a cruel and inhuman heart; for in this case you no longer have in you the marks of the heavenly Father's kindness."

Prayer to our Father should also foster in us a humble and trusting heart that enables us to become like children, for as

Jesus said in offering praise to his Father, "what you have hidden from the learned and the clever you have revealed to the merest children" (Matthew 11:25). The reason why we should put our trust and confidence in the Father was explained by St. Augustine: "What would he not give to his children who ask, since he has already granted them the gift of being his children?"

We call God Father because Jesus told us to do so and because God is the first origin of everything and at the same time the role model of goodness and loving care for all his children. We associate with fathers such good qualities as protective love, fidelity, leadership, strength, security, and stability, and we should not be swayed against using this term of endearment by those who promote negative images of fatherhood based on the failings of fallible human fathers

God our Father surpasses modern cultural images of him, and it would be wrong to attempt to create God in our image since that would be to fabricate an idol. "In no way is God in man's image," says the *Catechism* (n. 370).

As for those who think we should call God "our Mother," and there are places in the Bible where God is identified with such feminine characteristics as the tenderness and concern of a mother (Isaiah 49:15 and Matthew 23:37), the *Catechism* says that "God transcends the human distinction between the sexes. He is neither man nor woman: he is God. He also transcends human fatherhood and motherhood, although he is their origin and standard: no one is father as God is Father" (n. 239).

The *Catechism* says in another place that "God is pure spirit in which there is no place for the difference between the sexes. But the respective 'perfections' of man and woman reflect something of the infinite perfection of God: those of a mother and those of a father and husband" (n. 370).

Who Art in Heaven

Although we have been brought up to think of heaven as a place above the sky, the Church teaches that heaven is not a place or space, but rather a way of being. God is not elsewhere; he is everywhere. God is not "up there" and far away from us; he is close to us and dwells in the hearts of the humble and the contrite. We spend our lives here on earth, but we are citizens of heaven. In the words of the *Catechism*:

"Who art in heaven" does not refer to a place but to God's majesty and his presence in the hearts of the just. Heaven, the Father's house, is the true homeland toward which we are heading and to which, already, we belong (n. 2802).

Hallowed Be Thy Name

To hallow something means to make it holy. For example, the word "Halloween" actually means "holy evening" since it comes on the eve of All Saints Day, although many of the antics that take place on Halloween are anything but holy. Nevertheless, we are instructed to ask God to make his name holy and, as the second commandment tells us, to make sure that the name of God is not misused. How disappointing, then, it must be to God and to Jesus to hear those who claim to be believers, and even to be Christians, use these holy names to express anger, disgust, surprise, and other emotions.

Recall that when God appeared in the burning bush, Moses asked him his name. God responded with the Hebrew word *Yahweh*, which means "I am who am" (Exodus 3:13-14). This name was considered so holy by the ancient Hebrews that they never pronounced it. So, too, is the name of Jesus sacred, as St. Paul indicated when he said: "At Jesus' name every knee must bend in the heavens, on the earth, and under the earth, and every tongue proclaim to the glory of God the Father: JESUS CHRIST IS LORD!" (Philippians 2:10-11).

When we strive to make God's name holy, we immerse ourselves in God's plan of salvation. In Baptism we were called to a holiness of life, and both the glory of God and our life depend on the hallowing of his name in us and by us. "It is this name that gives salvation to a lost world," said St. Peter Chrysologus. "But we ask that this name of God should be hallowed in us through our actions. For God's name is blessed when we live well, but is blasphemed when we live wickedly."

But not only do we ask that God's name be made holy in us, we also ask that it be made holy in other people, especially in those who are separated from God. This is nothing less than following the Lord's command to pray for everyone, including our enemies.

The power of our good example can be seen in the actions of a woman we know who makes the Sign of the Cross every time she hears someone misuse the name of Jesus. She doesn't say anything to the offender, but simply blesses herself. People are puzzled at first, but then they realize what she is trying to tell them. After a few weeks, the woman says, the number of times her friends and co-workers abused the name of Jesus decreased dramatically — all because of her simple gesture. Perhaps more of us who love the name of Jesus should do the same.

One thing we can easily do is to recite every day the first four Divine Praises:

Blessed be God.

Blessed be his holy name.

Blessed be Jesus Christ, true God and true man.

Blessed be the name of Jesus.

Thy Kingdom Come

The kingdom of God has been coming since the Last Supper and is in our midst in the Holy Eucharist. St. Cyprian said that the kingdom of God may even mean "Christ himself, whom we daily desire to come, and whose coming we wish to be manifested quickly to us. For as he is our resurrection, since in him we rise, so he can also be understood as the Kingdom of God, for in him we shall reign."

The *Catechism* says that "thy kingdom come" refers primarily to the final coming of the reign of God when Christ returns at the end of the world. But this doesn't mean that we can sit back and do nothing but wait. On the contrary, we are called to take an active part in the ongoing battle between good and evil and to assist others in attaining lives of holiness so that they will truly be ready when the kingdom does come.

We must also make sure that we are working for "thy" kingdom and not "my" kingdom. Keeping to the spirit of the Beatitudes (cf. chapter 1 of this volume) will help us to stay on the right track and work as God's instruments while he in his own time and on his own schedule brings the kingdom to fulfillment.

Thy Will Be Done

There is a story about a teenager confined to a wheelchair whose livelihood for him and his mother was a small newsstand in Grand Central Station in New York City. Late one Christmas Eve, as the boy was getting ready to close up, two men came running down the concourse, hurrying to catch the last train. The first man came around the corner too fast and crashed into the stand, knocking the boy over and scattering his wares. The man jumped to his feet, cursed the boy, and raced off to catch the train.

When the second man, who was also in a hurry, came upon the scene, he stopped and helped the boy to his feet, asked if he were all right, and picked up some of the items that had fallen on the floor. He then gave the young man a $20 bill, wished him a Merry Christmas, and started jogging away.

"Mister," the boy shouted after him, "are you Jesus Christ?"

The man stopped, turned around, and said, "No, son, I'm not, but I try to do what he would do if he were here now."

Isn't that what it means to do God's will here on earth as it is already being done in heaven? We have the sterling example of Christ himself, who was obedient even to dying on the cross. "I have come to do your will, O God," said Jesus (Hebrews 10:7). "I always do what pleases him," Jesus said of his Father (John 8:29). And, of course, during his agony in the Garden of Gethsemani, when Christ was tempted to shy away from the cross, he declared instead, "Father, if it is your will, take this cup from me; yet not my will but yours be done" (Luke 22:42).

We are constantly tempted to do our will rather than God's will. The *Catechism* says that we are "radically incapable" of uniting our will to the Father so as to fulfill his plan for the salvation of the world, "but united with Jesus and with the power of his Holy Spirit, we can surrender our will to him and decide to choose what his Son has always chosen: to do what is pleasing to the Father" (n. 2825).

We can discern what is the will of God through prayer and at the same time obtain the endurance to do the will of the Father. It will not be mere words that will get us to heaven, but good deeds. As Jesus warned: "None of those who cry out, 'Lord, Lord,' will enter the kingdom of God but only the one who does the will of my Father in heaven" (Matthew 7:21).

We are also obligated to pray not just for ourselves, but for all those on earth, too. Jesus "commands each of the faithful who prays to do so universally, for the whole world," said St. John Chrysostom. "For he did not say 'thy will be done in me or in us,' but 'on earth,' the whole earth, so that error may be banished from it, truth take root in it, all vice be destroyed on it, virtue flourish on it, and earth no longer differ from heaven."

Give Us This Day Our Daily Bread

This petition teaches us how good and generous God is and how important it is for us not to be preoccupied about the things we need. In the Sermon on the Mount, Jesus urged us not to worry about our livelihood, or what we are to eat or drink or wear. He cited the examples of the birds of the air and the flowers of the field, noting how his Father takes care of them, and then gave us this good advice:

> Stop worrying, then, over questions like, "What are we to eat, or what are we to drink, or what are we to wear?" The unbelievers are always running after these things. Your heavenly Father knows all that you need. Seek first his kingship over you, his way of holiness, and all these things will be given you besides (Matthew 6:25-33).

Notice, too, that we are to pray about *today's* needs, not tomorrow's or next week's. "Let tomorrow take care of itself," said Jesus. "Today has troubles enough of its own" (Matthew 6:34).

As mentioned earlier, this and the three petitions that follow are not just for "me" but for "us." We don't ask God to give "me" my daily bread, but all those in the human family. Nor can we personally neglect the world's needy unless we wish to suffer the fate of the rich man in the parable about Lazarus (Luke 16:19-31) or the eternal damnation promised to those who failed to help the least of their brothers and sisters (Matthew 25:31-46). The abundance of some can remedy the needs of others.

"Our daily bread" refers not only to material hunger, but also to spiritual hunger since man does not live by bread alone, "but on every utterance that comes from the mouth of God" (Matthew 4:4). "There is a famine on earth, 'not a famine of bread, nor a thirst for water, but of hearing the words of the LORD,' " says the

Catechism. "For this reason the specifically Christian sense of this fourth petition concerns the Bread of Life: The Word of God accepted in faith, the Body of Christ received in the Eucharist" (n. 2835).

"The Eucharist is our daily bread," said St. Augustine, along with "the readings you hear each day in church and the hymns you hear and sing. All these are necessities for our pilgrimage." St. Peter Chrysologus also emphasized the importance of this food from heaven:

> The Father in heaven urges us, as children of heaven, to ask for the bread of heaven. [Christ] himself is the bread who, sown in the Virgin, raised up in the flesh, kneaded in the Passion, baked in the oven of the tomb, reserved in churches, brought to altars, furnishes the faithful each day with food from heaven.

How valuable and beneficial it is for us to receive this heavenly Bread daily at Mass if we are to have the spiritual strength to do the will of God in the midst of people who may insist that they believe in God, but who live as if God did not exist.

Forgive Us Our Trespasses...

The *Catechism* calls this fifth petition "astonishing" because it is linked to a second phrase, "as we forgive those who trespass against us." The petition recognizes that we are sinners before God, like the Prodigal Son (Luke 15:11-32) and the tax collector (Luke 18:9-14), but it also warns us that God's mercy cannot penetrate our hearts as long as we have not forgiven those who have wronged us. Here is how the *Catechism* explains this section of the Lord's Prayer:

> Love, like the Body of Christ, is indivisible; we cannot love the God we cannot see if we do not love the brother or sister we do see. In refusing to forgive our brothers and sisters, our hearts are closed and their hardness makes them impervious to the Father's merciful love; but in confessing our sins, our hearts are opened to his grace (n. 2840).

So important is this petition that Jesus develops it explicitly in the Sermon on the Mount. For example, right after giving the disciples the words of the Our Father, Jesus says: "If you forgive the faults of others, your heavenly Father will forgive you yours. If you do not forgive others, neither will your Father forgive you" (Matthew 6:14-15). Earlier in the same sermon, our Lord also said: "If you bring your gift to the altar and there recall that your brother has anything against you, leave your gift at the altar, go first to be reconciled with your brother, and then come and offer your gift" (Matthew 5:23-24).

When St. Peter asked Jesus how many times one should forgive another person, and thought he was being generous in suggesting seven times, the Lord responded: "No, not seven times; I say seventy times seven times" (Matthew 18:21-22). In other words, an infinite number of times.

By human standards it seems impossible to forgive those who have hurt us, but Scripture tells us that "for God all things are possible" (Matthew 19:26). The same Christ who told us to love our enemies backed up his words on the cross by extending forgiveness to those who were carrying out his brutal execution: "Father, forgive them; they do not know what they are doing" (Luke 23:34). The heart that offers itself to the Holy Spirit will experience the healing necessary to forgive others and even to intercede with God on their behalf.

Showing an example of genuine forgiveness, the *Catechism* says, "bears witness that, in our world, love is stronger than sin. The martyrs of yesterday and today bear this witness to Jesus. Forgiveness is the fundamental condition of the reconciliation of the children of God with their Father and of men with one another" (n. 2844).

Lead Us not into Temptation

It should be made clear at the outset that God tempts no one (cf. James 1:13). Nor does he allow us to be tempted beyond our ability to resist. "God keeps his promise," said St. Paul. "He will not let you be tested beyond your strength. Along with the test he will give you a way out of it so that you may be able to endure it" (1 Corinthians 10:13).

What we are really asking for in this petition is "do not let us *yield* to temptation." We are asking the Father not to allow us to take the way that leads to sin, to distinguish between trials, which are necessary for our spiritual growth, and temptations, which can lead to sin and death. Some Bible versions translate this petition as "subject us not to the trial," which is what Jesus had in mind since it would be impossible for God to lead us into temptation.

It is also important to distinguish between being tempted, which is not a sin, and consenting to temptation, which is a sin. We are constantly being tempted by the world, the flesh, and the devil to turn away from God and, in this battle, victory can be achieved only through prayer. Again we have the example of Jesus, both when he was tempted by Satan in the desert (Matthew 4:1-11) and in the Garden of Gethsemani, where "he prayed with all the greater intensity, and his sweat became like drops of blood falling to the ground" (Luke 22:44).

By including this petition in the Our Father, Jesus unites us to his battle and his agony, and he urges us to be vigilant, to keep watch, and to persevere in the final moments of our life. "(Be on your guard!" he tells us in Revelation 16:15. "I come like a thief. Happy the man who stays wide awake and fully clothed for fear of going naked and exposed for all to see!)"

Deliver Us from Evil

This final petition refers to the Evil One, to Satan, as Jesus indicated at the Last Supper, when he said to his Father about the disciples: "I do not ask you to take them out of the world, but to guard them from the evil one" (John 17:15). Evil is not an abstraction, but refers to a person, the devil, who tries to thwart the Father's plan of salvation. This is the fallen angel whom Jesus said "brought death to man from the beginning, and has never based himself on truth; the truth is not in him. Lying speech is his native tongue; he is a liar and the father of lies" (John 8:44).

But we are not to fear the devil, as St. Ambrose explains:

> The Lord who has taken away your sin and pardoned your faults also protects you and keeps you from the wiles of your adversary the devil, so that the enemy, who is accustomed to leading into sin, may not surprise you. One who entrusts himself to God does not dread the devil. "If God is for us, who is against us?"

Jesus won victory over the "prince of this world" when he freely gave himself up to death on Good Friday. When we pray this petition, we ask God to deliver us not only from the Evil One, but also from all evils, past, present, and future, of which Satan is the author or instigator, and we further pray for peace and for the grace of perseverance until Christ returns. Our plea is very well expressed in the petition that immediately follows the Our Father at Mass:

> Deliver us, Lord, from every evil, and grant us peace in our day. In your mercy keep us free from sin and protect us from all anxiety as we wait in joyful hope for the coming of our Savior, Jesus Christ.

And that should be our demeanor no matter what is happening in the world around us — an attitude of joyful hope as we await the coming of the Lord. For, as we say in the doxology after this petition, "the kingdom, the power, and the glory are yours, now and forever." The devil tried to usurp the three titles of kingship, power, and glory, promising them to Christ if he would but prostrate himself in homage before Satan, but Jesus rebuked the tempter in these words: " 'You shall do homage to the Lord your God; him alone shall you adore' " (Luke 4:6-8).

Vocal and Mental Prayer

Prayer is the link that brings us into contact with God. It is the lifting up of our minds and hearts to God. Vocal prayer, which the *Catechism* calls "an essential element of the Christian life" (n. 2701), does this by means of words. Mental prayer, which the *Catechism* says engages "thought, imagination, emotion, and desire" (n. 2723), does this by means of silent communication.

Saying the Our Father prayerfully and thoughtfully is both vocal and mental prayer. We should pray constantly since "prayer is both a gift of grace and a determined response on our part," says the *Catechism*. "It always presupposes effort.... We pray as we live, because we live as we pray. If we do not want to act habitually according to the Spirit of Christ, neither can we pray habitually in his name. The 'spiritual battle' of the Christian's new life is inseparable from the battle of prayer" (n. 2725),

Chapter 20

You Can Make a Difference

Every area of the lay faithful's lives, as different as they are, enters into the plan of God who desires that these very areas be the "places in time" where the love of Christ is revealed and realized for both the glory of the Father and service of others. Every activity, every situation, every precise responsibility—as, for example, skill and solidarity in work, love and dedication in the family and the education of children, service to society and public life, and the promotion of truth in the area of culture—are the occasions ordained by Providence for a "continuous exercise of faith, hope, and charity." —Pope John Paul II, *Christifideles Laici*, n. 59

When one considers the problems confronting the individual, the family, and society, the temptation is great to want to head for some deserted island somewhere. Or, like Pontius Pilate, to want to wash your hands of the whole mess. Or perhaps to wish that you had lived in earlier and more peaceful and less demanding times. While such thoughts may be temporarily soothing and dis-tracting, we seldom have much time to indulge ourselves in them. The waves of reality soon come crashing down on our seashore of dreams and wash away our idle thoughts, leaving us once again surrounded by a tide of troubles.

There are two courses of action we can follow in this situation. We can bemoan our fate, complain that "everything always hap-pens to me," and waste time and energy criticizing the present state of affairs. Or, recalling that the cross is the symbol of Christian life, and drawing inspiration from the crucified Christ, we can meet the difficulties of the day head on, propose Christian solutions for them, and work to see that the solutions are properly and perseveringly put into effect.

More than a century ago, Etienne de Grellet, a Quaker missionary, offered us these words of advice: "I expect to pass through this world but once; any good thing therefore that I can do, or any kindness that I can show to any fellow creature, let me do it now; let me not defer nor neglect it, for I shall not pass this way again."

What Can One Person Do?

Have you ever approached someone about dealing with some predicament involving your church or your community? You explain the circumstances to him and he says, "I'd like to help, but I'm only one person, and what can one person do?" Often this is another way of saying, "I don't want to get involved." But if the person is sincere, you might be able to convince him that "one person" can do quite a lot, even in situations that appear to be hopeless. A few examples to prove our point:

One person, St. Paul, despite floggings, shipwrecks, imprisonment, and frequent lack of food, drink, and clothing, preached the word of God throughout the hostile Roman Empire and caused thousands of people to reform their lives.

One person, St. Athanasius, was a bulwark of resistance to the Arian heresy that threatened to overwhelm the Church in the third and fourth centuries. And how many people today have ever heard of Arius and his heresy?

One person, St. Catherine of Siena, a young woman only in her twenties, helped to prevent war in Europe in the fourteenth century and later went to Avignon in France and persuaded the Pope to return to Rome.

One person, Joan of Arc, inspired the French people with her heroism in the fifteenth century.

One person, Juan Diego, a humble Mexican peasant, convinced the Bishop of Mexico City to build a church to our Lady in the sixteenth century. Today the shrine of Our Lady of Guadalupe attracts millions of visitors and devout pilgrims every year.

One person, Bernadette of Lourdes, a French teenager, was the prime instrument in the founding of the world-famous shrine at Lourdes.

One person, Mother Teresa, started an apostolate for the dying in the streets of Calcutta that has spread throughout the world and earned this humble nun the Nobel Peace Prize.

Now you might say that these people were different from the rest of us, that they were special, that they never had any doubt or hesitation about what they should do. But you would be wrong. They were human. They all had their moments when they wondered if it was all worth it. Even our Lord, true man that he was, asked his Father in heaven to spare him the ordeal that was to come. But then, as his followers have done ever since, Jesus went on to do his Father's will, giving us a perfect example to follow.

We are to be God's instruments in the world. If you leave your garden completely up to God, it will be overrun with weeds. Why? Because God helps those who help themselves. It is not enough to wish that things would get better; we must work to make it happen. God gave us a backbone, not a wishbone. He has given us the intelligence to recognize what must be done, and he will give us the courage to do it if we ask him.

Some Examples from American History

American history is replete with incidents where the vote of one person had a major impact on the future of our nation. Thomas Jefferson and John Quincy Adams were elected to the Presidency by one vote in the Electoral College. Statehood was granted to California, Idaho, Oregon, Texas, and Washington by one vote. President Andrew Johnson, who had been impeached by the House of Representatives, was acquitted in the Senate by one vote. The purchase of Alaska was approved by one vote. And the reason we speak English in America today is because a motion in the Continental Congress two centuries ago to make German the official language of the United States was defeated by one vote.

The next time someone asks what one person can do, or questions whether one person can make a difference, remind him of these examples and leave him with this thought: "I am only one, but I am one. I cannot do everything, but I can do something. And I will not fail to do that which I can do."

Everyone Needs Our Product

There is a story of two shoe salesmen who were sent to Africa to probe the possibilities for markets on that continent. After a few weeks, two cables came back to the home office. One read, "Forget it. Four out of five wouldn't know a shoe if they saw it." The other said, "Send immediate reinforcements. Almost everyone needs our product."

Can we not say the same thing about Christianity? Christianity is what the world needs. What are you doing to bring this product to the world? We have all been put on this earth by God to make a difference. It does not have to be a difference that affects the future of the world. It might be just to provide love, understanding, and encouragement to members of our own family. It might be to show compassion and kindness to a friend or neighbor in trouble. It might be to defend the right to life of everyone from the unborn child to the senior citizen.

It might be to work for racial justice, for a more equitable distribution of the world's goods to the less fortunate, for the election of moral and upright persons to public office, or to rescue someone from a cult. It might be to press for the freedom of our persecuted brothers and sisters in other countries. But whatever it is, someone ought to know that we have passed their way. Someone's life should be different for having come into contact with us.

To make a difference in this life will not be easy. No truly Christian life can ever be easy. Nor are we likely to receive the plaudits of the world for our efforts. We are called to be in the world but not of the world, a distinction that sometimes eludes us. Our reward is eternal, not temporal. But having responded wholeheartedly to the Christian call to holiness, we can then say with St. Paul, "I have fought the good fight, I have finished the race, I have kept the faith" (2 Timothy 4:7).

We are pilgrims on the road to heaven. We have certain responsibilities here and now but our destiny is the hereafter and forever. Christ and his Church give us the principles to follow in order to help solve the problems we face. We must put these principles into practice. We must do all that we can, individually and collectively, to exercise our Christian stewardship and to bring the true peace of Christ to families and society.

We must let the light of Christ shine through us, not dimly but brightly, hoping to dispel the darkness of sin from the world in which we are travelers. We must proclaim by word and example the Beatitudes and the other parts of Christ's blueprint for society which he spelled out for us in the Sermon on the Mount.

A Springtime for Christianity

We must do all of this with firmness, courage, and an abundance of Christian hope. Pope John Paul has given us an optimistic look at the future:

If we look at today's world, we are struck by many negative factors that can lead to pessimism. But this feeling is unjustified: we have faith in God our Father and Lord, in his goodness and mercy. As the third millenium of the Redemption draws near, God is preparing a great springtime for Christianity, and we can already see its first signs.

In fact, both in the non-Christian world and in the traditionally Christian world, people are gradually drawing closer to Gospel ideals and values, a development which the Church seeks to encourage. Today in fact there is a new consensus among peoples about these values: the rejection of violence and war; respect for the human person and for human rights; the desire for freedom, justice, and brotherhood; the surmounting of different forms of racism and nationalism; the affirmation of the dignity and role of women.

Christian hope sustains us in committing ourselves fully to the new evangelization and to the worldwide mission, and leads us to pray as Jesus taught us: "Thy kingdom come. Thy will be done, on earth as it is in heaven" (*Redemptoris Missio*, n. 86).

Epilogue

Pope
John Paul II

Basic human and Christian values are challenged by crime, violence, and terrorism. Honesty and justice in business and public life are often violated. Throughout the world great sums are spent on armaments while millions of poor people struggle for the basic necessities of life. Alcohol and drug abuse take a heavy toll on individuals and on society. The commercial exploitation of sex through pornography offends human dignity and endangers the future of young people.

Family life is subjected to powerful pressures such as fornication, adultery, divorce, and contraception, which are wrongly regarded as acceptable by many. The unborn are cruelly killed and the lives of the elderly are in serious danger from a mentality that would open the door wide to euthanasia.

In the face of all this, however, faithful Christians must not be discouraged, nor can they conform to the spirit of the world. Instead, they are called upon to acknowledge the supremacy of God and his law, to raise their voices and join their efforts on behalf of moral values, to offer society the example of their own upright conduct, and to help those in need. Christians are called to act with the serene conviction that grace is more powerful than sin because of the victory of Christ's cross.

Bibliography

Abbott, Faith. *Acts of Faith*
Alcorn, Randy. *Pro-Life Answers to Pro-Choice Arguments*
Angelica, Mother M. *Mother Angelica's Answers, Not Promises*

Balducci, Corrado. *The Devil ... Alive and Active in Our World*
Barron, John, and Paul, Anthony. *Murder of a Gentle Land*
Bonacci, Mary Beth. *Real Love Answers Your Questions on Dating, Marriage, and the Real Meaning of Sex*
Brennan, William. *The Abortion Holocaust*
Burke, Cormac. *Covenanted Happiness*

Carroll, Warren H. *70 Years of the Communist Revolution*
Carson, Clarence B. *Basic Communism: Its Rise, Spread and Debacle in the 20th Century*
Catechism of the Catholic Church
Catholic Almanac
Catholic Encyclopedia. Edited by Fr. Peter M.J. Stravinskas
Chamberlin, William Henry. *The Russian Revolution* (2 vols.)
Chambers, Whittaker. *Witness*
Ciszek, Walter J., S.J. *He Leadeth Me*
_____. *With God in Russia*
Clifford, John W., S.J. *In the Presence of My Enemies*
Cochini, Christian, S.J., *Apostolic Origins of Priestly Celibacy*
Connell, Francis J. *Outlines of Moral Theology*
Conquest, Robert. *The Great Terror*
Cristiani, Msgr. Leon. *Satan in the Modern World*

Dannemeyer, William. *Shadow in the Land: Homosexuality in America*
DeMarco, Donald. *Biotechnology and the Assault on Parenthood*
Dilenno, Joseph A., M.D., and Smith, Herbert F., S.J. *Homosexuality: The Questions*
Documents of Vatican II, The. Edited by Walter M. Abbott, S.J.
Drummey, James J. *Catholic Replies*

Encyclopedia of Church History. Edited by Matthew Bunson

Everett, Carol. *Blood Money: Getting Rich off a Woman's Right to Choose*

Flannery, Austin, O.P. *Vatican Council II: The Conciliar and Post Conciliar Documents* (2 vols.)

Fox, Robert J. *Fatima Today*

_____. *The Gift of Sexuality: A Guide for Young People*

_____. and Mangan, Fr. Charles. *Until Death Do Us Part*

Gesy, Fr. Lawrence J. *Today's Destructive Cults and Movements*

Grisez, Germain. *Christian Moral Principles*

_____. *Living a Christian Life*

Hardon, John A., S.J. *The Catholic Catechism*

_____. *Modern Catholic Dictionary*

_____. *The Question and Answer Catholic Catechism*

Harvey, John F., O.S.F.S. *The Homosexual Person*

_____. *The Truth About Homosexuality*

Hayes, Fr. Edward J., Hayes, Msgr. Paul J. and Drummey, James J. *Catholicism and Life*

_____. *Catholicism and Reason*

Hitchcock, James. *What Is Secular Humanism?*

Hoover, J. Edgar. *Masters of Deceit*

_____. *A Study of Communism*

John Paul II, Pope. *Christifideles Laici*

_____. *Crossing the Threshold of Hope*

_____. *Dominum et Vivificantem*

_____. *Evangelium Vitae*

_____. *On Human Work*

_____. *Letter to Families*

_____. *Mother of the Redeemer*

_____. *Mulieris Dignitatem*

_____. *Ordinatio Sacerdotalis*

_____. *Redemptoris Missio*

_____. *The Role of the Christian Family in the Modern World*

_____. *Salvifici Doloris*

_____. *On Social Concern*

_____. *Veritatis Splendor*

John XXIII, Pope. *Mater et Magistra*
_____. *Pacem in Terris*

Kasun, Jacqueline. *The War Against Population*
Kippley, John F. *Marriage Is for Keeps*
_____. *Sex and the Marriage Covenant*
_____. and Kippley, Sheila. *The Art of Natural Family Planning*
Kreeft, Peter. *Angels and Demons*
Kuharski, Mary Ann. *Raising Catholic Children*

Lawler, Ronald, Boyle, Joseph and May, William E. *Catholic Sexual Ethics*
LeBar, Fr. James J. *Cults, Sects and the New Age*

Marks, Frederick W. *A Catholic Handbook for Engaged and Newly Married Couples*
May, William E. *An Introduction to Moral Theology*
Miceli, Vincent P., S.J. *The Gods of Atheism*
Mindszenty, Jozsef Cardinal. *Memoirs*
Moody, John, and Boyes, Roger. *The Priest and the Policeman*
Myers, Bishop John J. *The Obligations of Catholics and the Rights of Unborn Children*

Nathanson, Bernard N., M.D. *Aborting America*
_____. *The Abortion Papers: Inside the Abortion Mentality*
_____. *The Hand of God*

O'Connor, John Cardinal. *Abortion: Questions and Answers*

Pacwa, Mitch, S.J. *Catholics and the New Age*
Paul VI, Pope. *Ecclesiam Suam*
_____. *Humanae Vitae*
_____. *Populorum Progressio*
Pius XI, Pope. *Casti Connubii*
_____. *Divini Redemptoris*
Pius XII and the Holocaust. Catholic League for Religious and Civil Rights
Pontifical Council for the Family. *The Truth and Meaning of Human Sexuality*
Pornography's Victims. Edited by Phyllis Schlafly

Pulling, Pat. *The Devil's Web*

Rader, Fr. John S., and Fedoryka, Kateryna. *The Pope and the Holocaust*

Reardon, David C. *Aborted Women: Silent No More*

Rice, Charles E. *50 Questions on Abortion, Euthanasia and Related Issues*

_____. *No Exception: A Pro-Life Imperative*

Rini, Suzanne M. *Beyond Abortion: A Chronicle of Fetal Experimentation*

Sacred Congregation for the Clergy. *Only for Love: Reflections on Priestly Celibacy*

Sacred Congregation for Divine Worship. *Christian Faith and Demonology*

Sacred Congregation for the Doctrine of the Faith. *Declaration on Certain Problems of Sexual Ethics*

_____. *Declaration on Euthanasia*

_____. *Declaration on Procured Abortion*

_____. *Instruction on Respect for Human Life in Its Origin and on the Dignity of Procreation*

_____. *Letter to the Bishops of the Catholic Church on the Pastoral Care of Homosexual Persons*

Sattler, Vern. *Challenging Children to Chastity*

Smith, Herbert F., S.J. *Pro-Choice? Pro-Life?*

Smith, Janet E. *Humanae Vitae: A Generation Later*

Solzhenitsyn, Aleksandr. *The Gulag Archipelago*

Steffon, Fr. Jeffrey J. *Satanism: Is It Real?*

Steichen, Donna. *Ungodly Rage: The Hidden Face of Catholic Feminism*

U.S. Catholic Bishops. *Basic Teachings for Catholic Religious Education*

_____. *Brothers and Sisters to Us: Racism in Our Day*

_____. *Sharing the Light of Faith: National Catechetical Directory for Catholics of the United States*

Willke, Dr. and Mrs. J.C. *Abortion Questions and Answers*

Wilson, Mercedes Arzu. *Love and Family: Raising a Traditional Family in a Secular World*

Wolfe, Bertram D. *Three Who Made a Revolution*

Index

Abortion, 95-101, 127-129
Anti-Semitism, 151-152
Arinze, Francis Cardinal, 186
Atheism, 173-174, 195-204
Authority, crisis of, 72-73

Beatitudes, 3-11
Birth Control, 89-95

Castro, Fidel, 221-222
Catechism of the Catholic Church, vii, viii, 4, 27, 30, 34-35, 40, 57, 67, 87, 91, 109, 148, 149, 162, 176, 183, 192, 196, 215, 217, 233-234, 235, 236, 237, 238, 239, 240-241, 244
Chamberlin, William Henry, 200, 201
Channeling, 192
Chastity, 44-46, 74-78
Children, discipline, 66-67; education and training, 63-66; role of, 61-63; sex education, 67-69
Communism, 209-213; vs. Christianity, 227; and morality, 223-224
Communist Manifesto, The, 198, 209-210, 212-213
Contraception, 89-95
Crowley, Aleister, 188, 190
Crystals, 192
Cults, 183-193

Day, Helen Caldwell, 155-156
Deacons, 19

De Sales, St. Francis, 70
Dialectical Materialism, 211-212
Divination, 192
Divorce, 33-36
"Dungeons & Dragons," 189-190

Economic Determinism, 212
Eighth Commandment, 181-182
Elderly, 137-148; obligations toward, 138, 173; reasons for institutionalization, 146-148
Engels, Friedrich, 197, 198-199
Enneagrams, 193
Euthanasia, 101-106
Evangelium Vitae, 88, 93, 101, 103-104, 104-105, 106, 122, 128-129

Family, four bonds of, 110-117; purpose of, 58-60
Fatima, Our Lady of, 205-206, 217, 230
Feminism, Radical, 127-129

Gesy, Fr. Lawrence J., 183, 184, 186-187
Gnosticism, 187
Gorbachev, Mikhail, 202-204
Graft, 178-181

Humanae Vitae, 91-93, 94, 95, 108-109

In Vitro Fertilization, 88-89

Jesus Christ, 3, 4, 5, 6, 7, 8, 9,
    10, 19, 30, 33-34, 48, 49,
    50, 54, 55, 60, 101, 109-
    110, 114-115, 123, 141,
    153, 156, 159, 160, 165-
    166, 171, 172, 174, 192,
    196, 228, 229, 230, 231,
    234, 236, 237, 239, 240,
    242, 243, 244, 249
John Paul II, Pope, ii, vii, 5, 7,
    11, 17, 18-19, 25, 28, 29,
    30, 31, 32, 34, 37, 40, 59-
    60, 62, 67, 83-85, 88, 90,
    91, 101, 103-104, 104-
    105, 106, 107, 109, 111,
    113, 121, 122, 124, 128-
    129, 131, 135, 136, 150-
    151, 158, 161-162, 163,
    168, 169, 172, 173, 174,
    178, 193-194, 195-196,
    217-218, 223-224, 245,
    249, 250
John XXIII, Pope, 63, 91, 129-
    130, 177, 195, 213-214

Kasun, Jacqueline, 90-91
Kolbe, St. Maximilian, 219

Lacordaire, Jean, 18
Lapide, Pinchas, 151
LeBar, Fr. James J., 183
Lenin, V.I., 199-201, 219, 224,
    229-230
Letter to Families, 28, 29, 30,
    37, 40, 60, 62, 107, 109,
    111, 131
Levey, Anton, 190
Liberation Theology, 222-223
Lincoln, Abraham, 175

Little Sisters of the Poor, viii,
    143-146
Lord's Prayer, 233-244

MacLaine, Shirley, 191
Mann, Nancyjo, 127-128
Marriage, Christian, 19-24, 27-
    37, 39-56; pillars of, 40-
    43; purpose of, 32-33;
    qualities for, 21-24, 44-49
Marx, Karl, 125, 197-198, 219,
    229
Mary, Blessed Virgin, 8, 47,
    109-110, 121, 122-124,
    132-135, 173, 205-206
Meir, Golda, 152
Michael, the Archangel, 191
Mindszenty, Jozsef Cardinal,
    125-126, 220-221
Modesty, 75
Mystical Body of Christ, 2,
    156, 157-158, 160-161,
    232

Natural Family Planning, 95
New Age Movement, 191-194
Newman, John Henry Cardi-
    nal, 15

Our Father, 233-244

Pacwa, Mitch, S.J., 183, 193,
    194
Parents, role of, 60-61, 63-69
Paul VI, Pope, 13, 24-25, 29-
    30, 40, 45-46, 91-92, 93,
    94, 95, 108-109, 195, 205,
    225
Paul, St., 4, 8, 9, 14, 16, 30-31,
    34, 47, 49-50, 54, 55, 62,
    84, 150, 153, 160-161,

84, 150, 153, 160-161,
164, 172, 192, 193, 226,
237, 242, 246, 248
Peter, St., 10, 19, 242
Pius XI, Pope, 29, 91, 108, 151,
195, 206, 208-209, 214,
221
Pius XII, Pope, 91, 102-103,
151-152, 157-158, 160,
195
Pole, Reginald Cardinal, 1
Politicians, principles for, 176-
178
Popieluszko, Fr. Jerzy, 218-
219
Population Control, 90-91
Prayer, vocal and mental, 244
Prejudice, 159-162
Priesthood, the, 18-19
Private Property, 213-214
Public life, morality in, 175-
182
Pulling, Pat, 189

Racism/Racial Discrimination,
149-162, 172
Radecki, Dr. Thomas, 189
Ratzinger, Joseph Cardinal,
223
Reincarnation, 192
Religion, persecution of, 217-
222
Religious Life, the, 17
Responsible Parenthood, 93-95

Satan, 243-244
Satanism, 189-191
Secular Humanism, 126-127
Senior Citizen, the, 137-148
Seventh Commandment, 178-
181

Sex Education, 67-69
Sexism, 127-128
Single Life, the, 15-16
Smith, Alfred E., 133-134
Socialism, 214-215
Solzhenitsyn, Aleksandr, 219
Solzhenitsyn, Natalia, 219-220
Steffon, Fr. Jeffrey J., 183, 190
Steichen, Donna, 188
Stepinac, Aloysius Cardinal,
150
Stewardship, Christian, 163-
174
Subsidiarity, principle of, 215
Suenens, Leo Cardinal, 135

Teenagers, 71-85; and dating,
74-78; and drinking, 78-
80; and driving, 81-83;
and drugs, 80-81
Tulin, Melissa, 128

Valladares, Armando, 221-222
Vatican Council II, vii, viii, 2,
10-11, 14, 16, 19, 29, 31,
34, 39, 40, 48, 59, 63, 64,
67, 71, 83, 91, 92, 94, 95,
100, 109, 113, 138, 152,
173-174, 176, 182, 195,
225, 233
Vocations, 13-25

Wicca/Witchcraft, 187-189
Woman, the modern, 121-135,
173
Women Exploited by Abortion,
127